Playwise

Also By Denise Chapman Weston and Mark S. Weston

Playful Parenting

and by

Denise Chapman Weston

Kidfriendly Parenting

Playwise

365 Fun-Filled Activities for
Building Character, Conscience, and
Emotional Intelligence in Children

Denise Chapman Weston, MSW
Mark S. Weston, MSW

A Jeremy P. Tarcher/Putnam Book
published by
G. P. Putnam's Sons
New York

We dedicate this book to our children, Arielle and Emily,
and all the children of the world, for whom
the future holds no limits.

Most Tarcher/Putnam books are available at special quantity discounts for bulk purchases for sales promotions, premiums, fund-raising, and educational needs. Special books or book excerpts also can be created to fit specific needs. For details, write or telephone Special Markets, The Putnam Publishing Group, 200 Madison Ave., New York, NY 10016; (212) 951-8891.

A Jeremy P. Tarcher/Putnam Book
Published by G. P. Putnam's Sons
Publishers Since 1838
200 Madison Avenue
New York, NY 10016
http://www.putnam.com/putnam

Library of Congress Cataloging-in-Publication Data

Chapman Weston, Denise.
    Playwise : 365 fun-filled activities for building character, conscience, and emotional intelligence in children / Denise Chapman Weston, Mark S. Weston.
        p.   cm.
    ISBN 0-87477-808-5
    1. Child rearing.   2. Child development.   3. Parenting.   4. Child psychology.   I. Weston, Mark S.   II. Title.
    HQ769.C3963   1996   96-3858 CIP
    649'.1—dc20

Design by Mauna Eichner
Cover design by Lee Fukui
Cover illustration © by Lorraine Silvestri
Interior illustrations by Ron Young

Printed in the United States of America

10   9   8   7   6   5   4   3   2   1

This book is printed on acid-free paper. ∞

Acknowledgments

P *laywise* is a book about character and of character. It began as a simple idea and grew in scope and work. It asked a lot from us, and we in turn asked a lot from others, whose help enabled us to devote the time, energy, and resources necessary to tackle this enormous undertaking. *Playwise* was, in other words, a team or community effort involving as much our children's teachers and baby-sitter as it did our associates and editors. To the many individuals who have shared their time, wisdom, and support, we extend a huge and heartfelt thank-you:

To our publisher, Jeremy Tarcher, who has been an inspiration and a guiding force in our writing careers, and whose challenge to come up with the most logical and best-fitting next book led us to conceive of and write *Playwise*; to his wife and partner, Shari Lewis, for her support and enthusiasm for us and playful parenting projects;

to Sharron Kahn, whose patience and unflinching good humor brought a sense of relief during times that were stressful and challenging, and for her efforts to bring order and brevity to some of our creative material;

to Robin Cantor Cooke, whose eye for detail and fluff kept us on our toes and focused, and kept this book neat and to the point;

to Irene Prokop, for her leadership and vision at Jeremy P. Tarcher, Inc.;

to the Putnam team, who have wrapped up all the multitude of parts to help create a classy book that we are immensely proud of: Jennifer Greene, Robert Welsch, Donna Gould;

to A. T. Birmingham at the Giraffe project, who shared with us a wealth of stories about special heroes both young and old, which now fill the pages of our book with hope and richness;

to Megan Collins, whose youthful enthusiasm, top-notch research, and warmth has made her a wonderful role model of great character both for our daughters and for ourselves;

to Rhode Island School for the Deaf and South Shore Mental Health Center, for giving us the insight and ability to understand play, children, and families;

to the families we have worked with, the parents and teachers who came to our workshops and lectures, trusting our skills and willing to listen, and who use our activities to make positive changes in their lives. It is truly an honor to have been part of so many people's lives.

To our new colleagues and friends in the "play" business, who spend days and nights creating products and places where families can come together to grow and play;

to Scott Nadel and his mother, Maria, for their honest and poignant story about their relationship;

to our supportive friends: Lauren and Dave Gansler, Fred and Cheri Ruffolo, Sharon Welk, Nuna Albert, Taunya Villcana, Rick Briggs, and Debbie Muther, who simply "know" what it takes to write a book and who extended their assistance at a moment's notice;

to the Knotts family: We thank you for your stories, your friendship, and your example. You are a family whose character we can always look up to.

To the McConnell family: Michelle, Dave, Kari, Colleen, Matt, and Annie. You make it possible for us to write and work because of the endless love and care you give our family.

To the superior teachers at Animal Crackers: Thank you for loving our children!

To both of our families: our parents Audrey and Cliff, and Hermine and Arthur, who provided us the childhoods we needed to develop strong characters. This gift we can now pass on to our own children. (And thank you, Mom and Dad, for giving special time to our children so we could spend the time writing this book!)

To our brothers- and sisters-in-law, who make our lives more full and complete. A special thanks to Terri, whose support is only a phone call away.

And, of course, a great big thank-you to our children, Arielle Mae and Emily Sarah Weston, who make it all worth it. Thank you for sometimes putting your needs aside so that Mommy and Daddy could devote time to writing this important book.

Contents

**Part II
Character Skills**

Introduction

After the release and success of our book *Playful Parenting*, we had become quite involved in conducting workshops for parents based on the book's playful approach. As with so many things in our lives, the inspiration for *Playwise* came from an encounter we had at one of these workshops. One mother, exhausted and desperate, had come searching for some help in handling her son. It seems young Will, at the tender age of eight, was well on his way to developing the skills of a con artist.

Night after night, the boy defied his mother's rule about being home before dark. But he was too clever to just come traipsing into the house at bedtime. He knew that if he did that, he would surely be punished. No, Will figured out that if he stayed at a friend's house until dusk, then *called* Mom to say he was on his way home, then lingered a little longer, then dawdled on his way home, he'd still get to ride his bike through the dark and his mother would have no grounds to punish him.

Will was becoming a skilled manipulator. But that wasn't all. His mother reported that her son had developed a mean streak. He would tease weaker children just to get a laugh from his peers. All of these things troubled her; her son who just a few short years ago was charming and loving had become mean and selfish. She worried that her son couldn't distinguish right from wrong, only followed rules when they served his purpose, and didn't have a clue about how his actions were hurting others—especially his mom.

Above all, Will's mother was worried about the type of person her son would grow up to be. After talking with her for a while, it became clear to us that she had come to our seminar looking for a lot more than creative discipline ideas. She was searching for something more profound. The focus of our discussion switched from behavioral problems to the more complex subject of raising children as moral and emotionally intelligent beings who are equipped to handle real-life challenges in a complex world.

The problem with Will got out of hand because his parent, as with many of us, was exhausted. She had become so wrapped up in the day-to-day power struggle with her son that she lost sight of her larger goal of shaping Will into a moral person who could understand how his actions were hurting himself and his relationships.

Although Will's mother felt things were hopeless, we helped her see that despite her son's behavior, Will was not a bad kid. He really did want to be liked, and he loved her very much. His character was simply out of balance; the different parts were not well integrated. Will had plenty of independent will, perseverance, and courage. He was also a sophisticated problem solver, as evidenced by his ability to manipulate. What was conspicuously absent were those other important traits of empathy, responsibility, self-awareness, and self-discipline, skills that are the foundation of emotional intelligence. In that hotel conference room that day, Will's mother found the last drop of fuel she needed to reexamine her goals. She decided to look for ways to help Will develop these other traits, and asked for our help in doing this. At that moment she became proactive instead of reactive.

We are raising our children in a morally ambiguous world and we have to do more than just discipline them and hope for the best. There's a huge misconception that discipline is the way to make your child a moral and successful being. The fact is, discipline may make your child behave well, but surface good behavior goes only so far. It has to be rooted inside, held in place by a range of skills and character strengths.

And that's what this book is: a manual for raising children who are emotionally and intellectually capable and confident.

What Really Is the Problem?

The most common complaints we hear from parents who come to our seminars, call in with questions, or come into our office, are that their children:

- ◆ don't listen to their parents
- ◆ procrastinate with their homework
- ◆ act without thinking
- ◆ pick on their younger siblings

- give up too easily
- ignore rules
- don't clean their bedrooms
- won't talk to their parents

When they've finished sharing their list of complaints, we ask them to think about what goals they have for their children. It's not surprising that this question initially draws a blank, for it is a question forgotten amidst the pressures of juggling work, marriage, car pools, discipline, and homework. After a while, they remember, and what they say goes something like this: My goal is to raise my child to

- be fair, honest, and kind
- respect laws and authority
- be an independent-minded person
- be successful
- live life morally and with principle
- be trustworthy and respectful
- be capable of love and generosity
- be disciplined and responsible
- be knowledgeable and motivated
- take care of his or her body
- solve big and small problems
- enjoy life and be happy
- communicate openly and with respect
- be a good person

Character Building Must Be a Priority

Like Will's mother, many parents lose sight of their long-term parenting goals and wind up putting a great deal of effort into the short-term ones; not because it is something they decided to do, but because these screamed out the loudest. What should be most important to us as parents too often seems to get pushed aside by the pressures, layers of deadlines, packed schedules, and endless demands.

We speak of this challenge not only as parenting speakers and family therapists, but as parents of two young girls, Emily and Arielle. We are committed to putting our long-term priorities first by taking the time to teach our children and help them develop their character skills, *but* we often experience how the daily grind takes hold of our family like a fierce tornado, spinning and twisting our best intentions and most well-laid plans out of control. But rather than spending time feeling like "bad parents," we find ways to reclaim control of our time and our parenting goals with creative solutions.

What Is Character?

Character is described as the internal knowledge, feelings, and values that guide us in life, driving our actions toward goals. Although we may be born with a set of predisposed traits and personality characteristics, this does not alone make up a person's character. Character is not a way of "being," but about "being able"; in other words, it is based upon an individual's ability to go beyond temperament by building a balanced repertoire of integrated skills, habits, traits, capabilities, and know-how, which can only be developed over a lifetime of *experience and learning*.

Foundations of Character Development

In order for children to develop these essential skills, traits, and know-how, there must be a nurturing environment for character development to take place. A character-building environment should embody these five foundations and be readily given to a child, including:

- ◆ knowledge and understanding
- ◆ stability and balance
- ◆ unconditional love and acceptance
- ◆ inspiration and good role modeling
- ◆ family and community connections

Children are not responsible for laying down these foundations: *we are*. We—meaning parents, caregivers, and educators—are our children's mentors. Our children's character development is dependent upon us to provide them with the knowledge they need to understand and make good decisions; the stability to help balance their lives in a fast-paced world; the comfort and security of being unconditionally loved; the teaching and examples of good role models; and a family and a community in which they will always feel they belong. Without these foundations, children have nothing upon which to build their character. Imagine a skyscraper built on weak and unstable ground. Your mind would conjure up scenes of chaos and disaster the day it begins to sink under the pressure and burden of its weight and structure. Children are just as vulnerable and cannot be left to sink under the pressure and burdens of growing up without foundation.

Essential Character Skills

There are many skills and abilities needed to navigate life's challenges; we've selected the most central of these and grouped them in a way that makes a daunting task more manageable. Each skill set will work in concert with others and will grow in relationship to a child's age and developmental abilities. We purposely call these *skills* rather than *characteristics* or *traits* to establish a mind-set that character is grown and learned by being taught. They are as follows:

- personal potential: self-knowledge, self-esteem, and internal motivation to persevere
- self-awareness: emotional management, personal insight and expression, and intuition
- social harmony (AKA people skills): communication skills, social competence, and teamwork skills
- sensibility: moral, conscientious decision making and independent thinking
- enjoying life: joy, stress management, and finding inner peace
- resourcefulness: crisis management and conflict resolution
- humanity: empathy, respect, and appreciation

If this list feels intimidating, look at it this way. These skills are yours and your child's weapons against adversity, negative social influences, and many of the other woes that keep parents up at night. Children need all of these character skills not just to become good, moral, and conscientious people, they need these skills to survive. You are reading this book because, like many others who care about our children's future, you are making the decision to make character building a priority. Your goals are our goals and that is why we wrote this book. A proactive approach does take time, but in the long run, it yields substantial rewards, and saves time and heartache.

Taking the Time to Teach

The time we take to enhance a character skill such as empathy pays off when we don't have to nag our child to be empathic or punish her every time she hurts someone's feelings or refuses to see another's point of view. If we take the time to build our children's ability to be thankful and appreciative, instead of having to be cajoled and chased to sign a thank-you card, they will take upon themselves the task because they feel gratitude and *want* to thank those who celebrated their birthday or gave them a gift. One less short-term thing for us to do, one more long-term character skill enhanced!

Our approach to building character and emotional intelligence in children does take time. Time seems to have become one of the most precious commodities available, one that people are not about to commit quickly to just any topic. When the question is raised regarding the amount of time it takes to do activities with children to teach character, we usually respond with the question, "Do you put sunscreen on your children when you go out in the sun?"

After the usual response, we ask how much time it takes to slather up the whole family. Five minutes? Ten minutes? Then we ask what happens when the kids come out of the water and need another application? Another five or ten minutes? Then we take out a calculator and do a little math. Those minutes add up to quite a lot of time during one kid's childhood, time that could be spent doing something important like paying bills. When we ask the parents what would happen if they didn't take the time to put on sunscreen, looks of understanding appear on their faces. The point they suddenly realize is that the five or ten minutes it takes to apply sunscreen is nothing compared to the time it would take to heal from a bad sunburn, or, in the future, be treated for skin cancer. Taking care of our children's emotional intelligence is no different from taking care of their bodies. Extra time taken to teach important character skills will save us precious time and prevent serious problems later.

Bringing up balanced and capable children should not be viewed as an unpleasant journey filled with endless lectures and lifeless instruction. On the contrary, this learning should take place in the day-to-day experiences of living, shared moments of discovery, planned and unplanned events and exercises, stimulating hands-on adventures. By this we mean teaching children through their most favored method of learning . . . *play*. One would think one can't play around with character, but that's the strength of our approach.

Becoming Playwise

Play is the most effective way to teach a child. With play, you can teach complicated concepts, philosophical principles, and emotions that are difficult to describe in words. You build your children's skills and show them how to solve problems when you play with them in engaging, child-tested ways that stimulate both the body and mind.

Unlike other teaching methods, play fully involves children in the lesson by engaging all their senses. They're not just hearing it or seeing it, they're doing it. Think about your own experiences with play. Imagine that you enroll in a class to learn how to make pottery and the instructor spends the entire time showing and discussing slides of clay pots. How much did you learn about working with clay? Now imagine that the instructor hands you a wet lump of clay and urges you to manipulate it, spin it, and experiment with different techniques as she explains and demonstrates. From which class did you learn more about making pottery?

Play is a child's realm. It's her natural method for figuring out the world. Consider, for example, how our daughter Emily learned to make a sand castle while simultaneously building her confidence and independence.

At first she filled her pail with dry beach sand. Turning it upside down, all she got was a big, loose mound. Being a natural problem solver, she didn't whine or ask for help. She looked around and noticed some children near the water who were using wet sand to build their castles. She walked over, lifted handfuls of heavy muck into the pail, and turned it over once more. This time nothing happened. The muck stayed cemented to the pail. Not ready to give up, she dug the wet glop out and discovered somewhere in between the ocean and the dry sand, a section of damp sand. When she filled the bucket this time, flipped it over, gave it the prescribed three taps, and lifted it with care, she revealed to her surprise a perfectly shaped mound that eventually turned into her first sand castle. Quite on her own, and through play, Emily solved her problem.

This was a learning experience that came about naturally and it would be great if they all worked that way. But they don't, so we need to inject some meaningful play experiences into our kids' lives. When we get past our tendency to view play as something trivial, or as a nice little *extra* that we don't have time for, we see how integral it is to healthy development. In addition to teaching, play reduces stress and it opens the mind to creativity. All of these things make play a wise choice for educating children about character.

Developing Character Through Play

We have always felt a special interest and affinity for monster remedies before and since writing *Playful Parenting*. In that book, one activity tickled the fancy of many people and to this day has drawn laughs and exclamations of thanks and praise from parents and children alike. It is called Monster Spray. And as you might expect it dissolves "monsters" on contact. It is just a simple spray bottle filled with "magic" water. With a few spritzes under the bed and in the closet by the fearful child—*poof!*—the *child* makes the monsters disappear! Well, we have another monster remedy to share, a true story, which we believe argues the point for play as a method to build character skills better than we could.

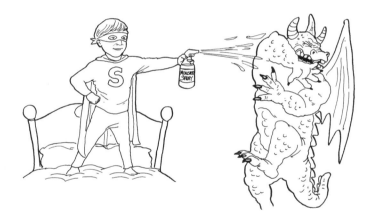

Four-year-old Roy developed a paralyzing fear of monsters. His mother tried using logic on her son, but he didn't want to hear that monsters don't exist. In fact, his mother's assurances made things worse because they convinced Roy that nobody understood him. Eventually he stopped complaining about monsters, but his fear grew worse. He couldn't sleep at night and he was afraid to try new things. The monster fear was invading his life and overall character-skill development as he felt unable to draw upon his courage and problem-solving skills to overcome this challenge. That's when his mother got playful. She decided that to help a child, you had to think like a child. She told her son that monsters don't eat children, but they do like raisins. Every night for a week, Roy went to bed clutching a handful of raisins. And in the morning, the raisins would be gone (courtesy of Mom, who'd pry her son's fist open each night).

Eventually Roy's entire demeanor changed, partly because he felt his mother believed him, but also because he was finally in control of the situation. Roy stopped seeing monsters. The best thing about the whole experience happened a few years later when Roy's little sister caught the monster frights. "Don't worry," Roy said to his sister, "did you know that monsters don't eat people? They eat raisins! Come with me, I'll show you what to do!" He turned to his mother and winked. Roy had developed courage and the ability to problem solve. On top of that, he had acquired empathy for his sister. And he built these important character skills through play.

That's what becoming playwise is about—gaining wisdom from play. Sometimes it happens naturally, as with Emily and her sand castles. Other times it takes more thought, as with Roy and the monsters. Most of the time it's up to the parent to create the play experience.

The activities in this book will provide a map for character development and emotional intelligence. We will show you ways to inject the five foundations to character and the seven character skills listed above into your children's lives through hundreds of practical and enjoyable activities. These hands-on life lessons will fuel your children's interest in their inner selves and personal skills, reinforce their self-worth, and enable you to have a terrific time being playwise together.

How to Use This Book

Because we understand how valuable your time is, we've constructed *Playwise* to be a ready reference. The material is organized into groups of closely knit foundations of character development and character skills that have practical application.

Part one (Chapters One through Five) describes these five foundations of character: knowledge and awareness, inspiration and modeling, stability and balance, unconditional love and acceptance, and family and community connections.

Part two (Chapters Six through Twelve) describes these character skills: personal potential, social harmony, self-awareness, sensibility, happiness, resolution, resourcefulness, and humanity.

Each chapter begins with a straightforward introduction about what you need to know to understand what is important about the character skill being discussed. We've developed a comprehensive but readable developmental table (for Chapters Six through Twelve only) that provides guidelines that will help keep your expectations in line with your child's age and developmentally determined characteristics. Use this table in combination with the descriptive information about the foundations of character development or character skill to help you evaluate the ability level in your child. These will help you prioritize which skills or foundations to focus upon, and help you organize what you already know about your child.

Remember, each child is unique, endowed with his or her own strengths, vulnerabilities, and gifts. This book is about making the most of those natural endowments, and overcoming natural deficits. Pay attention to who your child is. Inventory your child's skills and areas of need; then integrate what you know about his or her demeanor and style.

The chapter then continues, and the part you (and most definitely your child) will like the best comes next, the character-building activities. Each chapter offers between fifteen and forty activities that will playfully and proactively enhance the foundation and/or character development in your child. We describe the activity, clarify purpose, and identify appropriate ages for each.

Additionally, sprinkled in the margins throughout this book are enlightening stories about young heroes who show, through their actions and deeds, well-developed character skills at an impressively young age. These true stories come from a nonprofit organization called the Giraffe Project, which inspires people to *stick their necks out* for the common good. This organization has interviewed hundreds of people, of all ages, who are wonderful role models and a source of inspiration for children and adults alike. Use these stories to help keep your optimism about the potential of our children. Please take the time to read them to your children to inspire them as well. For more information regarding the Giraffe Project and their character-building curriculum for schools see page 279 in the Appendix.

We urge you to take a look at the Appendix at the end of the book prior to beginning your readings. Become familiar with this material because it contains some very helpful lists and information, including an extensive list of children's books that reinforce and help teach particular character skills.

And without further ado, let the character training *begin!* Play hard and have fun!

I

Foundations of Character Development

Knowledge

Knowledge is like eyeglasses for the mind: it clarifies personal experience, sharpens interpretations, and helps people focus on the world around them. Children build knowledge by interpreting their experiences and forming opinions. They store newfound knowledge for later use, retrieve it, apply it to the next situation, reinterpret it, and store it again. Each time children go through this process, they refine their understanding.

Children have a natural appetite for information, which is evident in their never-ending attempts to satisfy their curiosity. If we consider curiosity the seed of learning, it follows that it must be nurtured and fed in order to grow. Parents and other important adults are the ones who prepare the ground for a fertile learning environment. Your child's knowledge blossoms when you establish an open, noncritical learning atmosphere in your home. In this setting, your child feels good about learning. Remember that the learning process goes on twenty-four hours a day, seven days a week, throughout your child's life. It's not limited to scheduled lessons or school hours.

Nor does learning stop after a student graduates from school. There are opportunities to learn throughout life (consider the amount of information that a new parent learns during the first few weeks at home with baby). However, many adults don't take advantage of these opportunities. They close themselves to new knowledge, ending the learning process in early adulthood. Individuals who remain active knowledge seekers constantly refine their understanding of intangibles such as morality and love. The happy result is a richer, fuller life, one that serves as a model for young people.

The learning process starts with information input, but don't treat your child as a computer and simply enter data. A child must test out new information. That's why it's never enough to simply tell your toddler, "Don't climb onto the kitchen counter." He has to know what will happen if he does. Knowledge is forged from instruction and observation and honed through experience. For example, a child is told how to swing at a baseball. She tries and misses. Finally, she connects with the ball. The crack of the bat and the sensation of the impact is what clinches the lesson for her.

Learning is developmentally dependent, particularly in the early years when children leap from one new and exciting cognitive stage to the next (this is why infant and child development is first measured in weeks, then months, and eventually in years). Age affects how much a child knows and how she learns as well as the type of information she can comprehend. However, each child has a unique learning style with areas of strength and weakness. Some learn best through structured lessons while others do better when material is presented in a visual or demonstrative way. Learning requires effort and patience. Children need to know that effort is the path toward mastery, and that mastery is one of life's greatest pleasures.

With knowledge

- children can make better decisions. They use their knowledge to accurately assess a situation, visualize a goal, and figure out how to reach it—a series of actions that can occur in less than a second. They draw upon this knowledge again and again throughout childhood.

- children can interpret what goes on around them and understand their own thoughts, feelings, and behaviors.

- children can develop courage to work through fears ("Monsters are not real and that means there can be no monsters under my bed") and anxiety ("I know enough to get me through my first day at school").

- children can make split-second decisions rather than draw hasty conclusions, even under difficult circumstances such as a medical or fire emergency, or pressure from peers.

- children ask questions and challenge information that does not make sense or feels wrong, and develop high standards for truth. They trust their primary caregivers with sensitive and difficult subjects because they are convinced their questions will be answered honestly.

- children know the joy of feeling the pieces click into place—that moment of awareness when they say, "Aha! I get it!!!" In this moment, they realize learning is a self-affirming act and they thirst for more.

- children receive confidence and self-esteem, both of which fuel the child's drive to learn more. Knowledge is self-multiplying, because with it comes awareness of how much more there is to learn, as well as an appreciation for how much adults know.

- children possess something that cannot be taken away, something that can be embraced during difficult times.

Without knowledge

- children are likely to act impulsively, making hasty decisions without considering the consequences.

- children rely solely upon their intuition or direction provided by others.

- children may distort information, which may lead to misunderstandings, confusion, and fear. When children rely on faulty information, they may fail at a task, leading them to conclude that the information, rather than their interpretation, is bad.

How to Enhance Knowledge to Build Your Child's Character

- Be conscious of what you teach and how you teach it. Remember the adage about practicing what you preach. How many children of smokers listen to their parents' warnings not to pick up the habit themselves?

- Be mindful of your children's limitations. Consider what information your children can manage at their age and the best ways to convey it. Think back to your own childhood and try to remember what worked best for you.

- Become an expert on your child's unique learning style, strengths, and weaknesses. Be an unobtrusive observer. Watch him tackle a new task, assemble a toy, or explain how something works. Note when he becomes frustrated and gives up and when he glows with the pride of accomplishment. What was he working on each time? How did he approach each task?

- ◆ Emphasize learning over acquiring information. If you create a climate of openness and excitement, you will teach your child to love the process of mastering new things. Success is a powerful motivator; a child who learns through experience knows the pleasure of figuring something out. This child will never be short on motivation.

- ◆ Know yourself and your own motives. Are you helping your child learn something that meets his needs or yours? Hint: If your child is fighting you every step of the way, there may be something wrong.

- ◆ Control access to the information gateway. Just as you wouldn't hand the car keys over to your eight-year-old, you shouldn't give your child unlimited access to television, movies, video games, and computer on-line services.

- ◆ Consider your child's home and school environments as well as her learning style, age, and development.

- ◆ Children need to see their parents as teachers who are always willing to teach, who seek opportunities to keep learning fluid, and who consistently work toward finding answers. This belief gives children confidence in you and your ability to help them.

Activities That Enhance Knowledge

The Family Book of Knowledge

All ages   *A record book of information learned*

We're learning all the time. Our knowledge base expands each time we pick up a newspaper or debate a point with a friend. Our children have school-structured learning experiences. But as with adults, the most enduring lessons for children are those they stumble upon in unexpected places.

The Family Book of Knowledge helps your kids keep track of the learning process.

Use a large notebook to record all types of learning, facts, insights, realizations, etc. Include the practical (how to make a peanut butter sandwich), as well as the academic (the square root of seven; Ben Franklin's birthdate). It might be helpful to divide the book into categories, such as "facts about our world," "how things work," "facts about people," and "interesting information about our family." Consider customizing your book with chapters that pertain to you and your children's special interests, such as "great new music," "animals," and "baseball."

Treat the book like a journal: set aside times to discuss and record new learning and leave the book out for spontaneous entries. Date each entry. Your children will be fascinated to see how and when they learned various bits of knowledge. When they flip back through the Family Book of Knowledge, they'll be astounded by the sheer volume of information and proud to have this concrete symbol of their vast knowledge.

The Family Encyclopedia

A scrapbook of learning projects   All ages

This is the final repository for all those school reports, essays, homework papers, and newspaper clippings you and your children keep bringing home. Your Family Encyclopedia is similar to the Book of Knowledge, but is a scrapbook of your family's work and interests rather than a record of learned facts and skills.

Fill it with schoolwork as well as magazine and newspaper articles that reflect a family member's interest. Include your own work projects and hobbies. Model your encyclopedia on the traditional kind by organizing the contents into categories, such as "reports about family life," or "different cultures," or "holidays."

Your family can use the encyclopedia as a source of learning or inspiration. Keep this scrapbook within your children's reach so they can flip through it and admire or critique their own work.

Things-I-Know Book

An annual review of your child's physical and intellectual accomplishments   All ages

Begin a family ritual on your child's birthday by recording all the things he learned over the past year. This differs from the Family Book of Knowledge in that you review the last twelve months to assess what your child has learned.

Sit down together and recall physical feats, intellectual growth, and bits of knowledge your child acquired since his last birthday. Record it all in the book, then tuck it away until the following year. On each birthday make a new entry, and read the old ones.

The Family Library

2 years and up *A collection of your family's favorite books*

Even before we became parents, we began collecting children's books we loved. These span many themes. Some are heartwarming, others thought provoking. All are wonderful.

Our collection is enormous, and in constant circulation. Reading is a daily event in our family. It's something we can do together and an excellent way to teach our children about the world. Reading bridges entertainment and education.

We have so many books that the great little books got lost in the piles of great big books. Eventually, we organized a minilibrary. The books are shelved by category, such as "animals," "family life," "friends," "feelings," "funny stories," "being different," "you can do it!" (we review dozens of books a year on building self-esteem and personal triumph, so you can imagine how many we have on this subject), "scary themes," "holidays," and more. It's not the Dewey decimal system, but it's easier to find the book we're looking for.

You may want to round out your library with maps and a globe.

Library Love and Appreciation

All ages *Foster appreciation for your community library*

It's remarkable when you consider the treasure trove of information that sits in just about every community. If your children frequently mine the library for the riches it holds, they'll develop a reading habit that will last a lifetime.

It's easy to take a library for granted. To help your children appreciate how precious your library is, teach them to invest in it.

Each year, buy a few books to donate to the library. Or your child may want to give the library a few of his own books that are still in good shape. Help your library raise money by lending a hand with fund-raisers or join its expansion committee to plot out future growth.

Make sure your children understand that it's important to share their time, talents, and resources with the library, just as the library shares its knowledge with them.

Author, Author . . . Thank You for Your Great Book

Write to the author of your child's favorite book

4 years and up

Writers of children's books put in a lot of time and thought to create a story that your child will enjoy. Encourage your child to express her appreciation by writing a letter to or drawing a picture for the author of her favorite book. Address the letter to the author in care of the book's publisher and write the name of the book on the envelope. Authors love getting letters from their fans and usually write back, which will be a real treat for your child.

I Wonder

Probe your child's knowledge and ignite her curiosity about all those things you've always wondered about

All ages

On a long car trip, at the dinner table, or whenever you have time to sit and talk, give your child a crack at answering a few of those questions that have always bugged you.

Begin each sentence with "I wonder . . ." For example, "I wonder who invented pizza," or "I wonder how many teeth dogs have." (Consider your child's age when posing a question and let her use her own brain to come up with the answer.) See how your child answers,

> When eleven-year-old Janine Givens and Lee Palmer found out that their town wouldn't allow them unrestricted access to the library because they were not yet in seventh grade, they were perplexed. After all, they had always been told that learning had no boundaries.
>
> Janine and Lee circulated a petition among elementary school students urging the Library Board of Trustees in Andover, Massachusetts, to change its rules. The children were ignored. Undeterred, they turned to the media. They argued their case in radio, television, and newspaper interviews. Their campaign caught the attention of the Massachusetts Civil Liberties Union, which threw its support behind the children. Finally, four months after they started their effort, Janine and Lee succeeded in getting the library's policy changed.

and then switch, so she's the one doing the asking. Write down the "wonders" that you were not able to answer and try the next activity.

Wisdom Quest

2 years and up   *Spend a day researching a topic*

On a wisdom quest, you select a topic to explore with your child. If he's been wondering how a television works, spend the day researching the question. This may mean borrowing library books, examining your television, or scheduling a trip to the local cable television or news station. Even a look at the satellite dishes and television towers outside the station will be meaningful to your child. Take pictures and notes, then enter the findings and photos in your Family Book of Knowledge or Family Encyclopedia. Have your child share the information with someone who did not join the quest, such as a grandparent or a friend.

In the summer of 1990, high school junior Camellia Elantably took one look at her senior English reading list and decided the school system needed as much educating as she did. Of the fifteen writers listed, only two were women, and they were "optional." Not only was Camellia denied permission to substitute women authors for half of the books, the superintendent of schools told her that there are no good books by women because they are not writers by nature.

Camellia boycotted the English class as well as another one that deemphasized the contributions of women. Instead, she designed her own gender-balanced independent study course. This wasn't the first time Camellia protested sex discrimination in the curriculum. As a sophomore, she replaced her English class with her own program. The risk in taking such a stand was that Camellia might not have been able to graduate with her class. However, shortly before graduation, she and her faculty sponsor negotiated a compromise with the administration and Camellia got her diploma. Camellia's conviction has set an example for other young people and, one hopes, for the school system in her hometown.

Cultural differences are good fuel for a wisdom quest. Find out why Jewish people celebrate Hanukkah, or why some people eat Chinese food with chopsticks.

Anything can be turned into a quest for knowledge. Have you ever wondered how pencils are made, how people learn to juggle, or what the difference is between real and man-made diamonds? Grab your kids and find out.

Dictionary Dining

4 years and up   *Build vocabulary during dinner*

Throw out that faded wax fruit centerpiece and replace it with a dictionary. During meals, take turns selecting words and reading their definitions. Practice using the words throughout the meal in serious as well as humorous ways.

That's-Amazing Refrigerator Facts

Post newly learned facts on your refrigerator

3 years and up

Have plenty of magnets on hand for this activity. Select an interesting fact (from the newspaper, a magazine, or something you learned from television, school, etc.) or point of interest every week and post it on the refrigerator. Turn this into a family ritual so even kids too young to read will look forward to the latest fact. You'll probably want to put your older children in charge of finding each week's fact.

Wisdom Warriors

Show your appreciation for those who inspire your children

4 years and up

When Denise was in fourth grade, she had a bright and enthusiastic teacher who believed in every one of her students. Ms. Terchin fostered a lifelong love of learning in Denise simply by having faith in her.

If your child is lucky enough to have a wisdom warrior like Ms. Terchin, tell the teacher how great she is. Teachers need to know their impact on children and parents need to give them their thanks.

Anybody can be a wisdom warrior. Each week, review with your child the people in your family, community, nation, or world who have shared important information. This could be the police officer who talked about bicycle safety at school or a Nobel Prize–winning physicist who shared her research with the world. Write to your wisdom warrior with thanks for teaching your family something new, or recognize this person privately with your children by discussing the knowledge he or she has shared. (And a special thank-you to Ms. Terchin and teachers like her who bring wisdom to our children with enthusiasm and encouragement.)

Family Show-and-Tell

A regularly scheduled time for family members to show off something newly learned

3 years and up

Take time each week to have a family show-and-tell where everyone takes a turn showing off a new skill or piece of knowledge learned over the week. Make sure you, the adult, take a turn. Consider using your time in the spotlight to pass along some valuable information, such as, instead of buying prepared whipped cream or butter, show and tell your child how to make it from scratch.

The Specialist

3 years and up   *Designate each family member an expert at something*

Every person is especially good at something. Find and nurture the specialty of each member of your family, whether it be physically, intellectually, or emotionally oriented. Do this by giving specialty-enhancing birthday and holiday gifts that may include classes and workshops.

You may want to expand your circle of specialists by including extended family members and friends. This way, you'll have more opportunity to encourage relationships among cospecialists, such as a child and a grandparent who share an interest in sewing, cooking, or even juggling.

Be sure everyone is aware of each family member's specialty so they can solicit help when needed. Not only is it wonderful to recognize individuals for their personal points of excellence, but being considered an expert at something boosts self-esteem.

The Learning and Homework Center

4 years and up   *A special place for your child to do schoolwork*

If you want your child to take homework seriously, *you* have to take it seriously. One way to do this is to regard homework as at least as important as an adult's professional work. You will send your child this message by setting up an office to do homework.

Put it anywhere away from high-traffic areas and distractions. You don't want your child on the main route to the refrigerator or within viewing distance of the television when she's trying to solve math problems.

Make the area feel like a real workplace by furnishing it with office equipment. Here is a list of materials that we have found particularly attractive to children:

1. A desk with lots of drawers, files, and compartments. Fill the top drawer with pencils, pens, markers, crayons, and art supplies such as glue and scissors. Fill other drawers with a writing pad and colored paper, folders, index cards, and whatever else seems appropriate.

2. Hang a calendar on the wall.

3. Equip the desk with a children's dictionary and a thesaurus.

4. Include special touches, perhaps a tape recorder, a desk set with pen holder, or an inscribed nameplate. We also found that kids love appointment books.

Once the office is decked out, encourage your child to use it for homework. You might have your own office or area of the house where you pay the bills or do job-related work. By using your office for these tasks, you are modeling consistent work habits for your child.

Show your child how to be businesslike about schoolwork by planning out a weekly homework schedule in the appointment book. Let your child know that homework is his responsibility, but that you are available for help. Then pencil in times when you are available to tutor. That way, your child won't expect you to come to the rescue if he waits until the last minute to ask for help with an assignment. This will reinforce the consequences of not taking responsibility for homework.

A Family's Love of Learning

Fun learning games   4 years and up

Children are born to learn. But that innate curiosity can wilt if it isn't nurtured. Families that value education produce lifelong learners. The child who discovers early that the world is an endlessly engaging puzzle to be solved is a child who will always be motivated to learn.

The following games will provide you with several fun ways to make learning a family priority. Most importantly, your child will witness you learning and enjoying it, and will ultimately enjoy learning, too.

Get hold of your child's school curriculum, including specific themes and agendas so you can incorporate these topics into your family learning adventures. Have regular discussions with your child's teacher to find out how she is doing in school and what she needs to know for each subject. Now you're ready to turn your home into a learning environment of fun and games. Here are a few suggestions:

The Family Wheel of Fortune: Create television game shows modeled after *Wheel of Fortune, Jeopardy,* and PBS's *Where in the World Is Carmen Sandiego?* Questions should reflect what your child is studying in school. Take turns being the contestants, and don't forget to award prizes, such as a trip to the science museum or the local ice cream shop. (See pages 276–77 for a list of catalogs that sell academically focused games.)

Family Learning Adventures: Take your child on a family field trip related to a subject he is studying in school. Be creative and seek out places and activities that students wouldn't ordinarily visit on a school trip.

Family School Days: Make learning a family affair by taking a class together. Choose a subject you can study together, such as American Sign Language or conversational French. Learn to play the same musical instrument or take a course in astronomy. You can even take a crafts class together, like knitting, pottery, or painting. Most importantly, serve as a model student for your child. Show by example how to listen in class, ask questions, plan, and study. Your child will pick up your habits and enthusiasm. If possible, plan vacations or weekend activities that are related to your classes. For example, travel to a Spanish-speaking country or local community if you are studying Spanish.

Museum Magic

2 years and up   *Explore art museums with fun and learning in mind*

While writing this book, we met an interesting couple. Allen was the past director of the Museum of Fine Arts in Boston and is now the deputy director of the National Gallery in Washington, D.C. Nancy was a high school teacher for twenty years, became a lawyer, and now specializes in representing immigrants seeking asylum because of torture in their homeland. Allen and Nancy shared with us ways to use art museums to build character and teach life lessons. For instance, many museums have galleries specializing in artwork of one culture. These will enrich your child's understanding of other cultures and give him pride and insight into his own. There are obvious ways museums can be used as learning environments, but art museums are often overlooked. Use exhibits to show your child how artists interpret the same subject differently. Choose paintings of women from different periods and examine the ways these portrayals changed over the years. Have your child look at a few different styles of painting and see if there is one that interests him.

A Museum in My Bedroom

5 to 12 years   *Set up a private museum*

After visiting a museum, help your child turn a corner of her room into an exhibition site. Your child will be curator of the exhibit, which can be anything from a model car to a miniature solar system.

Encourage your child to be creative with the displays. If she's showing dinosaurs, help her build a landscape for them. Label the creatures and post fact cards about the various aspects of dinosaurs.

Have your child take you and others on a guided tour of the museum and rotate the exhibits so they change monthly. You can use the same museum concept for art. Just use your child's wall space to display her original art as well as reproductions of favorite works.

The Knowing Place
A special place to talk

2 years and up

Designate with your child a special spot to discuss important issues and share knowledge. Your knowing place can be a couch, a kitchen chair, in a den, or underneath a favorite tree in your yard or a park.

When your child asks a question that deserves a well-thought-out answer, such as, "Why do you have to go to work every day?" take her to the knowing place before answering. This acknowledges the importance of the information being shared. Children's questions aren't always easy to answer. It is important that we recognize the times they deserve our undivided attention.

The Parent-Teacher Connection
Establish a resource center for parents and teachers

5 years and up

Encourage respect between parents and teachers by spearheading a drive to create a parent-teacher resource center. A school library may be willing to donate a shelf or two that you can stock with donated books on parenting, health, medicine, and other subjects that help us all teach and raise happy, healthy children. Consider, too, establishing a fund to buy new books or to pay for workshops for teachers and parents.

By seeing this collaboration, your child will appreciate the importance of working together for a common cause.

Get the Facts

2 years and up *Say only what you know and show by example how to seek out the facts*

This is an activity for both you and your child. Sometimes we get carried away by our egos and rush to answer a question without really knowing the answer. Swallow your pride and establish a family policy stating that any and all information shared among members will be strictly factual. Facts are easy to find. Call a friend, go to the library, get on-line, but get the facts. This shows your child that it's smarter to admit when you *don't* know something . . . yet. Even more important is that you won't be steering your child wrong with incorrect information.

Things-You-Should-Know Memo

Ages 4 and up *Put important instructions in writing*

There are things children *must* know, like what to do if the house catches fire, and there are things your child *should* know, like how to use the stove, answer the phone, or do the laundry. Instructions for life's big and little challenges can be written out in the form of a memo. Make these simple, not lecturing, and to the point, item by item.

Things-you-should-know memos can be given directly to your child to be put in a book (see Family Book of Knowledge, page 6) or posted on the object it is intended for. For instance, the phone or laundry basket.

By the age of twelve, Aja Henderson of Baton Rouge, Louisiana, was a seasoned reader—a girl well acquainted with the pleasure a good story can bring. But instead of retreating into the pages of her books, Aja reached out and shared her love with other children, by convincing her family to turn their den into a public library.

The library is open daily and at all hours with Aja and her mother serving as librarians. For the children in her neighborhood, the library has become an alternative to using drugs and getting in trouble.

After five years, Aja's library grew to three thousand titles. The number of lives she has influenced remains countless.

Here's an example: A memo on how to answer the door would read, 1) Do not open door without seeing and hearing who wants to enter. 2) Do not open door if you do not know who it is. 3) If you know who it is, check with a parent to see if it is okay to open the door. 4) If parent is not home, then you may open door for: (list names of acceptable people).

Use humor when demonstrating a new memo. Even serious topics can be presented with a hint of fun. For instance, use a funny voice to pretend to be a stranger at the door and give your child the opportunity to practice how to respond. The memos themselves can be a source of humor if you give them out for silly topics, such as "How to give the best-ever good-night hugs," or "Six easy steps for removing toilet paper from the roll." These memos can become a significant communication channel between you and your children. But beware you may someday receive one from your daughter, say, on the proper way for a parent to act on the occasion of her first date.

Kiddie College

Prepare your child for a new experience   3 to 12 years

When your child is about to do something new, such as starting school or being admitted to the hospital, educate her beforehand in the same way we do young adults before they enter the workforce: send her to college. Kiddie College can be in session anytime, anywhere.

Little kids love playing school and it's an effective, nonthreatening way to prepare them for an upcoming event.

As your child's college professor, present clever, imaginative lessons that will really stick. The college experience can include "textbooks" (storybooks related to the topic) and an "internship" (visit the new school or hospital). On graduation day, issue your child a diploma and throw a party. The graduation gift should be related to your child's "major," such as a new suitcase for a hospital stay or a pencil case for school.

Your child's major doesn't have to be, well, *major.* You can send him to Kiddie College to learn how to bathe correctly, to go to bed on his own, or to behave properly at a wedding. Keep in mind that a Kiddie College graduate makes an ideal teacher later for a younger brother or sister who is facing a similar challenge.

Everyday Praise

Just what it sounds like   All ages

Don't let a day go by without praising those who enrich your lives. Don't overlook people who make your family knowledge grow such as child-care workers, the high school girl who baby-sits, the neighbor who bakes wonderful cookies or grows beautiful gardens. Children need to know that you respect knowledge no matter what form it comes in. Recently when a twelve-year-old boy named Matthew shoveled snow from our driveway, we paid him a little extra and complimented him in front of our children for doing such a thorough job. A few weeks later, while taking a walk after a snowstorm, our youngest stopped a gentleman shoveling his driveway and said, "You are very good at shoveling, did you learn how to shovel from Matthew?"

Balance and Stability

It's breakfast. You pour your child a heaping bowl of M&Ms and a glass of lemonade to wash it down. Lunchtime rolls around, so you bring out a couple gallons of ice cream and tell your child to dig in. For dinner, you're too tired for anything fancy, so you slap together a couple of marshmallow-and-potato-chip sandwiches. You figure that'll be enough, because after all, your child has been snacking on jelly beans all day.

Okay, that isn't you up there. In fact, that's nobody at all (except maybe your child's fantasy parent). Why? Because we know it's important to eat a balanced diet. What we tend to forget is the importance of balancing other areas of our lives as well. Most of us get so wrapped up in the daily business of living that we neglect to monitor our internal scales. Before we know it, our responsibilities have grown so heavy that we're out of kilter. The result: we're stressed out, cranky, or worse, physically ill.

Just as you balance your diet, strive to balance your emotional, spiritual, physical, and intellectual selves. Balance allows an individual to spring back from setbacks, move in new directions, and refocus energy.

For a child, balance is a proportionate mix of freedom and structure. The proportions change as the child matures, but the need to maintain the balance between the two remains constant. For example, the two-year-old craves freedom and autonomy while the seven-year-old thrives when rules and structure temper her newfound independence. Children need a mix of responsibility, discipline, frivolity, imagination, competition, cooperation, socialization, time alone, time with peers, excitement, peace, success, failure, frustration, physical challenges, and intellectual stimulation. When one area outweighs the others, the child may become confused and stressed. We have counseled children who have become so involved in sports and supposedly fun extracurricular activities that they have the stress level of a Wall Street investment banker. Figuring out the right mix of freedom and structure can be baffling. When considering a new activity or commitment for your child such as joining a youth group or participating in sports think about:

1. the child's age and developmental abilities

2. the child's disposition and current needs

3. practical matters such as scheduling conflicts

4. the bigger picture—how this activity or change will complement the other day-to-day aspects of the child's life

5. the needs of the entire family and how other members will be affected by this change

If saying no or imposing structure touches a raw nerve from your childhood, remember that setting limits and routines provides an external shaping and an internal sense of security and safety for a child.

Families require balance, too. This may mean there will be times when the needs of one person supersede those of another, and vice versa. For example, eight-year-old Sam may be asked to entertain his little sister while Mom cooks the family's dinner. This sort of sharing provides opportunities for others to shine (eleven-year-old Danny stops on the way to the kitchen to ask if anyone else wants a snack). A parent can also help a child reach an inner balance by showing that while he is certainly not the center of the universe, he certainly is a shining star. A child learns patience when his needs are balanced against those of others. The child who watches his baby sister for ten minutes while Mom cooks will come to understand there is more to life than his agenda.

With stability and balance

◆ children develop emotional intelligence and feel secure enough to stretch their limits, invite new experiences, and cope. Observable behaviors are the look of determination on the face of a child who is summoning up courage to face a challenge, the serene expression of a child who is enjoying her own company, or the pride in a child who has completed a task for the first time.

- children reflect their environment. Stable, well-balanced homes produce well-balanced children who weather change and hardship well.

- a stable child can deal with a lost basketball game, a squabble with a friend, or a difficult academic subject. Even life-altering catastrophes such as divorce or death of a loved one can become manageable.

- children think through problems and make better decisions. They remain true to themselves when their integrity and character are challenged.

Without stability and balance

- children are likely to feel anxious. Children whose lives suddenly change, say through a move out of state, may act unpredictably or out of control. They may be self-centered, moody, argumentative, and have a low tolerance for frustration.

- children who are pushed too hard to excel in one area (a promising gymnast training for stardom) may risk underdeveloping some other important skills and aptitudes—a potentially unhealthy way for a child to live.

- children may become emotionally askew, confused, or spoiled. Too little guidance and too few limits lead to a distorted sense of power. Too much structure and too many limits erode a child's self-esteem and confidence.

How to Enhance Stability and Balance to Build Your Child's Character

- Keep a clear head about the "big picture" in regard to your child's current and future lifestyle. Be sure the ebb and flow of his day, week, and year are well balanced and filled with as much excitement and activity as there is down time and relaxation.

- As a parent, you play multiple roles: playmate, disciplinarian, nurturer, teacher, superhero, coach, and role model. Allow your child to witness you in negotiating and balancing each of these roles. Doing so shows your balanced personality.

- Take inventory of your agenda and make sure there is harmony between your mission as a parent and your goals for yourself and your child and your other responsibilities.

◆ Balance your family lifestyle with the right mix of work and play, career and family, pain and joy, solitude and togetherness, reward and punishment. We are whole when we have seen both ends of the spectrum.

Activities That Balance

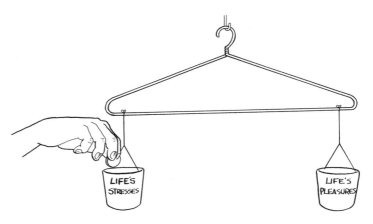

Life Scale

An actual scale to measure life's stresses against its pleasures

Materials:

paper cups or other small containers of equal size, string, clothes hanger, pennies or marbles to use as weights

5 years and up

This activity will help your children understand the need for a balanced schedule. Begin by having all participants list their activities, commitments, and daily responsibilities on sheets of paper. Activities should include structured ones, such as dance class and Boy Scouts, as well as the unstructured ones, such as watching television. Commitments would include visiting relatives and helping friends. Daily responsibilities are things like school, work, and chores. Next to each item, place a positive or negative symbol to indicate whether it is stressful or pleasurable. You can help your children think of their activities, but let them decide for themselves how each one makes them feel.

To assemble your life scale, use the string to hang paper cups from opposite ends of the clothes hanger. Label one container Life's Stresses, the other Life's Pleasures. Hang the scale from a pole or long hook so it balances freely.

Each penny or marble will represent an item from the list. Use masking tape to label each penny with its corresponding stress or pleasure. Each person takes a turn at the scale, placing each "weight of life" into the appropriate container. When all the weights have been placed, look at the scale. Is it balanced? If so, great. But if it is tipped by stress, discuss what you need to do to restore equilibrium to your life. You may have to remove some sources of stress. For example, nine-year-old Sally's schedule fills up faster than a corporate executive's. There's soccer practice, tennis lessons, and art classes, not to mention her responsibilities at home and school. Ironically, her fun pursuits have become a source of stress because there are too many of them. If Sally eliminates one of the activities, the others might become more pleasurable.

After everyone has examined their life's balance, combine all of the weights into a pile to measure the family's as a whole. Decide together which category each stress or pleasure belongs in. If your family is under too much stress, work together to balance the scale. If pleasure dominates, don't change a thing.

Too Many Pots on the Stove

Bring a well-turned phrase to life

5 years and up

Denise had a high school health teacher who transformed the expression "too many pots on the stove" into a memorable life lesson. Here's how it unfolded: The students were instructed to report to the home economics kitchen for class that day instead of the usual classroom. Denise and her classmates walked into the room to find their teacher boiling up eight pots of water on two stoves. With the steam rising behind her, the teacher began talking calmly about how too many pressures and responsibilities (represented by the pots) can cause stress, which adversely affects human functions (represented by the burners).

As the teacher lectured, she kept adding pots of water to the overcrowded stoves, sliding the boiling pots off the burners to heat up the new ones. She began muttering to herself about how some pots would just have to go cold while she tended to the others. Then she turned off the burners under two of the pots and began running around frantically, trying to keep her pots of water boiling. She turned off more burners and became increasingly overwhelmed. By the end of this life lesson, the health teacher had fifteen pots of water to boil and only one burner working.

With this exercise, the teacher turned a worn-out phrase into vivid theater that illustrated a body's limits. If you have a flair for the dramatic, try this lesson at home (you don't have to use a real stove to make your point). Ask your children to assign their own stresses to the pots and human functions and needs to the burners.

Spinning Human Tops

3 to 10 years *Demonstrates the dizzying effect of too much activity*

Little kids love to spin around in circles until they feel dizzy. Use this to show your child how muddled he can become by overstimulation.

Tell your child to spin to the speed of your voice. The faster you talk, the faster he will turn. Begin by talking slowly and calmly about a regular routine in your child's life, one that is evenly paced with equal parts responsibility and fun. Stop talking and ask how dizzy your child feels. Then give a rapid-fire recitation of an unstructured day that is jammed full of activities and re-sponsibilities. Your child should be spinning like a dervish at this point, so much so that at the end of this "day," standing will be out of the question.

Talk with your child about the experience and think of ways to stop a too-busy day from spinning out of control. Ask your child to do the same for you. You may be surprised by your child's version of a too busy/dizzy day for you.

Parent for the Day

5 to 12 years *Swap roles with your child*

You and your child have fallen under an ancient and mysterious spell that has switched your roles for several hours or a full day. You are the child. The child is the parent. Don't panic, enjoy the fantasy. Your child surely will.

Let your child plan the day, but provide a list of things that need to be done, such as laundry, housecleaning, and preparing meals. Have your child give you a list of things you need to do. At the end of this activity, discuss your experiences.

Plan and Prepare

2 years and up *Discuss the day's events with your child*

In some ways, a family is like a business. It operates most smoothly when everyone is working cooperatively. The skilled business manager unifies the work force through good planning, which requires accurate predictions of fu-ture challenges. It follows then that a good family manager should take the same approach to her duties at home.

By designing structured activities, daily rituals, and organized routines, you can eliminate conflicts. Think ahead about possible trouble spots. These may be periods when you cannot be flexible and when your child is likely to be cranky. When you have a good sense of your day at a glance, even an es-pecially busy one will feel more manageable.

Prepare your child for the day by explaining exactly what to expect in the next six hours ("First we'll go to the doctor and she will check to see that you're strong and healthy. Then we'll take Spot to the vet and then we'll visit Great-aunt Mimi and she will give you hugs and kisses."). By doing this, you head off the problem behaviors your child may exhibit when confronted with an unexpected change in routine.

Family rituals such as bedtime stories or Friday evening dinners at the local pizza place are other important ways to help your child feel more secure.

Stability and balance are born of routine and predictability. That doesn't mean we can't be spontaneous, merely that we need to know what's happening from one day to the next. Kids, especially, need the security of a routine. The following activities are a fun way to set that routine while teaching your children how to take responsibility for their own time and personal duties.

The What's Next Room Chart
A timeline depicting your child's daily schedule

Tape the paper to your child's walls, then divide it into half-hour segments spanning morning until night. Discuss the normal, daily routine with your child and together, draw pictures of each activity. Cut these out and paste them on the chart in their corresponding time slot. Include as many routines as possible, such as teeth brushing, dressing, and catching the school bus. This will literally give your child a clear picture of what is next in the day, what has to be done and how much time there is to do it. On days when your child's schedule changes, peel off the old activity and replace it with the new one. Each night before bed, go through the next day's schedule by asking your child to recite each activity as it appears on the border.

Materials:
wallpaper border or roll of contact paper or freezer paper long enough to wrap around the walls of your child's bedroom; construction paper

5 to 12 years

The Appointment Book

A daily planner for your child

Materials:
a homemade or store-bought
date book or wall calendar

6 years and up

Most of us feel lost without a visual record of what we have to do and when we have to do it. It is very difficult for anyone, children included, to fulfill daily responsibilities and commitments without planning them out.

Show your child how to maintain a daily planner. On Sunday nights, or more often if you wish, help record your child's upcoming responsibilities. Go through each day, stating times to wake up, catch the bus, and play. Include special chores or projects and help your child think of a plan to get these done on time. You may want to schedule times when you are available to help with homework or projects.

Planners are excellent not only for showing children what is happening day to day and week to week, but for helping them balance their activities. The best way to balance a child's life and reinforce stability is to teach the child how to do it himself.

The Big Family Calendar

All ages *A calendar for the whole family*

If yours is like most families, you probably have a calendar hanging in the kitchen. And we'll wager that it's packed with appointments, birthday parties, and get-togethers. A family calendar is an excellent way to organize time and commitments. The problem with most of them, however, is that the entries are usually indecipherable to all but the person who wrote them. A family calendar isn't truly a family calendar unless everyone can use it. It has to be big enough for everyone's appointments. If you can't buy one that big, make one. Attach a pencil or marker to it with a long string and get each family member to record his or her commitments, practice times, special events, celebrations, and project deadlines. For example, your son has soccer practice each Tuesday, a party invitation for the first Saturday of the month, and a big science project due on the fifteenth. Have him record these dates. And make sure you include your work-related duties so that your children and spouse know your responsibilities and time commitments. You can use family council meetings (page 57) to designate a time for family members to record their needs. In fact, post meeting times on the calendar. By the way, office-supply stores stock extralarge calendars that work really well for family calendars.

Activities That Enhance Stability

The Security Blanket

A safe place to snuggle

All ages

If you or your child ever had a security blanket, you know what a friend that "blankie" was during times of stress. So why is it that you can't wait for your kid to outgrow it? (Probably because it becomes so worn out and tattered that it looks like a poor excuse for a dust rag.)

Well, here's a security blanket that will never be outgrown (and one you can use even in front of the kids). Select with your child a special warm and cozy blanket or comforter in your home that's large enough for the entire family to cuddle under. Designate this as the family security blanket to be used during times of vulnerability, or simply when someone needs a little comfort. Wrap the blanket around those in need and enjoy. Whether it's one or five people under the blanket, make sure you talk with the user(s) about how nice and secure it feels to have a warm and cozy place to go when you're feeling needy. Bring out the blanket to someone who looks as though he needs a little security and offer a few moments of comfort underneath.

NOTE: The blanket can be a real boon when a child is feeling nervous about spending the night away from home.

The Home Security System

A toy security system to ease your child's fears

Materials:
a small box, construction paper and/or markers to decorate it

4 to 12 years

Think of how important it is for you to have a home where you can feel safe. For a child, the need for a secure refuge is doubly important. Young children need to be confident that you have done the most you can to protect their home from harm. Show your child the smoke detectors in your house, the high quality of your locks, and, if you have one, your burglar alarm. Involving your child in the home security process won't be frightening. Rather it will give your child a sense of control while emphasizing your attention to these details. So designate your child "official window checker," or "smoke detector testing assistant."

But keep in mind that children tend to harbor fears about things that we adults have outgrown (well, most of us), such as monsters. And a child's imagination is vivid, so what they see on television (or hear from an older sibling) becomes instant reality. For a young child, the bad guys on TV will be coming through the front door at any minute.

To help your child work through his fears, both real and imaginary, make a child-size home security system. Have your child decorate it to look like an alarm box and add colored round buttons labeled Possible Danger, and Not-Possible Danger. Explain to your child that a possible danger is one that could possibly happen, but there is a plan for handling it, and a not-possible danger is one that simply could not happen under any circumstances.

When your child voices a fear, have him "test" it on the security system by asking whether it's a possible or not-possible danger. If his fear is that the house will catch fire, guide him toward the "possible danger" button then remind him of the precautions you have taken, such as the smoke detectors and your family safety plan (see page 27). If his fear is that a tyrannosaurus rex will march down the street and eat your house, guide him toward the "not-possible danger" button. To put the fear in perspective without belittling it, use humor to explain why it's not possible. Pretend to be the alarm box, for instance, responding *"Beep! Beep!* This machine knows that it is not possible that a tyrannosaurus rex will come to your home and eat your family! *Beep! Beep!* Dinosaurs have been dead for a very long time and are only make-believe in movies. *Beep! Beep!* "

The Emergency-Stabilizer Kit

A kit to hold emergency-response plans

Materials:
index cards, a small box

4 years and up

There are lots of times when family stability is challenged by change. It can be something as important as a new baby or as seemingly trivial as a new guinea pig. These challenges can be less disruptive to your family if you come up with a plan to neutralize their unsettling effects.

The emergency-stabilizer kit encourages your child to prepare for emergencies by planning responses to them. Begin by making an emergency box to store your inventory of "stabilizers," your calm responses to challenging situations. You can use an empty tissue box painted red and labeled Emergency-Stabilizer Kit.

With your family, think of past situations that made family life unstable. These would include times when daily routines were disrupted due to illness, or because the baby-sitter didn't show up. Discuss with your family how you handled each of these situations. Try to think of something you did that seemed to help things go more smoothly. For example, "When Grandpa got really sick, even though Mom was gone a lot we still made sure we always had dinner at the same time." Your commitment to a regular dinner hour was a stabilizer. Write each stabilizer on a separate index card. If there are stabilizers that any of you have seen other families use, write these down as well. Next, discuss future challenges that could affect your family balance and write down possible stabilizers that might help. Place these in your emergency box where they will remain until your family needs some quick ideas for restoring stability during frazzled times. For a real emergency, such as a power failure or a tornado, make a few stabilizers for helping the family cope with the aftereffects. Although it may feel as if you are unnecessarily bringing up an unsettling issue, children are intrigued by talking about challenges such as these and need to know that your family has a plan should such an emergency occur.

Unconditional Love and Acceptance

When we love unconditionally, we love the people for who they are despite what they may do. If we claim to accept our children unconditionally, our actions must prove it.

It's just as important to tend to a child's emotional needs as it is to their physical ones. Just as a child needs to be fed, a child needs to be cuddled. Just as a child needs sleep, a child needs to hear loving words. A child's need for love and acceptance is instinctive and should not fall prey to rationalization and intellectual excuses. Too often people withhold physical and verbal expressions of love because they feel uncomfortable expressing affection. Expressions of this kind are vital—be generous with them. Altruistic love and acceptance convey an indisputable message of value and worth. Children who grow up with this have healthy self-love.

Don't confuse unconditional acceptance with permissive parenting. You should accept your child—not her behavior—unconditionally. Take a moment to look at the lives of children to understand how important their family's love is. At the playground, for instance, kids can subject one another to arbitrary, if not impossible, standards. If you act the right way, you gain acceptance in the group; if you act the wrong way, you are summarily dismissed. A child can do all the right things, but be rejected simply because his hair is red or curly, too short, too long, too brown, or too blond. Children spend a great deal of time among harsh critics whose acceptance they crave.

The classroom can be equally hard on a child's self-love. The very nature of our educational system is judgmental. Children quickly realize they are evaluated not by how much they care about learning, but by how high they score on exams. It doesn't take long before learning becomes secondary to pleasing the teacher.

With this in mind, consider how crucial it is for a child to have a place of refuge. A loving home provides children with serenity and security. It is a reprieve from the pressure to perform and be liked. Home is a place where a child is free to grow.

With unconditional love and acceptance

- children understand there are just consequences for their behavior. This keeps them focused on doing their best and taking responsibility for their actions.

- children don't fear losing their parents' love. This is a destructive concern that makes it harder to focus on responsibilities.

- children feel secure, safe, and validated. Their natural growth process is encouraged, paving the way for them to reach their potential and focus on being the best they can.

- children know where to turn for rest and refueling before jumping back into the judgmental and performance-oriented world of peers, academics, and sports.

- children have an inner peace and empowerment that allows them to take risks (asking another child to join in play, initiating a school project for extra credit, trying out for the hockey team).

- children keep their priorities balanced and maintain a realistic perspective on success. They are not likely to place achievement and material possessions above relationships.

Without unconditional love and acceptance

- children may deduce that love is dependent upon performance and behavior. Then there are two courses their lives may take: 1) They may blame themselves for not being loved. 2) They may become starved for acceptance but scarred by rejection and feelings of inadequacy. They become mistrusting and guarded and give up on love.

◆ children's sense of self-worth is fragile. They perceive even well-intentioned criticism as an assault on their character. Consequently, they become defensive and unable to benefit from criticism.

◆ children become dependent and insecure. Children who constantly have to prove themselves worthy of their parents' love become dependent upon others for approval. They base their opinions of themselves on what others think of them. They are prone to peer pressure because they do not think independently.

◆ children may never reach their full potential. If they don't believe in themselves, they will lack the conviction to press on despite adversity.

How to Enhance Your Unconditional Love for and Acceptance of Your Child

◆ Love, cherish, and accept your children simply because they are your children. They need to know your love is constant and unrelated to their behavior.

◆ This doesn't necessarily mean you have to accept your child's behavior, or stifle your feelings. You can be angry, furious, disappointed, saddened, even appalled with your child's behavior, actions, opinions, or attitudes. Altruistic love and acceptance imply that you consistently find ways to convey to your child that he is loved and accepted.

◆ We convey our love through words and actions. If you are uncomfortable with physical affection, look at your own childhood. If people weren't affectionate with you, then displaying physical affection with your child will be groundbreaking behavior. Be patient with yourself and with your child, who may respond warily. Find activities that allow for comfortable levels of touching, such as playful wrestling matches. If as a child your feelings about touching were ignored, violated, or dealt with insensitively, you will have to work to reach a level of comfort with your own kids. Seeing a therapist who specializes in this area may help you sort through this problem.

◆ If you feel awkward expressing love verbally to your child, again take a look at your childhood. The odds are that your parents had the same difficulty expressing their feelings verbally. Many people attempt to express love by giving gifts, although this is no substitute for expressing love with words and actions. Try writing letters or poems to your child. These acts may lead to a discussion later or they may develop into a warm family ritual. We know a woman who has continued a ritual she began while dating her husband of twenty years. She leaves an affectionate note and sometimes a treat in his lunch box. He then used this same approach to communicate with their teenage daughter when she was struggling with a boyfriend problem and feeling alienated from her parents.

Activities That Enhance Unconditional Love

The Runaway Bunny, by Margaret Wise Brown
Customize this classic storybook of unconditional love

This is a simply told, wonderful tale of a mother bunny's unconditional love for her child. We began reading *The Runaway Bunny* when our children were barely a year old. The story is a short one, so we've taken the liberty of extending it by inventing new scenarios for the little bunny and his mother. We've also added a loving father bunny.

2 to 5 years

This book has become such a part of our lives that when our kids seem upset, we find ourselves slipping into the mother bunny's manner of speaking to offer them reassurances of our love.

One evening Mark had to stay late at the office, so he called the children to say good-night. Arielle must have sensed his guilt at not being home because she told him, "That's okay, even though you had to run away to the office, I will find you and always love you!" The sweet result of unconditional loving is that you get it back.

Gold-Medal Love
Recognize selfless behavior

Hold a weekly gold-medal love award ceremony to honor the family member who gave most lovingly of him- or herself during the past seven days. Fashion the award after an Olympic gold medal and attach the ribbon or yarn so that it can be hung around the neck.

Materials:
cardboard, construction paper and glitter or gold foil paper, yarn or ribbon

3 to 10 years

Each week, select the person who performed the most generous act of loving. It can be something simple, like helping a sibling put on their shoes. Be sure every family member is a regular award recipient, including adults. And from time to time, give the award to a person outside your family, perhaps to a person you don't know, but only have heard about. This way you're acknowledging to your children that loving, good people are all around us.

Family Signature Hugs and Kisses

All ages *Personalized signs of affection*

We have special family hugs and kisses that we consider unique to us. We made them up with our children, and do our Weston hugs and kisses every time we drop our children off at school or simply want to say I love you. One is an air hug that Arielle invented because she didn't like throwing kisses. She squeezes the air as if she is really hugging someone, and we respond by squeezing the air back. Another is the I-love-you hand squeeze. When holding hands with our children we often squeeze their hands gently three times to say I love you. They squeeze back four times to say I love you, too! Make up your own family signature hugs and kisses. You can keep them a secret, or share your idea with other families. It's up to you.

Thanks, I Needed That

All ages *Acknowledge affection*

As parents of young children, we tend to take for granted some of life's little pleasures, like spontaneous hugs and surprise kisses. Then we remind ourselves how special it is to be on the receiving end of such an unself-conscious display of affection. When your children hug or touch you lovingly, tell them how happy it makes you feel. Don't let those small acts of unconditional love go unnoticed.

I-Love-You Tablecloth

Materials: *A family-made tribute*
markers, a tablecloth

All ages Make a special tablecloth for your child to bring out once annually, perhaps on her birthday. Spread it out, and with permanent marker, draw pictures and write about your love for your child. Get the whole family involved, including grandparents, and have everyone mark the tablecloth with a tribute to the child. These can be pictures of an actual event, a symbolic representation of your love, a quick poem, or anything else you can think of to express your true love.

You can save a section of the tablecloth for your child to express her own love for herself. (Get your child accustomed to doing this at a young age, before she becomes self-conscious about expressing a liking for herself.)

Why I Love You
Family members state why they love one another

All ages (yes, even teenagers!)

Bethelena and Timothy Knotts of New Jersey told us about a loving ritual they perform with their four children before they all go to sleep. Every night when they put each child in bed, Mom or Dad asks aloud, "Why do I love you?" then answers with at least three new reasons. Then it's the child's turn to ask himself or herself the same question about Mom and Dad. Bethelena explained that it's a challenge to come up with new "Why I Love You's" every night, but it forces her to remember the finer parts of her day with each child. Of course, Bethelena delights in her children's "Why I Love You" statements, but said that even better is something her children do on their own. For several months now, after she or Tim leaves the room where her two eldest sleep, she can overhear them telling each other, "Why do I love you? Because . . ."

Warm Fuzzies
Fill a prescription for love and comfort

Materials:
a jar, pompom balls

All ages

Wouldn't it be nice if you could buy a jar of warm fuzzy feelings and share them with someone who needs a little loving? Why not make it yourself? With your children, you can make warm fuzzies out of small pompom balls, which are available at any crafts store. Decorate the pompoms with little

smile faces, or leave them as is. Put them in a jar labeled Warm Fuzzies, and write up instructions on how to use them to express your love or cheer someone up. Some situations may require more than one fuzzy, so be sure to include a dosage chart in the instructions. Stick the instructions on the back of the jar, and put it directly in the reach of children so warm fuzzies can be administered whenever needed!

I-Love-You Poems and Songs

Express your love in rhyme

All ages

We both love to make up rhyming poems and silly songs. They're an entertaining way to express our love to our children, and a really special gift when written down and saved.

We suggest that you turn poem and songwriting into a family ritual for special occasions such as birthdays. Keep a scrapbook to store these family poems and lyrics.

I-Love-You Ping-Pong

A lighthearted, slightly silly way to profess your love

All ages

This is a fast-paced game of verbal Ping-Pong in which two players challenge each other to think of different backdrops or environments for their love for one another. Example: The first player says, "I love you on rainy days," the second player returns the serve by responding quickly with something like, "I love you when it snows." The game continues back and forth like a Ping-Pong match until someone misses. You can take this game one step further by coming up with a "theme" for the environment such as, at the circus, in the car, late at night. You and your child have to keep coming up with experiences of love within a chosen environment until someone misses.

I Love You in Different Languages

New ways to say I love you

All ages

The concept of telling someone you love them is universal and understood by people of all nationalities. Learn to say I love you in several different languages. Here are a few examples:

French: Je t'aime.

Spanish: Te amo.

Hebrew: Ani ohev otach.

American Sign Language: Extend the pointer finger, little finger, and thumb of one hand with your palm facing outward. Keep the two middle fingers curled down.

Valentines
Send your child Valentines all year long

3 years and up

Take advantage of post–Valentine's Day markdowns and buy a stack of cards to use for love notes to your child.

Fifty Ways to Believe a Lover
Think of different ways to express your love

Materials:
index cards

Gather your family for an enlightening activity in which you will try to come up with over fifty ways to express love in a believable manner. Anything from giving a warm hug to bringing chicken soup to someone with a head cold should be considered believable.

4 to 12 years

Write each idea on separate index cards. If you can't come up with fifty, expand on the ones you did think of, such as, "Hugging and saying I love you all at the same time" and "Hugging very tightly, but not too hard."

Be sure to keep adding to the pile as the days, weeks, and years go by. When you catch your child doing something loving, write it down on a card and add it to your pile.

Loving Ways
Choose a loving response to a theoretical situation

5 to 12 years

Use the deck of cards you assembled in the above activity to help your child understand how expressions of love may help others feel or behave better. Find books, magazines, or newspaper stories that depict people, animals, or any living thing in need of love (for example, a teenage runaway or an abandoned dog). Review the pictures and stories with your child and have her select from your pile of cards what the person or animal needs. If you don't have a card to match the situation, make a new one and add it to the deck. See if your child can find more than one card for a single situation.

You can also use the cards to help articulate the need for a special kind of loving during tough times. Flip through the deck like flashcards with a child who is unsure of what she needs. Go through the deck, card by card, asking your child to signal when you reach the expression of love that will make her feel better.

The Family Unconditional-Declaration-of-Love Poster

Materials:
poster board

All ages

A statement of unconditional love

Come up with a saying that respects the "laws" of unconditional love and acceptance. For example, "I may not always like the way you act or the things you say, but no matter what, I will always love you!" You can cite this "law" to soften punishment for bad behavior.

Then, make a declaration-of-love poster with your child. Write your family statement in big, bold letters, then decorate the remainder of the poster with photographs or drawings of your family.

Love Letters

3 years and up

Express your love in writing

Send a love letter to your sweetheart—your child sweetheart, that is. Write the letter in a kid-friendly style declaring your absolute love for him or her. For a special touch, dab the envelope with your favorite perfume or cologne. A father we know sends his daughter and son a special love letter on Valentine's Day. He writes the letter on real parchment paper and cuts up tiny red hearts to sprinkle inside the envelope. He started this family tradition because he feels that he expresses himself best in writing and the children adore receiving the valentines every year.

When Brianne Schwantes was born with a rare disease that makes her bones break at the slightest pressure, doctors told her parents they might as well "leave her to die."

Brianne was born with osteogenesis imperfecta. "OI" makes bones so brittle that they break even before birth. Brianne was born with more than a dozen breaks.

But thirteen years later, in 1993, Brianne was attracting national attention as a volunteer helping the residents of Des Moines, Iowa, clean up after devastating floods.

From birth, Brianne has been a research subject at the National Institutes of Health. She takes the responsibility seriously, hoping her experience will help other kids with OI. She also publishes a newsletter for them. In *Little Bones*, Brianne reports on research, shares stories, reviews books, answers letters, and shares tips and jokes.

For Brianne, staying busy is the best medicine.

"You should never give up on anything in life," she says. "Look at me. I'm proof!"

Mementos Box

A place to store gifts from your child

All ages

If you haven't already, set aside a special box to hold all those little mementos your child gives to you. It's got to be big and sturdy enough to hold it all— the tissue-paper flowers, the drawings, the homemade birthday cards, and the clay statuettes from art class.

You may want to write down moments when your child said something particularly loving and affectionate, and add these to the box as well.

Macaroni Golden Promises

A symbolic reminder of your commitment to your child

Materials:
tube-shaped pasta, gold paint, slips of paper

3 years and up

Children are always wondering (and usually out loud) whether their parents will always be there for them. What parent hasn't heard a tiny voice ask, "Will you love me even if I do something bad?" or, "Will you still take care of me if I get sick?" It seems that no matter how secure your child is, she'll always need to hear you promise always to be there, no matter what.

This activity not only says you will but lets your child hold on to your promise forever.

Get a box of tube-shaped macaroni such as ziti and paint the uncooked pasta gold. Next, write all your promises to your child on strips of paper. Roll these up and insert each into a "golden promise keeper." Explain to your child that each of these golden promise keepers holds a golden promise—one that will last a lifetime.

Give her a special box to hold her golden promises. Save the remaining painted macaroni and throughout the years, whenever your child expresses one of those fears that you will somehow let her down, promise her you won't, write it down, and roll it into a golden promise keeper.

Encourage your child to make golden promises to you. These should be saved for significant life choices. For example, your child can make a golden promise to consult you should a weighty problem arise. She can promise never to take drugs, and never to run away from home. You should also keep a special box to store the golden promises that your child gives you. And be sure to have extra golden promise keepers on hand for future promises from your child.

Love Stories

2 years and up *Tell your children about the evolution of your relationship with your spouse*

One of our children's favorite stories is the one about how Mommy and Daddy fell in love. We tell it to them often, adding more details as they mature. They're fascinated by how we met, and how our love, trust, and unconditional commitment grew. The best part of the story for them, however, is when we decided to get married and have children. They also enjoy hearing about how their grandparents, aunts and uncles, and good friends of ours met and fell in love.

The Day You Were Born

2 years and up *Tell your children the story of their birth*

Our children so love to hear the story of how they came into the world that this has become a bedtime ritual in our household. We begin with our decision to have a child, then describe Denise's growing belly and how our love for the baby inside grew just as big. Finally, we end with the grand finale—the birth. It's at this point that we tell each child that when she was born, we committed our love "forever and ever. No matter what you do or where you go we will always love you and try to be the best mommy and daddy we can be!" The kids know the story so well that if we skip a detail they inform us immediately, filling in the words themselves!

Take this storytelling ritual one step further by making a book titled The Day You Were Born using real pictures to highlight pregnancy and birth.

Just-Because Pictures

All ages *Keep your camera ready for spontaneous pictures*

Too often the camera stays tucked away until a special occasion comes up and reminds us to go dig it out. Don't limit your picture taking to birthdays and vacations. Take pictures of your child "just because," and let her know that you're doing it just because you love her.

Activities That Build Trust

The following games and activities are terrific ways to build trust because they teach children through real experiences that you will always be there.

Blindfold Trust

Players take turns wearing a blindfold and being led by others

4 years and up

Blindfold your child and lead him through the house (and possibly outdoors). Explain beforehand that he must trust you completely to keep him safe. Then take your child to different areas and encourage him to guess where in the house he is and to feel objects to figure out what they are. When you're done with the tour, ask your child to describe how it felt to have to trust you to keep him safe. Now for the hard part. It's your turn. Outline the rules and let your child know that you trust he will keep you safe. Blindfold yourself and have your child lead you through a similar experience. When your tour is over, let your child know what it felt like to trust him.

Graduate-Level Trust Walk

Same as above activity, only without physical contact

4 years and up

Here, one person is blindfolded and the other guides through verbal directions only. Of course both walker and guide should move very slowly. As trust and communication builds, the guide will be able to maneuver the walker around more difficult obstacles. Again, take turns trying each role and when you're finished, talk about the amount of trust the walker had in the guide and the deep sense of responsibility the guide felt toward the walker.

   With older children, you can use this as a metaphor for the limits you must set for them.

Trust Fall

Player falls backward into the arms of others

3 years and up

You need all family members for this game. Have your child stand while the rest of the family kneels behind her. Place your hands directly behind her back and encourage her to fall over backward, straight into the hands of her waiting family.

   The best way to do this activity is to let your child fall over and over again until she has gained enough trust that she simply lies back without attempting to break her own fall.

Activities That Help with Separation

Whether it's a few hours with a baby-sitter or a week at Grandma's, children find it hard to be separated from their parents. Learning to master their fears is an essential part of development. Here are some playful tips for helping your child feel secure and loved during a separation.

Puppy Love

A stuffed animal companion

Materials:
stuffed animal, cardboard or poster board, photograph of family

2 years and up

Ask your child to select a stuffed animal from his collection. Together, make a collar for it and attach a tag made from cardboard or poster board. On the tag, glue a photograph that reminds your child of his family. Your child now has a very special, cuddly buddy to help him feel loved and secure while you're away.

You can also use the animal to prepare your child for times apart. For instance, while you're getting your child ready to go off to day care, ask him to make sure his cuddly buddy is also set for the day. Provide props, such as a little blanket and pretend lunch box for the animal.

"It's Mommy—It's Daddy!"

Put yourself in your child's storybooks

2 years and up

Recently we went on a trip and left the children with their grandparents (who cared for them perfectly). Before we left, we decided to surprise the children by cutting out photographs of us and slipping them into scenes in their favorite storybooks. The results were hilarious! Mommy sitting in a tree, Daddy eating from a dog bowl. . . .

When Grandma and Grandpa read them the books, the children were delighted to see Mommy and Daddy right there in their favorite stories. And instead of feeling lonesome for us, they were warmly reminded of how loved they are, even from far away.

Framing Your Love

Your child makes a picture frame for you

Materials:
photograph of your child, picture frame, items to decorate the frame

2 years and up

A simple, loving way to remind your child of how special she is is to select a favorite picture of her and ask her to help you make a frame for it. You can fashion one from cardboard, or buy an inexpensive frame, then decorate it with paper hearts and bows. The essential part is to show your child that when you leave for work or go on vacation or a business trip, the framed picture is going with you and will remind you of how much you love her, even when you're apart.

4

Inspiration and Good Role Modeling

The word *inspiration* invokes the divine. We assume it takes a momentous event to inspire us, when in reality inspiration comes from the most ordinary of circumstances. Even the smallest of these leave their mark on us, and this goes doubly for children, who are so easily moved. For example, we have a pet, a black bunny named Sam. He broke his teeth one day when he jumped out of Mark's arms and hit his mouth. He couldn't eat for days and might have died had we not fed him a mixture of mashed-up bunny food and banana three times daily by hand. We cuddled him often and took him to the veterinarian. Our girls were so impressed by our dedication to this animal that they remarked for days about how we saved his life. "The bunny was lucky to be a Weston," Emily said.

We may not be consciously aware of this, but we inspire and model roles for our children every moment of our parenting days. Even little inspirations like black, furry bunnies that survive through care and affection are absorbed into our children's vision of how people should act. One of the most important requirements of a good parent is being and portraying a good person.

Role models serve as operational guides—they're examples of how to act and treat others. Children learn more from example than by being told. By observing and emulating you, your children acquire many of their mannerisms, behaviors, speech patterns, problem-solving and communication styles, attitudes, values, and moral standards.

It may seem simple to be an effective model for your child, but it requires thought and care. For it to work, you have to be consistent. There are two ways an adult can model desired behavior. The first is more a way of life than a technique. It entails taking stock of your values, then scrutinizing your behavior to see how well you are following them. For example, if you strive to be on time for appointments, you are teaching your child about honoring commitments. By easily expressing gratitude, you teach your child to appreciate others. The second way to model behavior is to identify which values you want your child to learn, then plan opportunities to demonstrate them. For instance, if your child has difficulty making friends, take him or her along when you introduce yourself to a new neighbor. Without saying a thing, you are modeling how to initiate a conversation and make a new friend.

With inspiration and modeling

- children have a blueprint etched in their unconscious mind. It's always there, available for a quick consult and internal guidance, even when there is no trusted adult nearby.

- children will have the sense of having been there before when situations involving morality arise. They'll know what to do.

- children know to whom to turn when confused or in need of guidance.

- children will be less likely to lose faith, give up, or act destructively during difficult or trying times.

Without inspiration and modeling

- children are lost, uncertain, and uneasy, and without positive role models will turn to anyone, even unsavory types, for inspiration.

- children are at a disadvantage, particularly when a situation requires decisions without guidance from a trusted adult.

- children are likely to adopt modeled behavior (your cigarette smoking) rather than your spoken guidance ("Don't smoke. It is bad for you") or even their own stated convictions ("I'll never smoke. It's a disgusting habit").

- children will give up easily.

How to Enhance Your Child's Exposure to Good Role Models

- Find inspirational figures to emulate and learn from.

- Be a living, breathing example of how to do things. Don't hide your own searching and learning process from your child.

- Be consistent. Do as you say and say as you do.

- Start as soon as possible, when the children are young.

- Make sure your positive character skills are constantly on display for your child, conveying messages about what you believe. Your example flows naturally from your true character. You have to live it for your children to believe it.

- Know what you are teaching. Sit down by yourself or with your parenting partner and take an honest inventory of your behaviors and characteristics. Consider whether they are consistent with who you claim to be, how you wish to live your life, and what you tell your child. If so, congratulate yourself—you're well into your child's single most effective lesson plan for life. If you find they are not consistent, then look closely at your wishes, expectations, and claims, and weigh them against your behaviors and character traits. Are your expectations of your child and yourself unrealistically high? Have you misrepresented your actions because you struggle to meet these high expectations? Whatever the cause of the discrepancy, develop a plan for change. Set a goal and a time frame for the change. You need not hide this process from a child—to embark upon a plan for change communicates a positive message about you, the possibility for self-improvement, and the courage to be honest.

Activities That Inspire and Illustrate the Power of Influence

Family Book of Inspiration

Materials:
a notebook

All ages

A record of your family's inspirational acts

Inspirations: On January 14, 1996, Dad picked up four empty soda cans in the park. Sue invited a girl who was new in the neighborhood to play with her, and Debbie cleaned her hamster cage without even being asked. Three great deeds—truly inspirational—now permanently recorded in that family's Book of Inspirations.

Create your own family book of inspirations to record actions of family members that you find enlightening, or simply thoughtful. You can decorate the front of a regular notebook, and title it Our Family's Book of Inspiration. Keep your eyes and ears open to all those inspiring things that family members do, but which often slip by unnoticed. Record the big deeds, like acing a test, or getting that promotion at work, as well as the little things, such as remembering Grandma's birthday by sending a card. The more you remember to write down, the better the book. And be sure to review the entries from time to time to remind yourselves of how truly inspirational your family can be.

Copy Me
A lesson on the power of persuasion

Materials:
two identical sets of crayons, drawing paper, an object to draw such as a vase of flowers or a bowl of fruit

6 years and up

Place the flowers or bowl of fruit on a table. Then sit down together with paper and crayons to draw it. Without revealing your motive, influence your child to draw his picture just like you do. Example: "That banana would look prettier if it were green. Let's use the green crayon to draw it in the picture. I'm going to make the bowl square in my picture. Wouldn't it be fun if you made your bowl square, too?" Try to influence your child to draw his picture exactly like yours, and go out of your way to make your still life look different from the actual object. When you're finished, discuss the experience with your child. Show him how your strong suggestions influenced the way his picture came out. Ask if he realized you were influencing him. Discuss how he would feel about his artwork if it was his entirely. If he didn't draw it your way, discuss how it felt to reject your suggestions. Explain that by your words and actions you can prompt and inspire another person to act a certain way. Talk about how people can influence others for both bad and good purposes.

Rub-Off-on-Me Statements
Acknowledge good deeds

All ages

Any time a family member does a good deed, or acts in an inspiring way, notice the action and proclaim, "I hope it rubs off on me!" We suggest that you add a little humor by rubbing your shoulder against the do-gooder's shoulder. This is a definite catch-'em-being-good activity. Notice both the big and the small actions.

Hero Poster

Materials:
poster board, photographs

5 years and up

A homemade poster depicting personal heroes

In this activity your child is going to make a poster of heroes who inspire him to be a good person. Have your child sift through magazines, newspapers, photo albums, and books to find people who have motivated him to succeed. (This can be done over the course of several weeks.) Sort through this material yourself and encourage your child to consider all types of heroes, not just sports figures and movie stars but everyday people, including family members and friends who did something really great. For example, point out that Grandma worked hard for forty-five years to make sure her family had enough money to be secure and happy—a far more heroic deed than sinking a twenty-foot jump shot.

When your child has selected a good number of heroes, have him photocopy their pictures and/or statements about them, then paste these on poster board. His hero poster will serve as a reminder of the heroic potential in us all.

My Hero

5 years and up

Tell your heroes why you admire them

Encourage your child to write to one of her heroes. In the letter, ask her to describe why she chose her hero, and how she tries to emulate her hero's behavior and deeds. (You can write the letter if your child is too young.) Be sure to send the letter. If you have trouble finding an address, a teacher or a librarian may be able to help.

Cherry-Tree Stories

6 years and up

Look for the seeds of success in your personal heroes

Every great adult started life as a terrific kid. Encourage your children to probe their heroes' childhoods for hints of the man or woman they would one day become. For famous personalities, this may mean reading biographies or news articles. If the hero is a friend or relative or a community figure, your child can interview them.

A Day in the Life

4 years and up

Spend time on the job

Does your child know what she wants to be when she grows up? Does she dream of becoming a doctor, a teacher, or an artist? Give your child a close-up look at her dream job by arranging for her to spend a few hours in the field.

Call on friends and family for help. Maybe you know someone (or know someone who knows someone) who holds your child's dream job and will let her tag along at work for the day. It's not so uncommon these days to see a young observer in the workplace. The experience can be invaluable.

By the way, you might be surprised at how much adults enjoy showing off their job to a child. Nothing reinvigorates a tired attitude as much as someone who believes in what you are doing.

Thought for the Day
Send your child to school, camp, or day care with a note of inspiration

3 years and up

There are thousands of books available that are filled with wonderful, inspiring thoughts. Here's a fun way to share them with your children.

Choose statements, thoughts for the day, pictures, poems, or meditations you feel will benefit or inspire your child. Jot them down on slips of paper or small notecards to tuck into unexpected places where your child will find them, such as a lunch box or ballet slipper. Make sure the statements are a mixture of serious and humorous ones. When your child is old enough to create inspirational thoughts of his own, encourage him to select his favorite sayings and put them in places for you to find.

The Great PAL Award
An award for excellent leadership abilities

Materials:
construction paper,
decorations such as glitter

4 years and up

PAL stands for positively awesome leader. We suggest that you make a PAL award, and bestow it weekly on a family member who inspired, motivated, or positively influenced another person. Explain that leadership comes in many forms. The older sibling who teaches his brother to play a new game is just as valuable a leader as the class president.

Inspire-a-Nation
Encourage your children to work for a cause they feel strongly about

5 years and up

Children have an unshakable faith that they *can* make a difference. When they find a cause that moves them, they often become committed activists. Read through the Giraffe stories in the margins and encourage your child to examine his or her potential for inspiring others.

If your child believes in a cause and seems to be committed to doing something about it, *do not disillusion him.* You may believe that one small child couldn't possibly make a difference and want to protect him from disappointment, but this is precisely the type of parental attitude that fosters malaise in children.

Throw your full support behind your child and make your child's cause a family cause (see Inspirations-R-Us, below). A child who believes in something can accomplish anything when others believe in him.

Great Gangs

5 years and up *Encourage your child to get involved with a group of like-minded people*

A gang is a powerful influence. Unfortunately, we tend to associate them with crime and violence. But the same gang dynamics that steer members wrong can also steer them right. It just depends on the gang's philosophy. Consider the number of healthy "gangs," such as Boy Scouts, Girl Scouts, youth groups, church and synagogue leadership groups, YMCA, and afterschool programs. Then consider the reason why children join gangs: they want to belong and need something to do with their time. We suggest that you get your child involved in the right kind of gang at an early age by encouraging him to join a youth organization. We also recommend that your child help choose the type of groups he would like to be affiliated with. Review material, interview group leaders, and learn as much as you can regarding the groups' missions, philosophies, and activities. Your child will need to decide whether his own visions and pursuits match those of the group he's thinking about joining. A boy we know chose not to join the Boy Scouts after learning that girls were not allowed to join. This went against his own beliefs that girls are equal and deserve the same opportunities. He joined Boys and Girls Clubs of America instead.

Inspirations-R-Us

2 years and up *Reach out as a family to those in need*

There are many ways a family can influence and inspire others—just think of all the things yours can offer. Maybe some of you can teach a trade or a skill, or serve as a mentor or a tutor in a literacy program. Your children can reach out to other kids through peer programs that prevent alcohol and drug use. A family member can become a Big Brother or a Big Sister. You may even want to consider becoming a foster family.

But there is much more to inspiring others than you might immediately conclude. When you reach out, a mutual exchange of wisdom and caring transpires. When our family has worked with the homeless, elderly, or physically challenged, our mission was not totally selfless. We got a lot in return. Each person we helped inspired us in one way or another. Their gifts were their unique wisdom, their power to overcome, their insight, and their gratefulness. So go ahead and inspire someone. You'll find it to be an inspirational experience.

Hall of Fame

Create an area of your home to display photographs of inspiring family members

All ages

Select a hallway in your home that will become your family's "Hall of Fame." Hang drawings or photographs of family members whose accomplishments, talents, and successes you and your children have found inspiring. You'll probably have to review your family history with your children to discover the hidden talents and unknown successes of your ancestors. Be sure to include pictures and accomplishments of your child in the Hall of Fame. Add new Hall of Famers as your family accomplishments grow. Your children will be proud to guide visiting friends and families through your Hall of Fame.

Kid Teacher

Turn the children into the teachers by establishing a student teaching program at your child's school

5 years and up

Watching a child inspire another child is like witnessing magic. When a child calls on his own resources to teach another, both children benefit. In this activity, your child will learn what a wonderful feeling it is to teach.

Approach your child's school about establishing a "kid teacher" program. Basically, this is an older child teaching younger children something he knows. It could be something as simple as the alphabet and a few nursery songs, or it could be something harder, like quadratic equations.

The "kid teacher" classes should be held regularly, perhaps weekly, but can be kept to a limited time frame, such as a four-week ceramics or Spanish class. Of course your child should keep his students' regular teacher updated on their progress. This will make the whole experience feel more valuable to him. The personal success your child feels from inspiring and teaching another child is unmatchable. You can imagine how this positive learning experience can benefit not just your child but his students, who will be getting attention from a kid who is smart and successful, just as they are.

Support Groups

3 years and up

Seek formal help when necessary

Sometimes we need a little extra help when our problems seem overwhelming. A good place to find it is at a support group. There are groups for children and adults for everything from divorce to the birth of a new sibling. The Appendix includes a list of national organizations that head up support groups for children and adults.

Family and
Community Connections

To understand today's families, it is helpful to examine how we got here. Our definition of family is dependent on the era and culture in which we live. During the early part of the century, immigrants to America extended the notion of family to include virtual strangers. They would open their homes and hearts to people who shared only the loose bond of having been born in the same country. People most often stayed put, living near grandparents, aunts, uncles, and cousins.

During the 1950s and 1960s, the ideal family became the *Father Knows Best* model, with homemaker Mom who doted on her children and always had supper on the table when Dad came home from his nine-to-five job. Girls were expected to help with housework and care for younger children while the boys got to play sports and have outside responsibilities such as paper routes.

Then came the women's movement, and more women chose to enter the workforce. Divorce became a socially acceptable alternative to an unhappy marriage and single parenthood became commonplace. Alternative lifestyles such as gay and lesbian households began to emerge. There was an increased awareness of child abuse, and consequently a rise in the number of foster homes, adoptions, and grandparent-led families. Most unusual was the advent of the commuter marriage where spouses live in separate households hundreds of miles apart and see each other only on weekends. Of all those changes, perhaps the most significant among them was the unraveling of the extended family. Increased mobility meant that families were able to leave the old neighborhood to seek better opportunities in other parts of the country.

By the 1990s, "family values" had made a comeback. Presidential campaigns were waged over the phrase. But at the same time as couples were reexamining their commitment to traditional values, it had become abundantly clear that they could not make ends meet on a single income. Women now make up the majority of job holders (though they still hold an inordinately high percentage of low-paying jobs). The *Father Knows Best* model has become obsolete because salaries have failed miserably to keep up with the cost of living.

Here's where we are today: At the same time as we're embracing the notion of strong family connections, we're living in a society where more than 40 percent of marriages end in divorce. Many families are either blended by remarriage or led by a single parent. This hasn't stopped us from refocusing on home and hearth, however. Despite the need for dual incomes, we are creating new solutions to balance the needs of work and family. New modes of working include the flexible schedule, job sharing, part-time hours, and working from home via computer linkups and other high-tech gadgetry.

It's important to be aware of societal forces that work against family unity. Contemporary society has increasingly encouraged individuality and material possessions over family or group needs and spiritual values. In this climate, the family becomes undervalued, creating for many a feeling of disconnectedness. But it's also important to keep in mind that in a thriving family environment, members should not only focus inward toward one another, but also encourage accomplishments and independence outside the family.

Depending on your family's lifestyle and beliefs, you can link a child to the community or alienate him from it. It is the quality of family members' interpersonal relationships that most significantly affects the child's sense of belonging and connectedness. Connectedness happens not in any one identifiable moment, but as a culmination of satisfying associations with the family and the individuals who make it up.

Though you may live far from relatives, keep in mind that extended family relationships forge a special link between children and their heritage. It's important to give your child a sense of his place in this vast family unit. Doing so will help him understand what came before him and what will follow. But it is just as important to help your child understand his place in the community. He begins this process by seeing similarities and differences between his family and others. Although every family has its own unique constitution, many rules and rituals are common to most, such as celebrating birthdays and tucking the kids in bed at night. This is why when a child sleeps over at a friend's home, he may feel a little uneasy but will have a good idea of what to expect. When children begin to attend school and visit the homes of friends, they get their first exposure to how other families operate. They may realize for the first time that things are done differently in their own home. In some instances this strengthens the child's appreciation for his family, while in others it weakens it.

It is these first outside relationships that a child develops, with his teacher or with the little boy down the street, that begin the process of becoming a part of a community. Communities operate much like families, with standards of behavior, commonality of belief, and shared investment in self-preservation. Remember that at the center is the family, the source of a child's knowledge about relationships, communication, friendship, and love. Children who internalize these values use them to better their community, and ultimately, the world.

With family and community connections

- children learn there is more to life than their own needs. They see that everyone has a role to play in the well-being of the family and community.

- children feel secure and cared for because they are linked to something that is tangible and stable.

- children's sense of identity and self-esteem become stronger.

- children are happier. They feel more important and stronger. The strength of the group—be it family or community—crosses over to the child.

- children build deeper relationships based upon shared experiences and efforts.

- children practice living by rules. Within the family, children must understand, interpret, and abide by the often unstated expectations and norms that govern behavior and relationships.

Without positive family and community connections

- children don't know what it means to belong and to contribute to a group.

- children are ultimately forced to find their own supportive relationships when they leave home—predictably too soon. Without firsthand experience in working out relationships between members in a family, they won't learn how to build friendships with others, making it difficult for them to build genuine and lasting relationships.

- children lack two valuable things: 1) an intangible, critical component of their inner core—a sense of belonging and a knowledge of family and community rituals, and 2) something that remains stable and constant and is always there to return to.

- children may blame themselves for not having had positive family and community connections and risk concluding that they deserve only low-quality relationships. Children are at risk for creating self-denying or abusive interpersonal relationships.

How to Enhance Your Family and Community Connections

- Creating a family climate of belonging and acceptance takes effort, courage, and patience. This is particularly true if you grew up in a weak family. It may be helpful to think about the activities and events (rituals and routines) as well as the personal and interpersonal factors that made your childhood positive or negative. Use this information to chart a method to strengthen your family.

- Family routines and rituals strengthen the sense of family personality and belonging, but they don't happen automatically. They are the result of parents' consciously initiating an event or activity time and time again until it seems it was always there. Create rituals that are uniquely yours. Don't worry what others think—your children will cherish the special things you do together. Try not to be limited by traditional activities although you may want to pass along some of the rituals from your own childhood, however insignificant or silly. When Mark was a child, his family would go to Perkins Pancake House for dinner after buying a new car, so this is one he has insisted our own family do.

- If older children resist your suggestions, charge them with the responsibility for coming up with family rituals or community activities they would enjoy. Then go ahead with your activity. Let the reluctant children stand on the sidelines and watch.

- Many family and community activities take some time but the effort is often gratifying and worthwhile.

◆ If you are shy and find social activities difficult, ask a friend or neighbor to join you, or see if she or he will bring you along next time she participates in one.

◆ Finally, don't force too much change at once. Change is always difficult, so be patient. If you envision and work at the type of family atmosphere you want, little by little and day by day—it will happen.

Activities That Enhance Family Connections

Family Council
A regularly scheduled family meeting

2 years and up

The family council meeting is a time to discuss relevant issues and concerns, to air grievances, and to share gratitude. The family council meeting supports the notion that all members of a family contribute to an atmosphere of cooperation and mutual respect. The meetings are scheduled weekly and follow a structured format.

Here are a few tips for starting and running a family council.

1. Meetings should be scheduled regularly and operate under established rules. These rules should include no yelling, no blaming others, and no speaking out of turn. They must be clearly stated and consistently enforced.

2. All members should share responsibility for running and contributing to the meeting. Rotate the jobs of chairperson and secretary.

3. Use meetings to address problems, distribute chores, and review family responsibilities. But also plan fun activities and be sure to encourage members to express their appreciation for each other.

4. It is important to bring to the family council communication techniques such as mutual respect, empathy, modeling, "I" messages, and effective listening, all of which are described in the chapter on communication.

5. Criticizing or disregarding members' ideas and suggestions must be scrupulously avoided so that everyone involved feels safe expressing his or her thoughts and feelings.

Another benefit of a family council is that it supports family unity, builds team spirit, and supports each member's sense of self-worth. Simply being heard on a regular basis is comforting, especially when busy schedules leave little time for family communication. This is an important enough reason to set aside some time each week to conduct your own family council, spend time together, catch up on what's happening in everyone's life, and plan future family events.

Family Ten Commandments

3 years and up *Rules for your family to live by*

Family rules are very important. They bond members by committing everyone to the same principles of conduct. Conveying these rules, or should we say family laws, should be done clearly and consistently but not so seriously that they scare a child into obedience. This activity will help you set your rules in a fun way.

Sit down together to make a list of the ten most important rules that family members should follow. You can phrase these like the biblical Ten Commandments and display them on a large piece of poster board decorated to look like an ancient tablet. Here is an example of the Ten Commandments of a family we know in New York with two teenagers and two preschoolers:

The Lamberts' Ten Commandments

1. Thou shalt be kind and courteous to family and friends

2. Thou shalt not hit or use hurtful words

3. Thou shalt do thy chores

4. Thou shalt be home at curfew or at least call thy worried mother if thou shalt be late

5. Thou shalt not eat, talk, and walk at the same time

6. Thou shalt plan to have dinner home with thy family twice a week

7. Thou shalt not throw a tantrum more than three times a day

8. Thou shalt read at least one good book a week

9. Thou shalt help a friend or family member once a day

10. Thou shalt tell a silly joke or say something funny and make at least one person laugh twice a week

Kid-Friendly Family Scrapbook

A scrapbook of real and imaginary adventures

3 years and up

We recently wrote an article for a magazine in which we shared our family scrapbook. Now, our family scrapbook is pretty unusual. Instead of the standard vacation photos and ticket stubs, ours is crammed full of stories—both real and imaginary.

We concoct our stories from mementos and photos of vacations, special events, and everyday routines. The kids help create our scrapbook stories by cutting and pasting the photos and collaborating on the text. One story the kids invented was a wild new Disney adventure that unfolded through a mixing and matching of family heads and bodies with those of Princess Jasmine and a tyrannosaurus rex. We recommend you try this kid-style version of creating a family scrapbook. It's loads of fun to conjure up different imaginary adventures and satisfying to record real ones.

Hint: There are some new books from Kodak that inspire some imaginative and creative family fun using pictures and humorous story lines. For more information about Kodak's Storyteller Books write or call: Eastman Kodak Company, 1100 University Ave, Rochester, NY 14607

Family Dreams and Goals Collage

Create a collage of your family's dreams and goals

4 years and up

We all have personal hopes, dreams, and goals. But we also share goals and dreams as a family. Too often we treat these group goals as less important than our personal ones. Creating a collage brings your family's dreams into the open where they can be examined and appreciated by everyone.

Start by discussing your goals and dreams for the family, then encourage your children to do the same. Agree as a group on the most realistic and reachable goals, then cut out magazine pictures to represent these dreams, or illustrate them yourself. Arrange the pictures on a large piece of poster board. Write at the top of the collage, "Our Family's Dreams and Goals." Hang your collage for everyone to see.

Your family may wish to focus on a specific challenge, such as "goals after divorce," or "dreams for ending violence."

Family Traditions

Start a family tradition

All ages

A family we know engages in an unusual annual tradition. For one week every January, the entire family celebrates chocolate, believe it or not. For seven straight days, everyone, including a relative from Germany, makes chocolate, buys chocolate, puts chocolate in almost everything they eat, and sends each other lots of chocolate.

A silly tradition? Not if you examine its roots. Almost a century ago, in the month of January, a great-great-grandmother (a teenager at the time) won a very big baking contest using chocolate—lots of chocolate. Her prize money was just enough to pay for boat passage to America. The trip saved her life and the future of her family.

Family traditions link generations. Traditions foster a sense of belonging and ensure the survival of family lore and culture.

If you don't have a family tradition, it's not too late to start one. Explain to your child the meaning of family traditions and then together come up with one of your own. Try and relate the tradition to a part of your family history. Traditions can commemorate specific events, they can involve the making and passing down of an heirloom, or they can revolve around a special activity or recipe that is unique to your family. If you can persuade relatives to take part, you will have more luck establishing a tradition that will last.

Family Dining Hour

All ages *Have dinner together*

There has been a lot of discussion about the problems associated with our frantically paced lives, not the least of which is the erosion of the ritual of sitting down together as a family for dinner.

We eat to fill our bellies, but mealtime is also a time to reconnect—to socialize and to communicate. We conduct important business during mealtimes and use food events to gather people for celebrations, observances, and even fund-raisers. The gathering of people around food is an important part of almost every culture.

Make a commitment to honor this important tradition in your family by setting a rule to have dinner, or even breakfast, together a certain number of times each week. Eat at the table, not in front of the television. Get members involved in the process of cooking and cleaning. Make this time important and use it to say hello, and to ask what's new.

Family Cheer

All ages *Spread cheer to those who need cheering up*

A single mother from a Boston suburb shared with us a wonderful family tradition her great-grandmother started years ago. She and her daughter make baskets of "cheer"—simple baskets filled with cookies, chocolates, jams, and crackers, which they give to someone they know who is a little under the weather. This mother-and-daughter team collects baskets from garage sales, and stores cookies and candies in their hall closet so that at a moment's notice they can bring someone a basket of cheer. They give baskets to friends who are sick, who lost a big game, who didn't get the job, or who simply had a bad day. They also give family cheer baskets for more serious reasons, such as a death in a family or a hospital stay. They do this because they love to cheer others, especially when they can do it together. Perhaps you can think of a similar way to spread a little cheer with your family.

Sibling Holiday
A day to celebrate siblings

2 years and up

Designate three or four times a year as Brother and Sister Day. Devote this family holiday to discussing with your children all the reasons why they appreciate one another. Reminisce about special times they had together and incidents when they behaved nicely toward one another. Have the children decide together on an activity or outing that everyone in the family can enjoy on Brother and Sister Day. Finally, hang your sibling flag (see next activity below) out in the front of your home to recognize the day.

Sibling Flag
A flag symbolizing your children's relationship

Materials:
fabric, textile paint, a wooden pole

3 years and up

Your children should design and make the flag together. Display the flag outside to let everyone know how terrific the brothers and sisters in your home are. Our girls made a beautiful "Sisters!" flag out of handprints, hand-drawn pictures of their favorite activities they both enjoy, and a big, gold heart, which symbolizes in our family the art of giving and caring. Our flag comes out often, especially when they need to be reminded that "it's better to be a sister team than to be sisters that fight and scream" (a famous saying in our house).

Family Team Chore Chart

4 years and up   *A chart listing each family member's household responsibilities*

Household chores bond a child to family and home. Chores give children a sense of value, worth, and accomplishment. This builds self-esteem and self-reliance and prepares your child for more demanding responsibilities in the future.

But let's face it, chores aren't a whole lot of fun. Unless, of course, you turn them into a game. That's easier than you may think, especially when you recruit the whole family to play.

First, create a chore chart that treats family members as players on a team. If everyone completes his assigned chore then the entire family wins— perhaps a mutually agreed-upon treat such as a trip to a favorite restaurant or a new household item that everyone will enjoy.

Family Chore Chart
Put an X or sticker in square when you do your chore.

Date:

	clean dishes	set table	take out garbage	walk dog	fold laundry	clean bathroom	dust clean vacuum	total points
George	Mon.	Tues.	Wed.	Thur.	Fri.	Sat.	Sat.	
Tammy	Tues.	Wed.	Thur.	Fri.	Sat.	Mon.	Sat.	
Suzy	Wed.	Thur.	Fri.	Sat.	Mon.	Tue.	Sat.	
Mom	Thur.	Fri.	Sat.	Mon.	Tue.	Wed.	Sat.	
Dad	Fri.	Sat.	Mon.	Tue.	Wed.	Thur.	Sat.	

To make your team chore chart, figure out chores that need to be done daily, then assign three to seven of them to each child, according to age and developmental ability. Explain that completing chores is no different from playing a position on a baseball, soccer, or football team. Encourage your child to remind other family members to do their chores for the sake of the team. You may want to include a "personal chore" section in your chart that requires your child to do homework, make his bed, or practice an instrument.

Family Emblem

An original emblem representing your family   2 years and up

The family emblem accomplishes three things: It teaches your family about its history, it identifies each member's unique contributions, and it builds family pride and unity. Your family emblem can be modeled after a coat of arms, or it can be an original design, but all family members must work democratically to decide what it will look like.

There are many ways to design a family emblem. Choose the one (or ones) that will work best for your family:

- Research your family surname and incorporate its meaning into your family emblem.

- For design ideas, interview family members, especially older relatives, about past accomplishments.

- Choose something that has been passed down from generation to generation to incorporate into your emblem. It can be something tangible, like an heirloom, or something intangible, like a prominent family trait.

- Take a trip to the library and research your nationality. Work into the flag a symbol of your family's country or countries of origin.

- Choose symbols representing each member's personal accomplishments or talents and integrate them into the design.

- Take a photograph or draw a picture of your family.

- Divide your emblem into two parts, one representing your heritage, culture, and ethnic ties, the other identifying present family accomplishments.

Once you have come up with a design, display it, perhaps by having it printed on T-shirts, coffee mugs, key chains, or the welcome mat in front of your home. You can put your family emblem on stationery and use it for letters and thank-you cards. One way to show off your family emblem is to draw your design on a banner, and hang it from a pole, like a personalized flag. Or how about painting your family emblem on the front door of your home? One family we know made a totem pole out of one-gallon cylindrical ice cream containers. Each person designed a container to reflect his or her personality and interests. Then the family put the containers together to make an eight-foot-tall totem pole that now stands in their living room.

Family Rituals

All ages *Establish a family ritual*

The family ritual is an important ingredient for building family unity. It can be virtually anything, from a weekly pizza dinner to an annual reading of "The Night before Christmas." The key to its success is that it be carried out consistently; a ritual doesn't happen only once or twice.

If you don't already have a family ritual, create one. A regular activity that is distinctively your family's will unify you and your children by giving everyone a sense of belonging to something larger than themselves.

Both of us have fond feelings for the family rituals we enjoyed while growing up. Each night at bedtime, Mark's father would make up another chapter in an ongoing adventure story to tell Mark and his brothers before they went to sleep. And to this day, Denise's family routinely performs a "magical act" of balancing spoons on their noses when they gather at restaurants, holiday events, even weddings. As you can imagine, this has become a unique family trademark. Depending upon what your family style and comfort level is, institute a ritual that will meet your needs. Get your family involved in the planning and invention of the ritual. Here are several ideas for family rituals:

- ◆ Choose a weekly activity at which all family members come together for a special night out at Joe's Pizza, a Saturday afternoon at the movies, or a Sunday mystery trip to a new place.

- ◆ Create an unusual family recipe for a main dish, side dish, or dessert. Name this secret recipe after your family and make it for parties, holidays, dinners, picnics, and special events.

- Make a family scrap album that recognizes special events, school achievements, vacations, birthdays, and the changing looks of family members. Bring out the album once a month to add new information and to reminisce over memories.

- Take a yearly vacation or trip that is planned and organized by the whole family.

- Have a family council meeting (see family council, page 57) or plan a weekly hour of time to discuss plans, grievances, chores, and accomplishments.

- Make a family time capsule in which your family collects items that signify the year's events and accomplishments. Place them in a container to be opened at a later time. This could be years or decades later. Make it a yearly ritual to collect the items and put them in the container. You may want to close up one time capsule and open a new one every few years.

Family Reunion

Host a family reunion   All ages

There's so little time today for just relaxing with the family that proposing a get-together of all the relatives is like suggesting a trip to the moon. Well, don't forget, we have made it to the moon—and back—several times. So everyone in your family should be able to manage getting to the same place at the same time for one day.

Family reunions are perfect for bringing generations together simply to celebrate being a family. Participating will give your child a sense of belonging. Involve your child in the process of setting up the reunion, from sending invitations to planning the activities and preparing the food. Ask her to come up with fun games that will help reacquaint people. Perhaps she can even pull together a talent show. Your child will come to understand the various relationships among relatives by creating a family tree. The book *Do People Grow on Trees? Genealogy for Kids and Other Beginners* by Ira Wolfman (Workman Publishing, 1991) explains how cousins, aunts, grandparents, and others are related to each other.

On reunion day, be sure to take plenty of pictures. You can add to the spirit of the occasion by ordering T-shirts with the family name or group picture on it. And when it's all over, suggest to your child that she keep the family spirit alive by sending everyone a newsletter that includes pictures and accounts of the reunion. She may want to issue it quarterly to keep relatives updated on interesting news and upcoming events—including, perhaps, the next family reunion.

Family Treasure Hunt

All ages　*A game to discover and uncover family facts*

This game is a natural for family gatherings and holiday celebrations. Its purpose is to engage your children in a historical and humorous treasure hunt for family secrets, stories, and folklore. Prior to the get-together, make a list of questions that will uncover interesting facts. Here are some suggestions:

1. How old is the eldest living relative?
2. What year was it when our family came to this country?
3. What were the names of your great-great-great-great-grandparents?
4. Who in the family had the most children?
5. Did anyone in the family do something famous?
6. Which family member got in trouble for doing something dangerous?
7. Which family member tells the best jokes?
8. What is the funniest story ever told about this family?
9. What countries did our family members come from?
10. What are some of your grandparents' favorite songs?
11. What does a dance from the old country look like?

Photocopy the list so every child receives his or her own. You may want to pair very young children with older children. Let the kids know that they must go from relative to relative to find out these bits of family treasures. Once they have written the answers to all the questions, they will receive a prize (perhaps a tasty dessert). When all the children return their list of answers, take time to read them out loud so that everyone can enjoy them.

Family Story/Family Folklore

All ages　*Investigate your family history*

Many cultures make a point of passing down to each generation their family history, traditions, lineage, and folklore. What is your family story? Do you know all the details? Take the time to investigate, then share your findings with your children. Enhance this activity by involving your child in the process of investigating your history through conversations and interviews with older relatives. You may want to record your findings in a book titled *Our Family Story.* Use pictures and illustrations to accompany the story. This will become a unique family heirloom to pass on to future generations.

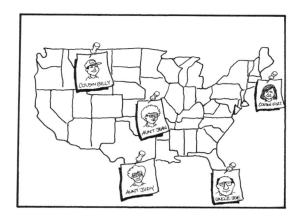

Family Map

Chart your relatives on a map

3 years and up

It's often difficult for a child to develop and maintain a sense of family when she sees relatives infrequently. Help your child visualize the size and breadth of her extended family by filling a map with pictures and statements about her relatives.

First select a map of the United States, or the world, if your relatives are far-flung. You can probably find a large enough map at a teachers' supply store. With your child, place pictures and/or names of relatives in their respective states or countries.

You may also want to map out your family's migration route to this country. For this you need a world map. Place pictures and/or names of ancestors in their countries of origin and trace the journey to their adopted homes with a marker. Include the year of their resettlement.

Family Handshake

Create a secret handshake that only your immediate family knows

2 years and up

Your handshake can involve a number of interesting moves—hand clasps, finger snaps, bottom bumps, and winks. Use your secret handshake whenever you greet each other, say good-bye, or say good-night.

Talking Pictures

3 years and up *Look at old family photographs*

This is one of our favorite ways to bring older and younger relatives together. Ask older relatives to bring old photo albums to family gatherings, with pictures from their past. During the get-together, the older and younger relatives should sit down together to leaf through the albums. Encourage the older generation to talk about the pictures, to tell stories, and to point out relatives the younger ones may have never known. Videotape this event. It deserves to be remembered.

Family Card System

3 years and up *A surefire plan to get greeting cards sent on time*

We are notoriously tardy card senders. Fortunately, our relatives are good-natured about receiving Christmas cards on Valentine's Day, and so far haven't kicked us out of the family tree for our transgressions. We do have a friend who (after asking if we own stock in a belated-birthday-card company) shared his method of getting cards out on time. Make a twelve-month file to hold pread-dressed greeting cards for the friends and relatives on your list. Of course, you need a master list containing all those important birthdays, anniversaries, and upcoming events, like weddings and graduations. Then, set aside a good chunk of a day to spend with your family in a card store. With list in hand, pick out cards for everyone on your list. You probably won't be able to buy holiday cards until they're on the store shelves, usually a month or so before the holiday.

When you get home, address the cards and pencil lightly on the envelope the date when each needs to be sent. If you want, stamp the cards, too. Finally, file the cards by month. At the beginning of each month, pull out the appropriate file and mail your cards.

We haven't put this idea to the test yet, but it certainly sounds like a good way to keep the greeting cards flowing (and our place on the family tree safe and secure).

> The Porter family extends way beyond the walls of their Houston home. Carol and Hurt Porter, Jr. and their children, Richard and Jamilhah, have embraced Houston's needy children with their program, Kid-Care. They run the program out of their kitchen preparing meals from both donated and government-subsidized food.
>
> The Porters answer fifty calls for help a day, distribute used clothing, and in a pinch, will provide a bed for the night. They have convinced a pediatrician and a dentist to provide free shots and dental care for "their" kids. Their goal is to establish enough kitchens to feed all the hungry kids in Houston.

Family to Family

Help out a family in need

2 years and up

It really puts things into perspective to step outside your own experience and glimpse someone else's. Strengthen your own family by reaching out to another.

Consider "adopting" a family in need by contacting a local shelter or social service agency. The Salvation Army, for instance, offers an adopt-a-family program at holiday time. Depending on the family's needs and your abilities, you may find yourself helping a family find a home, get jobs, or simply learn where to shop in your community. Teenage parents and immigrants are often desperate for some guidance and family connections. Give to other families as a family.

Family Comment Cards

Customized comment cards to evaluate how your family is doing

6 years and up

You know those comment cards tucked between the sugar and napkin containers at restaurants? They ask questions like "How was our service?" and "Was our food to your satisfaction?" Well, this isn't such a bad way to find out how your own family life is measuring up.

In this activity your family will make its own set of family comment cards. Devise your own set of questions about your family's performance based on your family mission statements (see activity on page 97). Here are some sample questions: "Rate our ability to meet your needs"; "Rate the amount of time we spend on you"; "Do parents listen to children?" and "Do children listen to parents?"

With your children, write these questions on index cards and leave space underneath for boxes to check indicating whether the family's performance is excellent, good, average, or poor. Think up as many questions as you can with your child and end the card with a section to write comments.

Make plenty of these comment cards, and leave them around so people can fill out comment cards whenever they get the urge. Keep an empty tissue box nearby to collect completed cards. Then from time to time read the cards and check out how your family is doing.

Family Gardens

Garden as a family

6 years and up

Mark loves to garden. He works in our backyard for hours and his efforts really pay off—in spring and summer it looks like a miniature paradise back there! Mark inherited his green thumb from his dad and our children are starting to show an early appreciation for backyard agriculture as well. The kids now have their own gardening tools and their own special patch of land to tend themselves. They love it and especially adore hanging out with their dad in the dirt (what kid doesn't like having permission to get dirty?).

Gardening is fun. But it's also inspiring and educational. The gardener sees the fruits of hard labor and glimpses the inner workings of nature.

If you haven't already, consider gardening as a family activity. You don't even need a backyard to do it. Find a nearby community garden or throw some dirt and seeds in a pot. We've seen some impressive coffee-can gardens that produce huge tomatoes and beautiful flowers on apartment balconies and even windowsills. Gardening is also a natural for teaching children about the life cycle.

Family Rings

3 years and up   *Forge family identity*

Extend the idea of the wedding ring to the whole family. Choose a ring for everybody to wear. Give family rings to favorite grandparents, aunts, uncles, and cousins, too.

Activities for Families of Divorce

Although you and your child's other biological parent may not live together, it's important to remember he still has both a mom and a dad, as well as an extended family including both sets of grandparents, cousins, aunts, and uncles. The following activities will help your child identify with his extended families by providing an image of their connection to him.

The Family Quilt

2 years and up   *Make a patchwork quilt from family clothing*

Stitch together scraps of clothing donated by new family members and biological relatives. For instance, use Grandma's old dress, Grandpa's favorite barbecue apron, Dad's dress shirt with the frayed collar, Dad's new wife's scarf, and her brother's old dungarees.

While cutting and sewing the pieces, talk with your child about how the pieces of cloth represent each person, and though you may all be separate from one another, you still have a common thread that connects you.

Picture Collage

Make a picture collage of family members

2 to 12 years

Using the concept of a family quilt, select photographs of family members or draw pictures of them and organize these into a collage. Include pictures from the past as well as the present so the collage depicts the changes your family has experienced over the years.

Family Calendar

Make a family calendar using twelve photographs that represent your family

2 to 12 years

Use one photograph per month. It can be of a family member, the place of a parent's home, or an activity shared with a parent. Enlarge the photos if necessary and attach each one to a month of the year. Use the calendar to mark the days the child is with one parent or with the other. Include where she will spend holidays, special events, and information that may help her understand what is happening throughout the year. This activity will provide your child with guidance as well as predictability in a sometimes confusing family structure. Explain to your child that the divorce makes things different, but just like the special calendar, your parental love and attention spans the year.

The Divorce Workbook

A workbook that helps explore feelings and situations that come about from divorce

2 to 12 years

Make a book in which your child can record the different processes, feelings, and changes the divorce has caused. You can use *The Divorce Workbook: A Guide for Kids and Families* by Sally Blakeslee, Michelle Lash, and David Fassler (Waterfront Books, 1985), which is actually a "write-in workbook" that encourages children to write and draw pictures of what they are thinking and feeling about the divorce.

Activities That Enhance Community Connections

Community Works

Visit places in your community

This is one of our children's favorite community activities. Each year we visit different work environments in our town. We visit the post office, library, electric company, fire and police departments, the hospital, houses of worship, municipal buildings, the court house, and even the garbage dump. We make an appointment ahead of time to meet the people who keep our hometown running smoothly. The employees are usually happy to show us around and tell us about what they do. At the end of every visit, we make a point of showing our gratitude to our hosts. Whether you live in a suburb, city, big or small town, this is a rewarding activity because it gives your child a close-up look at how your community functions, and at the people who make it happen.

Community Treasure Hunt

4 years and up *Use a map to find interesting places in your community*

Every community holds a treasure trove of history. Help your child unearth the riches in yours.

A good way to do this is by using a map to point out how your city or town was settled. Find the areas where the first homes, schools, and businesses were built (your local historical society or library can help you with this). Note interesting places, such as cemeteries and homes of historical figures. Extend your community treasure hunt to include the police station, hospital, and other places your child should know about in the event of an emergency. Have your child help you locate these places by using the map, then go out and visit them.

Family Common-unity

All ages *Seek out other families with interests similar to yours*

In every community, you will find people just like you. For this activity point out interests your family has in common with other families in your town. If you are concerned about the quality of education in your community, familiarize your children with organizations and political leaders in the community who support the schools. If your interests are in making playgrounds safe and fun for children, find others who are working toward this goal. Then get involved. Encourage your child also to join forces with others in your community to see your family goals met.

Millicent Mindfulness

Watch out for your neighbors' well-being

All ages The phone rings. "Hello, Denise, this is Millicent. How are you, dear? I don't mean to be a nosy neighbor, but are you using the dryer?"

"Yes, I am—is there something wrong?" Denise answers.

"Thank goodness. No. I thought I saw smoke, but it must be the steam from the dryer coming up the side of your house. I just wanted to be sure it wasn't something worse!" If only there were more Millicents in our neighborhood. It's a shame that our society has become so cynical and suspicious that we worry about being mistaken for a neighborhood spy. We're glad Millicent doesn't worry about that. She calls when our dog gets loose and lets us know when our garbage can blows into the street. Millicent is mindful; she minds her own business but luckily for us, she minds ours as well. We have learned a lot from our good neighbor and we hope others will, too. Take the time to look out your window. Care about your neighbors' welfare. Be nosy and welcome others to be nosy about you. . . . One day that steam could be smoke.

> David Cox knows how it feels to need help, so he has made it his mission to provide that help. David was born with cerebral palsy and is paralyzed on his left side. Even so, he has been finding ways to help others.
>
> Since he was twelve, David has been offering his services to the elderly and the disabled, shoveling snow, taking out the trash, shopping, and doing home repairs. Since he's been old enough to drive, David has also chauffeured his neighbors to doctors' appointments.
>
> David truly knows how to make his community a nicer place in which to live.

Community Volunteering

Become involved citizens

2 years and up

Get the whole family involved in supporting your community. You can volunteer in your schools, hospitals, community centers, preservation societies, and zoos. Take part in fund-raisers, and bring your children along when you vote. It's important that they see how much you care about the people and the needs of your community.

II

Character Skills

Personal Potential

Our daughter Arielle has often been described as a little flower petal, an angel, and a peanut. She's small and her spirit is gentle. Insightful and attuned to others, Arielle has, since birth, shown an affinity for animals and a sensitivity to her surroundings. All qualities that make her special and a joy to be with.

However, these same qualities have worked against her in other ways. Like all people, she has been naturally endowed in some areas but less so in others. Being small and somewhat slow to develop physical strength has, at times, been frustrating for her. Some activities haven't come easily for Arielle and she would often give up, crying "I can't do it." We felt her pain and frustration and wanted to help her become stronger than any problem she might encounter.

Knowing this, we embarked upon a plan to help our daughter build her self-confidence. We encouraged her to try, try again, and urged her not to give up. We tried to recognize every accomplishment, especially if it was one requiring strength or courage, and we seized every occasion where she stood up for herself or attempted a new task.

There were times when we doubted whether we were making progress, but upon closer inspection, we would see signs that Arielle was developing confidence. One morning, she mustered the courage to tell the waitress her breakfast order. Another day, she powered her tricycle up the incline of our driveway for the first time, and on still another she taught a friend how to draw a tree. Despite these successes, Arielle still struggled to keep up physically with her playmates. But seeing our efforts pay off gave us the encouragement we needed to press on.

The beauty of consistent and unwavering support is that our faith in Arielle eventually became Arielle's faith in herself. Our words of encouragement had gained a momentum of their own, one strong enough to carry Arielle through her greatest physical accomplishment to date: the monkey bars.

Arriving at her preschool one afternoon, we were astonished to hear her announce that she would cross the monkey bars without help. She fixed a brave, determined expression on her face and marched over to the metal contraption. The bars loomed over our tiny daughter. She climbed to the top and grabbed the first rung. Through sheer determination, Arielle drove herself forward, swinging from bar to bar. She lost her grip and fell. Our hearts sank, then swelled with pride when she brushed herself off and returned to try again.

Apparently Arielle had been quietly practicing the monkey bars for weeks leading up to that moment. For some reason we may never quite understand, she had decided on her own to tackle this as her biggest challenge. She did it by summoning up a reserve of strength, courage, and perseverance.

After that day, our daughter was more confident. For weeks, she was uncharacteristically tolerant of her strong-willed younger sister, and she dealt head-on with situations that she would have shied away from just a short time earlier. Arielle had achieved a major feat and was basking in her private glory.

Given Arielle's nature and her small size, the monkey bars presented her with a considerable challenge that she wouldn't have mastered or even attempted had she not had confidence in herself. Arielle's story is a perfect example of what using one's personal potential can do for a child and how it grows. In this chapter, we will talk about the components of personal potential: self-esteem, courage and confidence, and perseverance and optimism. Personal potential isn't something that we are born with. It grows from experiences such as Arielle's on the monkey bars, experiences that allow children to test their limits, to push on even after failing, force out negative self-perceptions such as "I can't do it, I'm not strong enough," and replace them with positive ones. These confidence-building events create a deep-seated belief that says "I can do it, I have the abilities, I believe in myself." For this reason, children who develop their personal potential are more likely to reach their goals despite seemingly insurmountable odds.

In decades past, children were given little power and few rights, and they were sheltered from difficult decisions and tasks. This practice undoubtedly made children more obedient, and on the surface made parenting easier . . . until children wanted to explore their rights and power. Today's children are expected to be independent at a younger age, for example latchkey kids who are charged with the job of supervising themselves and sometimes a younger sibling, or preparing a meal. In addition, they are exposed to more situations that require mature decision-making skills and knowledge. Parents have responded by giving their children more rights, more power, and more information. Children in this position need to feel good about who they are and have confidence.

Self-Esteem

At every stage of life, self-esteem affects our ability to make good decisions in times of need. Self-esteem can be defined as respect, faith, and love of oneself. Self-esteem is derived from our self-concept, and self-concept is the set of ideas that define how we think of ourselves. When we're comfortable with these ideas, our self-esteem is high. These ideas begin to be developed in the first years of life and are shaped by the input of parents and other significant caregivers in the child's life.

Children who grow up with a positive sense of self-worth are fortifying themselves even against circumstances that are beyond their control, such as divorce, death, or absence of a parent. A high sense of self-worth causes a child to hold himself in high regard, thus discouraging self-destructive and reckless behaviors, such as drug use or sexual promiscuity. A child with healthy self-esteem will value her life, her goals, and her body over approval of peers, and media influences.

Courage and Confidence

By recognizing that their children feel a kind of personal power and potential, parents and educators will help children develop courage and confidence. A confident and courageous child will take the appropriate risks necessary to tackle physical, intellectual, and emotional challenges with enthusiasm rather than dread. Fears and uncertainties will be worked through and overcome rather than given in to, such as when a child who is afraid of the water learns to swim. These successes not only make the child's life fuller, they act as a catalyst for other challenges.

Perseverance and Optimism

Children who exercise their personal potential are goal oriented, acting with a purpose and a plan when aiming for a goal. They can visualize a far-off re-

Over the Years
Guidelines for the Development of Character Skills

Note: This guide is meant to serve as a general orientation to what you can expect and when to expect it. While there are no absolute norms or limitations regarding how and when characteristics within a developmental period appear, and every child is unique, there is a range of similar and expectable periods of development, each marked by patterns of behavior and capabilities. Keep in mind that the nature of personality development is dynamic and repetitive, meaning that it is ever-changing and traits and/or skills seem to appear, disappear, and then reappear throughout development.

Personal Potential—Self-esteem, Courage, Confidence, Perseverance, Optimism

Stage I Infancy: Birth to 24 Months
The stage of life from newborn through toddlerhood

Foundation period in which many behavior patterns, attitudes, and patterns of emotional expression are being established. Much of the first 12 months of this period are affected by instinctual drives for nurturing, food, and basic care.

Expect baby to: exhibit increasing confidence in the form of decreasing dependency, as early as 10 months (i.e., self-feeding, self-undressing); exhibit increasing mobility and independent gross motor activities from 12–24 months (i.e., sitting, crawling, retrieving a desired object, pulling oneself to a standing position, and eventually walking); show increased interest in other people and tolerate brief separations from primary caregivers; make known wants and needs, express curiosity, and interest in play; from 20–24 months use newfound mobility to assert emerging needs for independence (running away from a chasing parent). These early behaviors are an indication that baby is feeling positive about himself and his potential.

Do not expect baby to: show any overt or obvious signs of any of these skills at this stage.

Stage II Early Childhood—The Preschool Years: Ages 2 to 6
The stage of life from toddlerhood through kindergarten

This is often called the play age because it is the peak period of interest in play and toys, marked by exploration, discovery play, creativity, magical thinking, fierce strivings for independence, and acquisition of social skills. This is a time of preparation for learning the foundations of social behavior needed for the school years to come.

Between the ages of 2–4, expect children to: exhibit dramatic growth of personal potential; want to do everything for themselves; show little fear or apprehension in tackling new tasks or activities; take pride in newly discovered motor skills, even those things that they have not mastered (tying shoes, pouring a drink, self-dressing and -feeding); interpret adult proposals as a threat to their integrity and autonomy, and stubbornly resist in every way they know how, earning this period the title "terrible twos."

Do not expect children to: understand the often self-defeating dynamic of these behaviors; recognize the dangers and risks of some of their shows of independence (climbing on a counter to retrieve a glass, running across the street).

Between ages 4–6, expect children to become: more competitive ("I beat you, I am faster"); more socially confident and astute (separating for kindergarten, inviting a playmate to visit); willing to try new things (organized sports, ordering meal at restaurant, going overnight with a friend or relative); more secure about their place in the world and their rights ("If you are mean to me, I will go home," "This is my house and my family").

Do not expect children to: cope with separations easily (even if they had before); win or lose graciously; develop these traits without support and infusions of a caregiver's love and support.

Stage III Late Childhood—The School Years: Ages 6 to 11
This stage of life begins with entrance into first grade and extends into preadolescence

This period is marked by major interest and concern for social involvement with peers; participation in rule-based group play; and increased motivation to learn, acquire technical knowledge, information, and achieve academic success. This stage is very important for establishing attitudes and habits about learning, work, and personal potential.

Expect children to: experience challenges and even setbacks to their skills in personal potential; struggle with feelings of inferiority, inadequacy, and loss of confidence due to teasing, name calling, rejection by peers, racism, prejudice, academic difficulties, or gender stereotyping; find their personal potential through academic success and affiliation with friends, teammates, and neighborhood playmates; derive positive feelings from relationships with special adults and mentors outside of their family (i.e., teachers, coaches, scout leaders).

Do not expect children to: develop personal potential in an environment of ridicule, criticism, or instability, without school success and advocacy by caregivers.

Stage IV Early Adolescence: Ages 11 to 15
This stage of life begins around the time a child finishes elementary school and concludes by the time he graduates middle school (junior high school) and enters the world of high school

This period is marked by change and turmoil, the onset of puberty, growth spurts, increased interest in peer relationships and the opposite sex, and fierce strivings for self-identity and independence.

Expect adolescents to: feel misunderstood and alienated from their parents; at times be unrealistic and overly optimistic in their aspirations and expectations, causing them to suffer disappointment and disillusionment about themselves and their parents in particular, and to some degree about their world; experience dissatisfaction with their bodies and the physical changes they are undergoing, and their perceived attractiveness, causing decreased self-esteem, confusion, irritability, and despondency; show confidence and courage to tackle challenges independent from assistance of their parents (i.e., applying for a job); experience positive personal potential skills from a part-time job and school success.

Do not expect adolescents to: remain as confident and self-assured as they had been in the previous stage; remain optimistic after a failure; to feel much better from a parent's positive appraisal of their attractiveness (but do not let this stop you from commenting positively).

ward, will set expectations optimistically and realistically, and will persevere, whether it is studying all semester to make the honor roll or enduring months of painful medical treatment to beat back a life-threatening illness. Through the experience of persevering in pursuit of a goal children learn patience, emotional control, organization, creative problem solving, responsibility, and independence.

Evaluating If a Child Has Difficulties with Personal Power

Use the "Over the Years Guidelines" on the preceding pages to be sure your expectations are in line with your child's age and developmental capabilities. Use the "Questions to Ask Yourself" as a checkpoint and a way of evaluating the child's strengths and weaknesses. If you answer yes to any of these questions, it will be beneficial to help the child develop these skills further.

Questions to Ask Yourself

Does the child often express feelings of inadequacy? (She says, "I can't do it, I am not smart enough to put this puzzle together.")

Does the child respond to frustration with aggression, anger, or violence directed at herself or someone else? (She breaks a toy that she can't make operate effectively.)

Does the child equate personal power with physical aggression and violence, aggressive characters and play figures? (The child idolizes TV and cartoon characters who fight and use aggression to solve problems, and these are his only heroes.)

Does the child have consistently low expectations of herself? (She doesn't make the extra effort to reach a goal or gives up after encountering a setback.)

Does the child procrastinate and leave school and projects until the last moment? (She waits until the day before a term paper is due to start this project.)

Does the child focus upon past failures and obstacles? (He approaches a new activity with trepidation anticipating all of the possible things that may go wrong.)

Does the child seem compelled to control others and "hog" the spotlight? (She is manipulative or bossy with playmates and refuses to play when she can't be the leader.)

Does the child have difficulty acknowledging and enjoying his successes? (He may become upset or becomes uncomfortable when given praise or recognition for accomplishments.)

Does the child seem to need immediate gratification? (She prefers to take on only those tasks and projects that provide immediate reward, and if they don't deliver, gives up.)

Does the child follow others seemingly without awareness of what his own thoughts are? (She will adopt the style of dress, behavior, and language of her peers, frequently changing to fit in with others.)

How to Enhance a Child's Personal Potential

1. As a parent, caregiver, or educator you can help children discover the potential they hold by evaluating their strengths and weaknesses, then helping them turn these strengths into skills to overcome these weaknesses. Keep in mind that children will need to discover for themselves what they can accomplish. You might create the opportunity, point the way, and then step far enough away so you will be there to cushion the hard landings. Your children will do the rest.

2. It helps to get to know your feelings and beliefs regarding your personal potential, and separate your issues from your child's. Most of us have struggled at one time or another to develop our own self-esteem, confidence, or courage; through this struggle we've gained insights that will help us share these skill-building experiences with our child. If you are a natural worrier, keep a check on your tendency to overprotect; children need to be allowed to take appropriate risks such as swinging high or climbing up a tree to a precarious perch to achieve courage and confidence.

3. Our children are exposed to negative influences and misleading information perhaps more than any generation before them. Our sons and daughters, students, and grandkids need to learn that results aren't instantaneous and automatic. Teach them patience and perseverance by modeling these behaviors. Use yourself as an example and talk about the rewards of hard work and the sweet payoff of patience.

4. Handed the opportunity, children are bound to test the limits of their power and your rules. Believe it or not, the four-year-old who says "No, I

won't" for the fifth time at the checkout counter, or the thirteen-year-old who strolls in after curfew are not purposely trying to upset you. Don that coat of armor, shield yourself from these actions so that you don't overreact, and then deliver whatever consequences you feel are appropriate. The goal is to avoid getting entangled in the child's quest for control and to see his experiments at autonomy and power for what they are.

5. If you start to feel threatened by the child's emerging independence and power, do a reality check. Look beyond these instances to how she gets along in general, how well she has incorporated your rules and structure, and how she behaves out of the home in other settings. Also compare her to other children her age and incorporate what developmental and environmental challenges might temporarily be affecting what is happening.

6. Encourage your child to chase his dreams and endure, even when quitting seems so much easier. Be a resource and remind your child of when he was courageous or overcame an obstacle to reach a goal. Over time, your children will begin to define themselves by their successes and the result will be a positive self-concept.

Activities That Enhance Self-Esteem

Skill Cards

3 years and up   *A deck of cards containing the admirable traits of family members*

These skill cards will become a major component of other activities in this book. When you play with them, you help your children develop a fuller understanding of their capabilities. This insight is the backbone of personal power.

Each family member gets their own set of one hundred or two hundred skill cards. Allow enough time (several days, if necessary) to explore each person's unique abilities. These should include everything from being good at sports to petting the dog gently. Thoroughly audit your family members' characteristics, traits, and talents. Probe what they can achieve with their minds, bodies, and feelings. Take a close look at their hobbies, appearance, and their smile. Break apart a single talent to discover the various skills it employs. A good baseball player, for instance, can catch, throw, run, work cooperatively, and withstand the heat of the day. Look hard enough and you'll discover something to admire in even the most questionable pastime. Your child has developed great hand-eye coordination from endless games of Nintendo, for instance. If you still need help, check out the Appendix in this book, which includes over five hundred skills and capabilities a child may possess.

Write down each skill on a card. Each family member should accumulate a deck of cards by the end of this activity.

Most of the families and schoolteachers we've taught this activity to found their own best uses for their skill cards, but following are three ideas to get you started.

Backpack of Skills
The child carries the skill cards in a backpack, a literal reminder of the child's capabilities

4 years and up

Place a selection of cards into a backpack. Slip it over your child's shoulders and explain that with her skills right behind her, she will have the confidence to handle any challenge thrown her way.

Role-play situations in which your child has felt insecure. In each instance, encourage her to reach into the backpack for the skills that will restore her confidence. Add new cards to the deck daily to increase her awareness of her many abilities.

Have your child wear the backpack whenever she needs a boost of confidence. Most importantly, let her know that her skills are always with her, regardless of where the card deck is.

King or Queen for a Day
Treat your child like royalty by designating a day to honor their attributes

3 years and up

Bedeck your little king or queen in crown and robe. Family and friends choose from the skill-card deck the qualities they admire most in the child, then tape these to the imperial garments. The royal highness will reign throughout the day, wearing the robe, crown, and a plenitude of noble qualities.

Great-Me Wall Hanging
A poster that illustrates your child's skills and capabilities

Materials:
poster board, film, camera

3 to 12 years

With your child, pick at least twenty-four skills from his skill cards. Include the everyday activities, like brushing teeth, sharing toys, and making Dad laugh, as well as special talents like sports, dance, art, and music.

As your child goes about his week, take pictures of him engaged in these pursuits. When the film is developed, arrange the photographs on a poster entitled "Great Me."

Both of our daughters have great-me posters in their bedroom. We find ourselves referring to these often when the kids are feeling frustrated or when their confidence is running low.

Pat on the Back

A whimsical way to remind your children to be generous with self-praise

Materials: glove, shirtsleeve, stuffing

3 years and up

Here's that third hand you've been wishing for. Only this one is reserved solely for congratulating all the work the other two do. Fashion a hand from a glove attached to a stuffed shirtsleeve. Keep it handy (sorry, couldn't resist) for all those undervalued and overlooked achievements. When your child comes home from school with an A in math, hand over the hand and tell her to pat herself on the back.

Pick-a-Praise

Store compliments in a jar, then dole them out like cookies

Materials: jar, slips of paper

4 years and up

Decorate a jar and label it Pick-a-Praise. Whenever your child receives a compliment, jot it down on a slip of paper and drop it in the container. Keep the jar handy for those times when your child needs an ego boost.

You Make a Difference

Show your child the effects of desirable behavior

2 years and up

When your child does something praiseworthy, expound on your compliment. Explain the consequences of your child's deed. For example, when you get help setting the table, let your child know *why* you appreciate the effort.

Little Memos

Surprise love notes

4 years and up

Think about all those things you love about your child, then write them down on self-adhesive notes. Leave these in unexpected places, like the bottom of a cereal bowl, or in the medicine cabinet next to the toothbrushes.

Your child will get a kick out of discovering them. Turn it into a game by challenging him to collect the notes to stick in even sillier places for you to find. At the end of the day, see how many of the messages your child can remember.

Fortune Cookies

Fill fortune cookies with examples of the good fortune your child possesses

Bake fortune cookies or buy them and carefully pull out the slips of paper inside with a tweezer. Put statements about your child inside. For example, a message might say, "You are a great kid and know how to tell jokes that make people laugh."

Materials:
a recipe and ingredients for fortune cookies

4 years and up

Once-a-Year Letter

An annual review of your child's life

On each birthday, write your child a letter recalling everything during the past year that was special to you. These will become treasured keepsakes for your child.

All ages

PC Self-Esteem

Home computer fun that enhances self-esteem

If you have a home computer you're probably aware of the magical hold it can have on your child. We're still mystified by how deft our children are at manipulating the keyboard and mouse.

There are some terrific educational programs available. Check out software reviews in parenting and computer magazines to find out which are best for your child. Computer mastery is a source of personal power for children, and in many cases, the one thing kids feel good at. The following activities build on the ego-enhancing properties of computers. Keep in mind, any of these can be adapted for those old reliables: pen and paper.

4 years and up

Newspaper Front Page

Your child makes the front page

Plaster your child all over the front page with a computer publishing software that has a kid-friendly newsletter program. Concentrate on a single accomplishment like learning to ride a bicycle or clinching a spot on the all-star debate team.

Study front-page articles with your child to get a feel for how news stories are structured. Write a straight story about your child's recent success, then round out your coverage with a profile piece, an opinion column, and interviews with proud parents and grandparents. Don't forget to include a byline and dateline on each article. Save room on the page for a picture of your child and photocopy this very special edition for friends and family.

5 years and up

Great-Achievement Book

4 years and up *Publish an autobiography of your child*

Sit down with your child to list her achievements. Start with her birth, then go on to those significant milestones of babyhood, such as the first smile, the first tooth, and the day she learned to walk. Encourage her to remember her various accomplishments. She should include the major ones, like capturing the lead in the school play, without neglecting the mundane triumphs such as figuring out how to pump her legs on the playground swing.

Almost everybody in Laura-Beth Moore's neighborhood agreed there should be curbside pickup for recyclables but nobody was doing anything about it. So, when the seventh-grader circulated a petition calling for a program to recycle glass, aluminum, plastic, and paper, she easily filled it with signatures. But when she sent her petition to the mayor, nothing happened. The mayor said recycling would be too expensive.

Laura-Beth came up with a new plan. She vowed to find a drop-off site where people could take their recyclables. But this proved harder than she thought. Laura-Beth approached a number of people with her request, but no one took her seriously because of her age.

After a year and a half of persistence, Laura-Beth finally got the city to devote a portion of the schoolyard to her recycling project. There people drop off tons of materials that otherwise would end up in landfills.

Laura-Beth Moore says that the most important thing she's learned from her experience is that you can do anything if you just refuse to give up.

Your child will arrange these achievements in book form using a book-publishing program. Consider this book a work in progress, one that will be periodically updated as your child grows.

A Chicago couple we know who does this activity with their three children found a way to convey how precious these autobiographies are. On each child's twelfth birthday, their parents presented them with a personalized, engraved leather book cover.

Banners, Certificates, and Home Decorations

4 years and up *Create customized decorations to honor your child's achievements*

Turn out professional-looking banners and certificates with programs such as BannerMania from Broderbund Software. Have your child come up with an empowering statement about herself and hang these fun reminders in your home.

Great Kid Business Cards

5 years and up *Calling cards that state your child's name and specialty*

On precut business cards, write your child's name, talents, or attributes. For example, "John Roberts: knock-knock jokes a specialty," or "Sarah Tyler:

bright and loving." Your child will feel important handing these out to friends and relatives.

Activities That Build Courage and Confidence

Fear-a-lizer

A roller machine that smashes fears on contact

Fear is a powerful emotion that can crush a child's self-confidence. The fear-a-lizer gives your child the power to crush his fears, and in the process, shows him how to extract courage from his innate abilities and talents.

Discuss what frightens your child, then carefully write each fear on a cracker. Consult your child's skill cards to come up with a list of all his weapons against fear (for example, "eager to try new things," "smart," "quick thinker"). Write these skills down on a piece of paper and then wrap this around the rolling pin and secure it with tape.

Place a cracker on the table and explain to your child how each quality listed on the fear-a-lizer is stronger than the fear itself, and when conscripted into service and strategically deployed, will conquer his fright.

To activate the fear-a-lizer, your child grasps the handles firmly and confidently, recites his fear-fighting abilities, then crushes the cracker with all his might.

A memorable way to show your child that anxiety is more easily defeated after it has been broken down, is to ask him to blow away a fear cracker. It can be done, but not easily. Now ask him to crush it with the fear-a-lizer, then blow it away. It's nothing but pixie dust in the wind.

Materials:
rolling pin, markers, soda crackers

5 to 12 years

Chunking

Materials:
poster board, markers,
scissors

5 years and up

Obliterate fear by breaking it apart and taking on its components

Before you begin this activity, help your child understand that fear is actually a collection of anxieties that have accumulated over time and that have become incorporated into our personalities. For example, a fear of swimming may be the result of a number of disturbances that most of us get over pretty easily, such as the distress of not feeling firm ground under us, and the discomfort of having to hold our breath. Add to these a bad experience, such as slipping under the water in the bathtub and choking, and you have a full-blown fear.

Chunking shows your child how to stomp out fear by breaking it up into crushable chunks.

Write what frightens your child in huge letters on poster board. Explore the various elements of this fear with your child, listing the situations, experiences, and anxieties that feed it. Write these on the back of the poster board, leaving enough space to cut these out later. Together, examine each element objectively. Figure out where it came from and how to make it go away. If that's not possible, decide how your child can live with it. Finally, cut it out of the poster board. When you're through, that big, overpowering fear on the other side of the board will be literally reduced to shreds. Next time it makes an appearance, your child will be ready to tear it to pieces figuratively.

Courage Amulet

3 years and up

An object to give a child courage

When Arielle turned four she suddenly became fearful of new things. We were concerned her timidity would seep into other areas of her life and damage her confidence. It was clear that Arielle needed some help rediscovering her courage. We found it, in the form of a rock.

It was plain and gray, small enough to fit snugly in a child's fist. We spotted it in our garden and made up a story about its magical properties. We told Arielle that she would become courageous just by holding it in her hand. She took the rock from us and felt its weight. She examined its color and texture. Then she brought it inside, washed it, and painted it her favorite colors.

Arielle took that rock everywhere. It accompanied her to doctors' appointments and rode along in her pocket when she learned to roller-skate. Over time the rock found its way to Arielle's dresser, where it sits as a memory of her outgrown need. When we asked her why she stopped carrying it around, she said, "Because the rock juices spread into my insides and I don't need to hold it anymore."

If your child is going through a shaky period, we suggest you find an equivalent of Arielle's rock. Anything will work, and it helps all ages. A friend of ours carried a small wooden lion in her pocket the summer she was fourteen because a relative insisted the carved figure would give her the strength to endure her parents' recent divorce. More important than the object is the faith of the person who bestows it and the faith of the one who accepts it.

Magic Power Shield
Enhance a child's additional confidence

Materials:
paper plate, magazine pictures, family photographs

5 years and up

Plains Indians decorated rawhide shields with pictures of spirits who they believed would protect them during battle. These magic power shields gave the warriors confidence in times of trouble, thus reinforcing their belief in themselves.

　　With your child you can make a Plains Indian magic power shield. Using a paper plate, have your child draw pictures or paste photographs of her personal protectors, such as parents, the family dog, a smoke detector, and the police. On the back, ask your child to write his skills for coping with danger. Finally, glue a handle to the back.

　　To show your child how the shield works, pose a hypothetical dangerous situation and ask how the pictures on the front and the skills on the back would keep him safe from harm just like the Plains Indians.

Activities That Teach Perseverance and Optimism

Chitchat Hat
Your child learns to think positively by verbalizing inner thoughts while wearing the hat

5 years and up

One of the best methods for increasing children's self-esteem is to encourage them to talk positively to themselves. We're not suggesting they go through life cheering themselves on, but that they tune in to their inner voice and train it to be pleasant.

　　When we talk about the inner voice, we're referring to that "self" in our head that narrates our days. The voice is powerful. It can build us up ("I can do this!" "I look great in this shirt!"), and it can tear us down ("I'm such an oaf!" "I shouldn't have tried!"). That's why it's essential that your child learn to listen to her inner thoughts and train them to work for, not against, her.

　　Label a hat Chitchat Hat and treat it like a loudspeaker that broadcasts the wearer's thoughts. For example, your child is struggling with math homework. You know those equations are careening inside his brain like pinballs so you plunk the hat on his head and ask him to think out loud so he can hear those thoughts. Negative thoughts aren't as insidious when they're verbalized.

It's a good idea to do this activity yourself so your child will see how it works. Wear the hat while you're watching television, making dinner, or getting ready for work.

Rhyme and Rhythm Self-Talk

4 to 10 years · *Make a rhyme out of self-affirmations*

Show your child how to program her inner voice with self-affirmative statements, then help her memorize them by turning them into a rhyme. For example, "You are nice, friendly, smart, and fun./New friends don't have to make you run./Say hello and you will show/the kids at school that you are cool." Here's another one sung to the tune of "Twinkle, Twinkle, Little Star": "Jeffrey is so smart and strong./It's okay to do it wrong./Do your best and really try./That's what matters, you know why./Jeffrey is a little star/and it matters who you are."

Seeing Pictures

4 years and up · *Children visualize their thoughts as pictures*

While working with deaf children, Denise learned that people who communicate through sign language talk to themselves through a combination of sign and visualization. She had a group of deaf students teach hearing children to do the same. The hearing children were given paper and asked to draw their thought process during a specific situation, such as buying five items at the grocery store or learning to ski.

The purpose of the experiment was to help the deaf children feel good about their method of communicating while giving the others insight into the ways people who don't hear might get their message across. The unexpected result, however, was that the hearing children found that their thoughts were more concrete when in picture form, which made the thoughts easier to deal with.

Eyes on the Prize

4 years and up · *Visualize a goal*

Build upon the foregoing exercise titled "Seeing Pictures" to help your child perfect the technique of visualization. Visualization is a powerful method for focusing on a goal, and one that is used by business executives and Olympic athletes alike. While the executive will picture herself over and over closing a deal, the figure skater may spend months envisioning himself landing that perfect jump. The key is to imagine with such clarity that it feels real. You don't need to become a meditation guru to use this technique successfully. The following activity will help even a very young child foresee her potential.

Begin by having your child decide on a single goal, for example learning in-line skating. Explain that you will tell a story, but she has to illustrate it in her head. Ask her to close her eyes while you tell a detailed and realistic tale of her successful skating lesson from start to finish. Repeat the story, only this time ask your child to help by deciding what she will do next. Have her describe what she's wearing and how she's feeling. Finally, have your child tell the story herself.

This next part is optional but seems to help a child visualize without the story. Next time you or your child tells the story, "capture" it in a box and seal it up quickly so it won't escape. Wrap the box with pretty paper and a bow. Next time your child can't picture her goal, all she has

> It was more than a decade ago that Ocean Robbins starred in the play *Peace Child,* but he took the role to heart. The experience convinced the then ten-year-old that a child could make a difference in the world. He has since served three times as a youth ambassador to the USSR. He and three hundred other young people from all over the world wrote position papers on global issues such as famine and economic parity and sent copies to every chief of state in the world.
>
> Robbins shifted his focus to what he called the leaders of the future—the children—and embarked on a city-by-city tour of the United States. He and his four companions, all volunteers, called themselves YES (Youth for Environmental Sanity) and performed an environmental-awareness show at elementary and high schools across the country. Their message is that each person can make a difference, that the world belongs to all of us, and it is up to us to care for it.

to do is hold this prize, close her eyes, and remember what's inside. Whenever your child feels unsure of herself, remind her to "keep her eyes on the prize."

Ayyyak!

A personal power word   3 years and up

When Arielle is confronted with a new challenge, she yells "Ayyyak!" as if she's karate-chopping a board. She tells us it means "Good for you! Go for it! Good job! You can do it!" She invented her personal power word when she was a toddler and uses it to push her way through new challenges and endeavors. We've heard Arielle use it for everything from jumping into a swimming pool to applying the finishing touches on a drawing. We love to hear her power statement, but we get even more satisfaction when we realize from her self-assured facial expression that she's saying it silently to herself.

Take-Charge Words

All ages   *Teach children to speak well of themselves*

Negative and immoral influences threaten your child's sense of right and wrong as well as his ability to overcome personal challenges. Your child may someday be urged by peers to take drugs, hurt someone, or steal. He may be faced with a life-threatening situation or confronted with a difficult choice.

Help your child come up with four or five statements about himself that rekindle his self-confidence during these times. Phrases such as "I am in charge of my destiny," "I know I can," and "I am capable of telling right from wrong" are simple statements that mold positive self-perception. These take-charge words will echo in your child's mind and activate the inner voice that gives him strength and direction.

Positive "Software" Self-Talk Mindputer

Materials: *Replace negative self-perceptions with positive ones using a play computer*

shoe boxes, computer magazines, computer disk labels, four-by-six-inch index cards cut in half

7 years and up

If you have trouble understanding where your inner voice gets its material, it may be helpful to think of your mind as a computer. Your brain is the "hardware" and your life experience is the "software." The inner voice is our brain interpreting our experiences. The hardware is running the software.

Software is being installed from the first day of life. In the beginning, it's supplied entirely by others, which is pretty frightening because it means that as very young children, we don't choose what to think, it's chosen for us. As we mature, we learn to become more discriminating. We accept some things as truth and discard others, but still, we're working with an inner voice that was shaped by others. This activity will help your child reshape that inner voice.

The mindputer symbolizes the thinking mind. It's a concrete way for your child to examine his inner voice and discard negative self-talk statements. Adults can benefit from this activity as well, so we suggest you make a mindputer for yourself.

Present the metaphor of mind as computer to your child once he has a good feeling for his inner voice. Draw or paste magazine pictures on the box to turn it into a play computer. Cut a four-inch slot for the floppy-disk drive.

Examine the programs your child runs in her mind. Start with the negative ones because they're easiest to think of. These will include bad experiences that influence self-concept. For instance, if your child repeatedly strikes out at softball, she may think of herself as a poor athlete. Think of a name for each program and write it down on a computer label. Stick the label on an index card. On the back of each card, write the self-talk statements the programs generate. For example, "I'm a klutz," "I hate softball," "No one wants me on their team." Next, think of positive software programs and do the same. Keep in mind that experiences create both positive and negative self-talk, so try to remember both.

When you're through you should have a stack of "software program disks." Have your child install these software programs into the mindputer by slipping them through the floppy-disk drive.

Continue this activity over the course of several weeks, making new disks as your child thinks of additional programs. Once she feels she has "copies" on disk of most of the software programs that have been installed in her head, open the mindputer and examine what's inside. Does your child like the programs? Should there be some changes? Do the negative statements outnumber the positive ones? Are some programs outdated? Is an upgrade in order? Have your child ask herself what software programs she would buy if she walked into a mindputer store. By all means, "buy" these, but remember, you can't install them until the hardware can accept them. If your child wants to buy the "I draw beautiful pictures" mindputer program, enroll her in a sketching class or check out a pile of art books from the library. Only then will her mindputer be able to run the new software.

> Amber Coffman doesn't have much money. Her family is small—it's just her and her mother—and they have few possessions. Yet she is rich in ways that go beyond the material world.
>
> When she was eight, Amber started to do odd jobs at a homeless shelter until her mother could no longer afford the gas money to drive her there and back. Still determined to help out, Amber found an organization closer to her home of Glen Burnie, Maryland. There she volunteered to help make sandwiches every weekend.
>
> It was after doing a book report on Mother Teresa that Amber decided to start a group exclusively for children who wanted to help the homeless. Helpers for the Homeless meets Saturdays at Amber's apartment to make four hundred bag lunches. Amber does the recruiting, organizes the packing, and delivers the bags personally to hungry street people. At her twelfth birthday party, Amber was once again on the giving end. She hosted a dinner for the homeless and gave gifts to all of her guests.

The Hurdles
A poster representing real-life challenges

Draw a race track on a large piece of poster board, including a starting line, hurdles, and a finish line. Explain to your child that his progress toward a goal is like running a race. If the goal is writing a report for school, the starting gate represents the teacher giving the assignment, the hurdles are the steps toward completing the report (choosing a topic, researching it, and writing a rough draft), and the finish line represents when the final report is handed in. Tape a picture of your child onto each hurdle as he "jumps" over the task it represents. When your child reaches the finish line, celebrate!

Motivation Map

6 years and up

Like "The Hurdles," with additional incentives

At each imagined obstacle toward a goal, add a relevant incentive. For instance, if the goal is to write a report on aquatic life, and your child has an aquarium, reward him with a new tropical fish when he clears each hurdle.

Punch Out

Knock down a wall of boxes symbolizing obstacles to a goal

Materials:

a pack of plain four-by-six-inch white stickers, a few dozen shoe boxes and/or empty tissue boxes

5 years and up

Ask your child to list his objectives in life. Together, imagine possible obstacles to the goals, write these on the labels, and stick the labels on the boxes. Stack the boxes into a wall representing the barrier between your child and his goals. Refer to your child's skill cards and mark the rest of the labels with those abilities that will help him overcome the obstructions. Press the stickers directly on your child. Equipped as he is with his skills, have him quietly face the barricade and gather his strength to break through. When he has psyched himself up, your child will barge through the wall to meet his objectives. Encourage him to let loose and really stomp, pummel, and pulverize his obstacles.

Pillow Punch

Engage in pillow warfare against the destructive forces that interfere with success

Materials:
pillow, plain white pillowcase, permanent marker, paper

5 to 12 years

This is similar to "Punch Out," except that you, the parent, get to play a major role. List your child's skills directly on the pillow case, illustrating them if desired, and slip the pillow inside. List some of your child's goals on the paper (become a ballerina, ace a math test) and tape it to a wall. Your child stands facing the paper holding the pillow.

Now, get ready for an all-out battle pitting your child's capabilities against the obstacles, with you, of course, representing the obstacles. When your child starts the long walk toward a goal, jump in the way and yell out a challenge ("Long hours of practice!" "Paying attention in class!"). Your child beats you into retreat with the pillow while shouting out the skills she is using (perseverance, concentration). The older the child, the more you should challenge her. Have other family members take turns playing the part of the obstacles.

Personal Mission Statement

Summarize your personal mission

5 years and up

Most companies have a mission statement that summarizes their philosophy and sets the direction for future growth. People should have their own mission statements to guide their lives.

Explain the concept of a mission statement to your child. Have your child think up his own mission statement. Remember, this should be phrased in general terms, focusing on overall achievement rather than a specific goal. (Have your child save his specific goal statements for the next activity, Personal Goal Book.) Examples are, "Strive to make happiness happen!" and "Have fun, learn new things, be good to people and animals and the earth."

The best way to come up with a mission statement is to establish personal goals and figure out what behavior is required to meet these. Work alongside your child to create your own mission statement. Ask the rest of your family to do the same and weave these into a family mission statement.

Personal Goal Book

A record of goals and accomplishments

5 years and up

You can start this activity as soon as your child understands the nature of goals and the steps required to reach them. This usually occurs around the age of four. The personal goal book will help your child determine his goals and outline the means to reach them.

Begin by explaining goals to your child. Tell her about yours and point out ones she has reached. For example, giving up a pacifier, learning to do a cartwheel, and mastering long division.

Use construction paper to make a book in which your child will write or illustrate her goals. Date each entry and update the book monthly, at least. Record the date each objective was met beside the date it was set. Be creative and add photographs of your child reaching the goal.

Remember that the message here is not about defining success as winning. It's about the quality of effort your child puts forth.

Half-Empty and Half-Full

4 years and up   *Shows how a positive affects our perception of reality*

This is (more or less) a simple technique for teaching your child the meanings of optimism and pessimism. By optimistic we mean hopeful, cheerful, happy, enthusiastic, and encouraged. By pessimistic we mean cynical, doubtful, distrustful, and discouraged.

Illustrate the half-empty, half-full metaphor by filling a clear glass halfway. Show your child that depending on how he looks at the glass of water, he could call it half-empty or half-full. If he sees it as half-empty, he is thinking pessimistically; if he sees it as half-full, he is thinking optimistically.

Incorporate this figure of speech into your family's language by pointing out times your child is seeing the metaphorical glass as half-empty or half-full. This will help him reexamine a situation from the other side.

Get-Real and Get-Positive Sunglasses

Helps children grab hold of a new perspective

Designate one pair the "get-real" sunglasses, the other the "get-positive" sunglasses. Pretend with your child that the glasses have the power to change her outlook, so that when she loses her fifth straight soccer game, she should slip on the get-positive sunglasses to see her situation more brightly. If she distorts reality by insisting you don't love her because you won't let her ride her bike on the street, give her the get-real glasses to wear. In either case, ask your child what she sees. If she doesn't want to tell you, put the glasses on yourself and tell her how *you* see it.

The Inside Story

Reveals the good in bad situations

4 years and up

We carry volumes of stories in our heads. These tell us about our past, they review our present and imagine what is to come. Some of these emerge from experience, others are fed by a stream of wishes and desire. The tone of the story depends less on its theme than on our self-concept. If our self-concept is positive and strong, our stories also are positive.

Talk with your child about your stories and hers. Offer a few of your happiest, then ask your child to do the same. Next, tell your child stories that aren't so happy. Be sure they're appropriate for your child's developmental age and reveal something about you and your ability to find good in even a bad situation. You may want to practice framing your stories in a way that won't upset your child.

Encourage questions and ask your child to help you decide how the experience affected your life for the better. Now have your child share her unhappy stories and work together to shape them so they have positive angles.

Into the Future

Plot a plan for your future self, then record it in a book

5 years and up

This is similar to "The Inside Story," except this story hasn't happened yet. Your child taps in to her imagined future and weaves a tale of the person she dreams of becoming. Begin by telling her what you see yourself accomplishing ten years from now and how you plan to get there.

Record your child's story on an audiocassette or write it down. If she gets stuck, help her out by reminding her of the skills that will satisfy these future desires. Be sure, however, that your child's story comes entirely from her.

Her dreams will come alive if she "publishes" them in a book. Make the book by stapling pages together using a heavier-weight paper for the front cover. On the bottom of each page, write key phrases from her story sequentially for her to illustrate.

This book is a real keeper. Bring it out whenever your child needs to be reminded of the wonderful future that's in store for her.

Dream Makers

Make a mobile of personal goals and aspirations

Materials:
yarn, clothes hanger, poster board, scissors

4 years and up

We find that kids love to imagine their grown-up selves, and when prodded, will ride their boundless imaginations far into the future.

In this activity, your child will create a "dream mobile" to remind her of all the fantastic things she hopes to accomplish. Have her draw at least five billowy clouds on the poster board to cut out carefully. Ask her to think of future goals (become a doctor, have a family, travel overseas), and write or draw descriptions of each of these on a cloud. Punch a hole near the top edge in each cloud and thread them with yarn of varying lengths. Tie the dream clouds to the bottom of the hanger, spacing them out so that when hung, the weight of the poster-board clouds is evenly distributed.

Hang the dream mobile over your child's bed. At night, before she drifts off to sleep, she can gaze upward and dream of the possibilities that await her.

Note: For a child who has nightmares, draw calming, peaceful images on the clouds.

The Interview

6 to 12 years   *Your child meets his older self at a one-on-one interview*

You and your child can script a mock interview between a reporter and your child's "older self," the adult he envisions he will become. The questions should probe the interviewee's feelings about his present life, inquire about his everyday activities, and ask how he achieved his goals.

If you want to (and you don't have back problems!), turn your child into an adult by putting him on your shoulders, plunking a hat and glasses on him, and covering yourselves with an oversized topcoat. Have another person play the reporter and use the script to interview your adult. (Don't forget the video camera.)

Garbage Gab

Materials: *Toss away detrimental thoughts*
a large pile of scrap paper,
a large trash can   This is the ultimate exercise in teaching your child to control self-defeating thoughts.

5 years and up   Explain to your child how a negative outlook can damage her opinion of herself. Ask her to write down on scrap paper all of the hurtful things she thinks about herself and others. (For example, "I'm fat and ugly," "My nose is too big," "My family is weird.") Encourage her really to let loose and shake those observations out of her psyche where they can contaminate her self-esteem.

Sort through the pieces of paper, critiquing each statement (see "Get-Real and Get-Positive Sunglasses"). If together you conclude a statement is untrue, have your child crunch it up, with passion, and throw it in the trash. By the end of this activity, your barrel will be overflowing.

The Thomas Edison "No One's Perfect" Award

Teaches children to accept and learn from mistakes
6 to 12 years

As adults we have a hard time accepting how little in life is perfect. For children, it's even harder.

If your child reacts to setbacks with extreme disappointment, if she gives up too easily, then it's time to activate The Thomas Edison "No One's Perfect" Award. By the way, Thomas Edison made two thousand unsuccessful attempts before he invented the lightbulb, a fact your child should know.

Buy a loving-cup trophy and have it engraved The Thomas Edison "No One's Perfect" Award. Explain to your child that you will place a penny (or a poker chip or a marble) in the loving cup each time she accepts a mistake and tries again with good spirit. When the trophy is full, it's hers.

Engrave the trophy with your child's name before you give it to her and be sure she gets the message that mistakes can lead to great things if people follow Thomas Edison's lead and allow themselves to learn from them.

Find Your Song

Help your child find his or her "song" of courage
4 years and up

A singer by the name of Desiree came out with a song that describes dozens of children we have known over the years as therapists. The song is called "You Gotta Be," and the chorus sings out loud and strong, "You gotta be bad, you gotta be bold, you gotta be wiser. You gotta be hard, you gotta be tough, you gotta be stronger."

Desiree must know the same kids we do. Either that, or she was one herself, because the traits she sings about are the ones those kids must summon up simply to survive their mixed-up lives. We call these children "survivors" because they emerged from seemingly impossible situations with the will to live and the *courage* to make their lives work. Their ability to be courageous is built on their instinctual need to be good and capable people. These kids are amazing and truly personify the meaning of the words *personal potential*. We have been honored to grow with a young person who was a you-gotta-be kid.

Her name is Taunya and we met her when she was a spunky eight-year-old at an afterschool day-care program where we worked. She was a bundle of fury! Her face said it all: "I'm tough and rough and I will survive!" Challenges and crises came in and out of Taunya's life with the frequency of weekly laundry (which is what she slept on when we first met her—on a pile of dirty clothes).

With all the abusive and neglectful things that happened to her, Taunya had good enough reason to be mad at the world, but somehow she always found a way to see past it all. Throughout Taunya's life she was told, "You're no good!" But being the survivor that she is, she would respond to the statement by saying, "You don't know me!"

Over her young years, Taunya's rough exterior softened and she put all her powers into surviving. She was a quick thinker and learned to negotiate difficult situations at home by coming up with makeshift solutions. She was also quick on her feet—literally! This girl could run! She discovered her ability to run fast and used it to satisfy her mother by winning almost every race she entered.

She was just one of those kids who believed that life had a lot to offer, and the sampling she got during childhood was simply bad luck. The same tenacity that makes her win race after race is what gets her to the finish line of each goal she sets for herself. Taunya throws every ounce of her being into a challenge, whether it be a race or a problem at home. And each time she flies across the finish line, ready to collapse, but smiling ear to ear with pride in the knowledge that she can do anything if she puts her heart and mind to it.

Taunya is in her mid twenties now, finishing college, holding down a great job, and mapping out a very fine life for herself. During a recent phone conversation, we told Taunya how impressed we are that she was able to win a big bicycle race despite being distracted by some family problems. We told her that she is a tough, strong, and smart woman. Her response? "You gotta be!"

Social Harmony
(AKA People Skills)

There's a lesson in the importance of communication in the story of seven-year-old Jay and his family.

Jay was attending a summer camp for deaf children where Denise once worked. On parents' night, which occurred only once during a camper's stay, families gathered at tables with their children. Little was said, however, because most of the parents did not know sign language, the primary language spoken by the children at this camp. Children sat there smiling at their parents, parents smiled back, but virtually nothing was being communicated. Except for one family. Tucked away in a corner of the room was Jay, his mother, father, and younger sister. Hands were flying as family members vied for the floor. Jay spotted Denise staring and invited her over. "Meet my family," he signed with pride. Jay had told her a lot about his family, but left out one big detail: Every member was deaf.

Parents only stayed a few hours with their children; they didn't have communication to keep them together. Except for one family that actually got larger. Nearly three quarters of the campers had gathered around Jay's table. Jay's warm and friendly family stayed late until the evening, long after many of the parents had left. They stayed to hear the stories from the other campers who were eager to tell someone about all their experiences at camp.

As Denise learned, many of the parents and children were unable to share

Communication

Social Competence

**Teamwork and
Cooperation**

their thoughts, feelings, and even their experiences from the past weeks of separation because they lacked the ability to communicate in the most basic way (the same language!) with one another, while those few parents who knew sign language were able to share with their children the excitement of the day, and the zest and enthusiasm that children bring to life.

Effective social communication is an area of competency that has been overlooked until only recently. Today it is understood that the ability to communicate well and work together as a team is a key to professional success. So great is the need that the last five years have seen the creation of a microindustry of professional communication trainers who promise to improve worker efficiency and help salespeople boost commissions. Knowing that communication is a teachable skill, we would like to see it taught in more schools, right along with arithmetic and geography. There is no doubt that with improved social skills, our children will enjoy better relationships. Through teaching and practicing these skills with their children, many parents will receive these benefits also.

The tools for social competence are

1. the ability to express one's thoughts and feelings

2. the ability to effectively listen and understand others

3. the ability to understand and interpret the rules of social relationships

4. the ability to cooperate and work as a member of a team

Communication

At Denise's camp, language itself became the obstacle to communication. However, the kind of communication we are speaking about is more than language; it is what happens between people when they interact in a meaningful way. Language is just one of the ways we express ourselves. Other means include gestures, posturing, tone, facial expressions, eye contact, and actions. We are dependent upon this repertoire for conveying information, thoughts, and feelings. And it is through exchanges like these that we have opportunities to build rapport with loved ones, teach our children, seek assistance and answers, and even interact with total strangers.

For the communication process to work, the participants must be as adept at receiving (listening and understanding) the signals of social communication as they are at sending (expressing or demonstrating) them. When people find themselves saying "I had no idea you felt that way," this is a sign that effective listening is not occurring. For even if the speaker has not overtly shared these feelings, chances are he has expressed them in other ways. The effective listener enlists her eyes, ears, and heart to understand what another person is communicating, looking beyond what is said to capture the person's thoughts and feelings. Some of the most important messages are wrapped in anger or pain, and are never truly heard because they push the listener into a defensive stance. To listen effectively at these times, the listener must put aside his need to rebut or refute what is said, ignore or overlook the hostile words or tone, and instead focus upon understanding the feelings behind what is said.

Social Competence

To find satisfaction in relationships, children need to learn a multitude of social skills. This doesn't happen by chance; in fact, when left to chance, most children will not develop the interpersonal abilities needed to understand, negotiate, and manage social living. Social competence is a prime component of emotional intelligence and an ongoing process of acquiring skills, practicing them, and refining them. Every child needs to be able to read the social landscape: the rules that govern how to behave, as well as the exceptions to the rules. They also need to bring with them an ability to cooperate, share, compromise, and manage their impulses and emotions. Social competence is raised even higher when a child can negotiate creatively, resolve conflict, and empathize with others.

It is important to remember that children bring their temperament and style into social situations, and these affect the way they interact. Some children seek high levels of energetic social involvement with large groups while others prefer quiet play. What is important to take away from this chapter is the fact that with these skills, no child is limited by natural predisposition or temperament. A shy child can find ways to reach out and participate, and a leader can find ways to sit back and relinquish control. Parents should attempt to enhance, rather than change, their child's temperament or natural style.

Teamwork and Cooperation

Teamwork and cooperation are skills of interdependence, which means we all need one another to survive. Teamwork is what makes the difference between a group of talented athletes and a winning team. In the family, it means the individual needs of the members are balanced against what is best for the group.

Note: This guide is meant to serve as a general orientation to what you can expect and when to expect it. While there are no absolute norms or limitations regarding how and when characteristics within a developmental period appear, and every child is unique, there is a range of similar and expectable periods of development, each marked by patterns of behavior and capabilities. Keep in mind that the nature of personality development is dynamic and repetitive, meaning that it is ever-changing and traits and/or skills seem to appear, disappear, and then reappear throughout development.

Social Harmony—Communciation, Social Competence, Teamwork, and Cooperation

Stage I Infancy: Birth to 24 months
The stage of life from newborn through toddlerhood

Foundation period in which many behavior patterns, attitudes, and patterns of emotional expression are being established. Much of the first 12 months of this period are affected by instinctual drives for nurturing, food, and basic care.

Expect baby to: exhibit beginning signs of communication and social competence as early as 3 months by distinguishing people from inanimate objects, and by crying for attention (to be picked up, with a wet diaper, hungry); by 6 months by differentiating "friends" from "strangers" (smiles at the former and shows fear in the presence of the latter); by 9 months by attempting to engage people (i.e., eye contact, smiles, touching); by 12–16 months by attempting to imitate speech and gestures (baby talk, smiles, look of surprise); by 18–24 months grasping the concept of language (shows understanding of simple words of caregivers and uses simple words and gestures to express himself).

Do not expect baby to: exhibit beginning signs of teamwork until at least 20–24 months as baby imitates adult activities and engages in parallel play (pushes toy replica while parent vacuums).

Stage II Early Childhood—The Preschool Years: Ages 2 to 6
The stage of life from toddlerhood through kindergarten

This is often called the play age because it is the peak period of interest in play and toys, marked by exploration, discovery play, creativity, magical thinking, fierce strivings for independence, and acquisition of social skills. This is a time of preparation for learning the foundations of social behavior needed for the school years to come.

Between ages 2–4, expect children to: show explosive growth in communication skills; exhibit rapidly increasing vocabulary and improving pronunciation; begin to imitate adult gestures, postures, and facial expressions; better comprehend the meaning of what others say to them; show increasing interest in talking and playing with other children through parallel play—independent activity of a similar or identical nature to that of a nearby child.

Do not expect children to: share toys or other possessions easily; understand or buy into the concept of teamwork and shared responsibilities.

Between ages 4–6, expect children to begin to: engage in cooperative play—activities in which children take turns using a toy or playing a role, share in the development of a story or theme, or play according to mutually agreed rule base; understand the rudiments of team play and teamwork; be conscious of others' opinions and feelings, as well as the rules for acceptance within the peer group (fewer disagreements and fights, increased cooperation, compliance with rules, and focus on group success).

Do not expect the child to: exhibit these newly acquired skills consistently or under adverse conditions such as when tired, or feeling shy; always play fairly or honestly.

Stage III Late Childhood—The School Years: Ages 6 to 11
This stage of life begins with entrance into first grade and extends into the beginning of adolescence

This period is marked by major interest and concern for social involvement with peers, participation in rule-based group play, and increased motivation to learn, acquire technical knowledge, information, and achieve academic success. This stage is very important for establishing attitudes and habits about learning, work, and personal potential.

Expect children to: increase the amount of time they spend with other children primarily of the same gender in organized team sports, informal groups or clubs, and with best friends; understand and follow prescribed social rules for relating to peers; experiment with social conformity, even rejecting parental rules and standards in the name of acceptance; expand their vocabularies to include slang and swear words, and secret vocabularies with intimate friends.

Do not expect children to: listen well to others if they are not listened to at home, or understand the rules of social relations without frequent exposure and practice within their family.

Stage IV Early Adolescence: Ages 11 to 15
This stage of life begins around the time a child finishes elementary school and concludes by the time he graduates middle school (junior high school) and enters the world of high school

This period is marked by change and turmoil, the onset of puberty, growth spurts, increased interest in peer relationships and the opposite sex, and fierce strivings for self-identity and independence.

Expect adolescents to: communicate their wants adeptly and also their opinions and beliefs; experience friction with most family members (even a favorite sibling); pay close attention to their social group's expectations for prescribed gender-role behaviors (i.e., crying is acceptable for girls but not for boys) and the implications for noncompliance; develop social interests in sports, clubs, and activities that bring opportunities for social time with peers and social acceptance; view their relations with family as less positive than with their friends, resulting in an attitude of hostility or ambivalence about family activities.

Do not expect adolescents to: develop social competence easily if they had not participated in opportunties for practice as a school-aged child; invest the same effort toward family communication and teamwork as they do toward their peer group; apply their improved communication skills when they are experiencing heightened emotions.

However, children are selfish by nature. Before they learn to be coopera-tive, they must develop an awareness of the needs of others. Parents and other caregivers model this by unselfishly subordinating their personal needs to those of the family. A child learns cooperation and teamwork while satisfying personal needs. For instance, when a two-year-old helps her parent in a chore of folding laundry, she is following her instinct to belong and be useful while engaging in an experiment to see what role she can play within her family.

Evaluating If a Child Has Difficulties with Communication and Social Skills

Review the "Over the Years Guidelines" to be sure that your expectations are in line with your child's age and developmental capabilities. Use the "Ques-tions to Ask Yourself" as a checkpoint and as a way of evaluating the child's strengths and weaknesses. If you answer yes to any of these questions, it will be beneficial to help the child develop these skills further.

Questions to Ask Yourself

Does the child behave impulsively, or without considering the consequences of his actions? (Statements you may hear are "I didn't mean to do it," or "I forgot what you said," or "I didn't know that would happen.")

Does the child seem immune or blind to the discomfort others around him feel? (He comes close to or touches people without gauging their approval or interest in this level of intimacy; he continues with behavior that is clearly causing stress to someone else; he plays loudly or roughly with no awareness of how he affects others, perhaps asking, "What did I do?")

Is the child avoidant or unwilling to consider participation in social events, team sports, even situations you suspect she is interested in, without any reasonable explanation? (You may hear statements like "I don't know why, I just don't want to go," or "I don't like school," or "I know I said I wanted to take gymnastics, but I don't like the coach.")

Does the child frustrate easily, get into fights, or blame others for things that go wrong? (He always seems to say, "He started the fight," "I couldn't help it, he got me mad," or "I didn't do it really, they're lying, I swear.")

Does the child have a difficult time asking a question, raising his hand, or joining a group discussion? (When asked he will say, "I don't know," or just look confused and say nothing.)

Does the child strive excessively to gain attention by acting silly, rude, or behaving dangerously? (He seems to think this is the way to make friends, and looks for validation through laughter.)

Does the child seek friendship and acceptance from children considerably older or younger than himself? ("They're fun to play with," "Kids my age are immature," or "They like me a lot.")

Does the child see his wants and needs as more important than those of other family members? (He is happy only when he gets his way with peers; he marches away, declaring, "I don't want to play," or "You're not fair!")

Does the child see every situation involving more than one person as a competition, a situation where the outcome is either win or lose? (In team situations he focuses upon his own performance and seems to derive little satisfaction from the team's success.)

How to Develop a Child's Communication and Social Skills

1. Begin thinking about teaching these skills from the time your child is born and do not stop, ever. The reality is that to become effective communicators, listeners, and social beings, our children need extensive and frequent education in these areas.

2. Be a model of effective communication and positive social behavior with your children, spouse, family, and friends. The way you treat people and how we communicate with them has as much to do with your attitude as it does with the way you act. In fact, children often learn more by observing what happens around them than by what they are taught or told to do. Children are vigilant observers, always watching and learning from what they see and hear (even what is not said).

3. Balance your family's needs with your own so your child will see that a good team member doesn't lose sight of his or her own welfare.

4. Remember that in the normal course of growing up, every child will experience rejection, frustration, and social disappointments. Show the child

that to err is human and that you are as human as anybody. Use your own communication mistakes and social blunders to help teach this attitude. Whether the incident occurred in or outside of the child's presence ask her to discuss it with you. You'll find that children, even those reticent about sharing their thoughts or feelings, will be more than willing to discuss a parent's or teacher's mistake, and you'll be surprised to find that discussing a mistake with a child can be surprisingly easy. Children are often less judgmental than adults. Discuss how you feel about what you did, and what you might do to repair the damage or correct what is wrong. Ask the child what she thinks, and for her ideas about what to do. By including her in your real-life mistake, you show more powerfully than you could verbalize that you are fallible and willing to admit your mistakes. In addition you teach that through good communication, a person can make something good come out of something not so good.

5. Conflict is a normal part of every adult relationship. Don't hide your disagreements from your children, use them as an opportunity to model how to resolve them. If you do this with discussion, humor, and love, you are teaching your children the most important thing about teamwork—that if people remain committed to working things out, they will maintain a positive team environment.

6. Take time to listen to your child. This may sound obvious, but time is a commodity for which there is no substitute. Distractions from TV, interruptions from the telephone, shortage of time, competing demands (cooking dinner) all serve to reduce the amount of quality listening that takes place in a family, during the few hours that parents and children spend together.

7. Be an effective listener; listen with your eyes, ears, and heart. Notice the child's posture, facial expressions, body tension, and fidgeting. Practice sitting face to face and making eye contact.

8. Keep your expectations reasonable and age appropriate. A child's ability to communicate effectively and know how to act in a particular situation will grow as his body does—gradually and over time. Use the "Over the Years Guidelines" in this book and other developmental information to adjust your expectations accordingly.

9. Look at the big picture. Be sure to take into account environmental and circumstantial issues, as well as your child's historical track record. For example, what has already been required of the child preceding the time in question? Was he sitting in school all day, or in church all morning? Did he have a fight or disappointing experience? Was he upset or frightened the last time he was in a similar situation?

10. Make learning fun and filled with kinesthetic (body senses) experiences. Get down to the child's level and means for understanding the world by playing with her. Use props and toys, puppets, and stuffed animals to role-play the issues, have a nonthreatening conversation, or simply get your point across. The child will appreciate your playfulness, making it easier to get your point across.

11. Be flexible, patient, and sensitive to your child's needs, timing, and surroundings. Find a place to be together that is free of distractions, and comfortable, such as your lap, on the bed, the floor, or up in the treehouse. Gauge the child's comfort with closeness, eye contact, and touch. Use this insight to determine how close to sit, and when and where to have the meeting time. For example, trying to discuss a difficult subject with an eleven-year-old at the dinner table with her younger siblings present is usually not a good idea; however, that same table and chairs, later that evening, alone with Mom or Dad and some chocolate cake might be the perfect setting.

12. Give appropriate feedback. Avoid the temptation to lecture or recall stories that have little relevance to your child. Be a sounding board to your child, a person she can depend upon for honest information. Don't give advice, guide your child toward her own solutions.

13. Reward positive communication and appropriate social behavior with praise, encouragement, and a heartfelt smile; and discourage undesirable behaviors with a clear expression of your feelings, a look or a touch, or in some cases by ignoring it. Simply and briefly let the child know what he did and how it made you feel. Use "I" messages to deliver this communication effectively.

14. Help your child become more aware of how his behavior affects others by turning the tables on him. For instance, if he uses a loud voice, then talk loudly during his favorite TV show. Don't forget to do this with humor and compassion. Develop a system together for alerting him discreetly to obnoxious behavior, so that he is able to take corrective action without being embarrassed.

15. To address aggressive behavior and negative modeling, express your feelings about violence as a solution. Teach nonviolent conflict resolution through games, stories, hypothetical situations, and examples from sports or the behavior of other public figures. Be sure that your children are exposed to more prosocial behaviors and solutions than antisocial ones. This means limiting their access to violent movies, cartoons, and video games.

16. To address shyness, use role-playing to practice basic communication techniques and skills such as making introductions, effective listening, showing interest in another's idea, expressing one's opinions, or making suggestions. Talk about body language and the way other children act. Go to the mall or the park and sit together watching and learning. Pose questions that cause the child to analyze what she sees. Gradually introduce your child to "safe" situations to practice newly learned social skills (with a known child and with an adult present). Take a few minutes to review situations that took place, what the child enjoyed, and what she found difficult. Try not to provide the analysis yourself, rather guide her to helpful conclusions about what worked and what didn't.

17. Establish talking, listening, and social behavior guidelines in your home and for your family, and post them in a central location. Do your best to hold everyone to them—adults included.

Activities That Build Better Communication

The following eight activities are essentially a crash course for parents in play techniques for understanding and talking with children.

2 to 9 years **Communicating Through Play Props**

Talking through play using props such as dolls, puppets, and stuffed animals is the all-time favorite communication technique used by play therapists who are trying to get through to a young child.

The technique is simple, and requires time and compromise. However, it is worth every second. Play is nonthreatening because it occurs on the child's own level. If you're flexible and engaging, you'll learn a lot more about your child through play than you will in conversation. When you encourage play, your child uses his or her imagination, creative thinking, and body expression to communicate.

Use play to gain insight into your child's behavior or when you need to explain something important. To begin, sit back and watch your child play. You'll probably pick up a theme or two. You will be amazed by how much you will learn about his thinking. Children's make-believe play is an extension of real life. Even if your child is reenacting a Disney movie, the situation or "scene" he chooses to play is most likely about his own feelings. For example, a child Denise worked with for years who was in a very bad car accident loved to play "magic carpet" from the movie *Aladdin*. He would take stuffed animals on the magic carpet ride of their lives—always narrowly avoiding walls and furniture—but never crashing. He was in control and this time nothing bad was going to happen.

Once you have a good feel for how your child likes to play, it's time for you to join.

Play to Understand

Gain insight into your child's thoughts through play   2 to 9 years

Invite yourself into your child's play by using a prop such as a doll or puppet. Use the prop (and a silly voice) to become a character that fits in with your child's play theme. Communicate only as the character you have created (stay in the third person) and if you have questions about the direction of play, ask the other play props, rather than your child.

Come up with imaginative interactions, but let your child lead the play. Chances are, your child will be very excited to have you join his world. Unless he has never seen you play before, he will immediately give you all kinds of directions and things to do. After a while, you will feel the flow of the play, and know when it's possible to throw in a few probing questions. But don't do this too quickly, you don't want to make your child feel as though he is being tricked. Here's an example:

Real-life drama:
New baby sister has invaded the life of a four-year-old

Pretend drama:
"I just want to be king!"

Play scene:
A bad guy and a good guy are having a fight over who gets to be king

Cast:

Parent: bad-guy bear

Four-year-old: good-guy lion

Act I:
After ten minutes of fighting about being the king, the bad guy (parent)
speaks in his very best bad-guy voice:

Parent:
"I think I should be the king! You have been here too long and I'm new here and I can growl real loud to get the queen's attention! I wanna be the king!"

Child:
"I was here first and the queen loves me more than you."
(Bites the bear's head for emphasis.)

Parent:
"Do you think the queen can love both of us? She's a very good queen and is especially good at loving lots of people at the same time."

Child:
"Maybe—but I still want to be the king." (Bites head again.)

Parent:
"Okay, you can be the king. I just need a little more attention from the queen. I'm not as strong as you and I need the queen to help me."

Child:
"Okay, the queen can love you, too!"
(Then takes a few more bites to show the bear who's the boss. . . .)

Did you understand what was really going on? The new baby sister was the "bad guy" and the child was playing himself. He felt dethroned and the play reassured him that he is still king. The parent could summarize what happened during the playful interaction by stepping out of character at the end and saying something like, "I love playing with you, you're so much fun. You're a real good guy at home, too, just like the lion. Son, you've been very kind to your new baby sister. Sharing your mommy is very hard to do. But you know something, you're still my big boy king!"

Play to Teach

2 to 9 years ◆ *Pass along information during play*

To teach a child a lesson through play, you need to be more directive by setting the scene, the characters, and plot. Establish your goal from the beginning. Tell your child what you will be playing as well as its purpose. For example, tell your child you will be teaching her what to do in the event she were to become separated from you in a public place. Set the scene with play props and assign your child and yourself roles. ("Okay, you be the mommy doll and I'll be the lost baby doll.") Then, together, act out the entire situation, from getting lost, to becoming upset but remaining calm, to finding a "safe" person to help the lost baby doll. Though the message may be serious, be playful about it. If you act too solemnly, your child may feel threatened and you risk scaring her or losing her interest.

Communicating Through Dress-up and Role-Play

2 to 10 years

Kids love to play dress-up. They can get lost for hours trying out new roles. But there's more to dressing up than play. When your child pretends to be an animal, a superhero, or a mommy, she's expressing herself. As with toy play props, you can use dress-up play to explore your child's thoughts and to teach her new things.

Dress-up Trunk
Play dress-up

2 to 10 years

Stock a trunk with adult clothing, hats, and accessories. Over the years, we have collected an array of children's Halloween costumes, which we buy a few days after the holiday when they are marked down. Try not to be influenced by gender. It's important to allow your child to try both masculine and feminine roles. We have two girls, but they enjoy their superhero and cowboy outfits as much as the ballerina and princess costumes.

Playing Dress-up with a Child to Encourage Communication
Learn about problems through dress-up

2 to 10 years

As with prop play, you should observe your child playing dress-up before jumping into the fun yourself. Ask your child what he wants you to be and have him help you dress for the part. Step into character and try your best to match the pace of his play. Use your child's cues and follow his directions. If you recognize a theme that echoes real life, you can ask a few questions (in character). Use the answers to guide the play gently to help your child work through a problem. You will know if you made a wrong move or pushed too hard if your child suddenly wants to stop playing. If so, give up your secret mission and have your child get you back into the character he wants.

Using Role-Play to Communicate with a Child
Teach through role-playing

All ages

Role-play is much more directive than dress-up. Often the parent lays out the scene with a specific goal in mind. You can use props and costumes, but you may not need to. In role-play, you assume a role and act it out as if you were following a script. For example, if the neighborhood bully is bothering your daughter, pretend to be your daughter and tell her to play the bully. Throughout the play, offer support and suggest ways to handle the situation. This helps your daughter understand the dynamics of the conflict and gives her practice resolving it. Role-play is most effective when you switch roles back and forth.

Communicating with Older Children Through Humor and Play

3 years and up   *Invent a family problem-solver*

This activity is called What Does Thelma Think? Thelma is a pretend family member who knows everyone's problems. Whenever there's a conflict, ask, "What do you think the problem is, Thelma?" Encourage your child to answer for her. "Thelma" gives your family an extra, neutral voice, which helps you and your children think of alternative ways to define a problem.

Activities That Improve Talking and Listening Skills

The You-and-I-Statement Chairman

3 years and up   *Designate a you-and-I-statement chairman in your family to draw attention to accusatory statements*

The you-and-I-statement chairman will help family members tune in to the subtle ways people assign blame. A statement that begins with the word "you," as in, "You broke my toy!" is considered accusatory. A statement that begins with "I," as in, "I wish you didn't play so roughly with my toy," is a more effective way of communicating the same thought. Write on an index card "I Statement." On the back of the card, write "You Statement." During a family discussion, the designated you-and-I-statement chairman acts as a neutral listener and signals with the card when appropriate. If the speaker is flashed a "you" by the cardholder, he should think about what he just said, and if necessary, rephrase it. If the statement is rephrased in a positive way, the cardholder will flash an "I."

Before engaging in a real family conversation you might want to give the cardholder a few practice runs to get the hang of it. If there are enough people in your family, assign a team to hold the card. This is the good way to teach a younger child what to look for. If a person disagrees with the card-holder, talk it over and decide as a family how to classify the statement.

Listen-and-Find Scavenger Hunt
Improve listening skills with an old-fashioned scavenger hunt

4 to 9 years

Call out a list of household items for your child to find. This means your child has to listen carefully in order to remember what to look for. Later when your child is not listening to you, remind him of how well he played this game.

Listening Cap
A listening aid

3 years and up

"Put your listening cap on." Turn this familiar saying into a tool to help your child remember the rules of being a good listener. Draw big ears on a baseball cap and label it Listening Cap. When you need your child to concentrate on what you are saying, give him the listening hat. Pretend the hat has super-powers that are activated when the wearer looks into the eyes of the speaker and focuses on what is being said.

Pay Attention
Reward your child for paying attention

5 years and up

This activity will get your child to pay attention, literally. Write the word "Attention" on an empty glass jar and fill a second jar with pennies or nickels. Label the second jar with your child's name. Each time your child fails to listen to you, tell her to put a coin from her jar into the "attention" jar. At the end of the week, she can keep the coins remaining in her jar.

The Listening Place

3 years and up   *A special place for special conversations*

This activity is for the whole family. Designate a special listening place in your home to discuss important issues, ask meaningful questions, or tell special stories. It can be anywhere—a corner of a room, a cozy chair, a stairway, even under a big blanket with a flashlight. Being led to the listening place is a sign that something significant is about to be shared.

Walk and Talk

3 years and up   *Clear the air with a talk*

We know firsthand, as well as from talking to other families, that the very best talks happen during walks. Walking removes you from a noisy place and stimulates conversation. It is energizing and revitalizing. Talking while walking allows people to be physically close without the intensity of facing each other. Make conversational walks a weekly ritual. If possible, send your children out for a walk with an older relative. You may consider taking a walk by yourself. Denise always goes out for a brisk walk when things get too hectic. She mumbles to herself a lot and returns refreshed and ready to roll.

Magazine Chat

4 to 10 years   *Imaginary conversations*

Stockpile a variety of magazines, then with your child pick out pictures of people (and/or animals) interacting. Ask your child about the animals: What are they saying and feeling? Are they being honest with one another or are they hiding their true thoughts? Ask your child to suggest ways the figures in the picture can communicate more smoothly. Choose pictures depicting a variety of communication challenges, such as one of a baby and a parent. (How can the baby tell the parent what he wants?) If your child came up with some good suggestions for helping the magazine people communicate better, write them down and put them on a special communication card to help your family next time they're in a communication jam.

     Also, try turning off the television sound and imagining what the characters are saying. Check in from time to time to see how you're doing. Use this activity to show your child how much we are able to understand what people are saying through body language.

The Kooky Conversation Game

Say a lot without words

4 years and up

Not only is this game hilarious, but it teaches kids how much people rely on body language and voice inflection to make themselves understood. To begin, each player imagines a scenario that requires communication between two or more people. (Some examples are a father and child shopping at the grocery store and one suddenly has to use the bathroom, or breaking the news to Mom that you just broke her favorite vase.) Each person secretly writes his scenario on a piece of paper and puts it in a box. Next, each player chooses one word or sound that will become his sole means of verbal communication. The word or sound can be anything, from "kneecap" to "moo," to "skally-waggy," but keep in mind the word or sound is an entire language. Everyone takes a turn picking a scenario from the box, then acting it out in his own personalized "language." He'll have to rely on body language and inflection to make himself understood.

If you have enough players, work in teams. The other players have to guess what is being said.

Add more spice to the game by adding a box of feelings. When players choose a situation to act out, they also pick out a feeling to convey, such as angry, frustrated, happy, or silly.

When the game is over, discuss how much can be said without words. Highlight the skills your child used in getting a point across and acknowledge how good he is at making himself understood. Most important, enjoy the game!

Telephone

Teach children how scrambled a message can become when it's passed along through many people

4 years and up

Players sit in a straight line. The person at one end whispers a brief message to the next person, who whispers the same message to the third in line, who whispers it to the fourth, and so on. The last in line repeats the message out loud. Is it correct, or is it completely different from the original? Talk with your kids about the results. Mention that it's better to deliver significant messages directly, or in writing.

The following activities help families increase opportunities to communicate with each other during the bustle and bustle of everyday life.

Letter Writing

6 years and up *Set up an internal mailbox for communication among family members*

Some people fare better at written than at verbal communication. Letters give the writer time to consider what to say and the luxury of reworking a thought until it is phrased right. When you write to someone you don't have to worry about being interrupted, or worse, tuned out. Preteens and teenagers seem to take naturally to writing letters and notes to friends (especially in class), and memos are a tried-and-true way to communicate at the office. See if you can extend this method of communication to the home.

Buy or make a mailbox to keep in the kitchen next to a supply of paper and envelopes. Encourage family members to use your personal mailbox just as they would the U.S. Postal Service. Parents and kids can write notes to one another, seal them in envelopes, and leave them in the box. Remember to respect the privacy of your family mail. Don't open letters that aren't addressed to you.

Parents may write letters to supplement regularly scheduled talks. The family mailbox is a good way to broach problems and raise serious issues, but it's also a fun way to congratulate each other on achievements or simply to tell someone how much you love them.

MESSAGE CENTER

NOTES

SCHEDULE	SUN	MON	TUES	WED	THURS	FRI	SAT
MOM		PTA		PTA		PTA	
DAD			CLASS		CLASS		
JIM	SOFT-BALL		SOCCER		B-BALL		SOCCER
DIANE		COMPUTER CLASS		DANCE		GIRL SCOUTS	T-BALL
SUE			DANCE		DRAMA		SOCCER

BE BACK AT 3:00 MOM

Message Center

3 years and up *A centralized place for messages*

Post a message center right below your family calendar (see page 71). Use a blackboard, bulletin board, or dry-erase board and hang it low enough for the littlest ones to reach.

Family life gets pretty hectic sometimes and important messages get lost in the shuffle. Use the board to highlight appointments, important meetings, things needed, special love notes, and good luck wishes. Also use the message center to post issues for the next family meeting (see family council, page 57).

The following communication techniques are designed to help people who are having problems expressing themselves or listening to others. They work by imposing actual guidelines, which encourage positive interactions and limit negative ones. Think of these as medical treatments for unhealthy communication patterns.

Three Minutes, Please!

A surefire way to get through a conversation uninterrupted   4 years and up

Give each speaker three minutes to talk and use a stopwatch or egg timer for accuracy. During that time, everyone must pay attention. This means no interjecting, no making faces, and no lapsing into daydreams. In fact, the only gesture the listener can make is a nod when appropriate. If the speaker finishes talking before the time is up, the listeners must remain silent until the full three minutes have passed. Then another participant has a turn, and so on, until the issue is resolved. This technique works especially well when an important issue is being discussed.

> When he was in seventh grade, Franklin McCabe started a music and light show called Chaskae D.J. taken from his Sioux name, which means "First Son." His goal was modest—to have something fun to do on weekends—but the popular show soon took on a serious purpose when Franklin, a Navajo/Sioux who lives on the Colorado River Indian Tribes Reservation, realized his show could help reconnect his fellow Native Americans to their heritage. Through Chaskae D.J., Franklin has sparked no-alcohol social events for Native Americans in Arizona, Idaho, Wyoming, Colorado, and Montana.

Back-to-Back

"Three Minutes, Please!" without eye contact   5 years and up

This is to be used only when emotions are running so high that it's impossible to discuss delicate matters without displaying negative body language.

It's hard to hold a meaningful conversation with someone who is smirking or rolling their eyes. Therefore, you must avoid eye contact in order to air your feelings. Standing back-to-back should be used as a last resort because communication is at its best when you are looking into each other's faces and talking and listening without restrictions.

You Say, I Say, We All Say

5 years and up

Gets to the heart of an issue

This technique helps you summarize the important points of a conversation, much the same way that a reporter boils down an issue for a newspaper article.

Take notes during an important conversation that takes place during a family meeting or when you are problem solving a difficulty with your child, taking care to jot down crucial statements and salient points. For example, your notes may look like this:

Jenny: Mom and Dad treat me like a baby.

Mom: Jen doesn't act responsibly.

Dad: Maybe we aren't giving Jen enough responsibilities so that she can learn to be independent.

After you have collected enough statements, read them aloud and look for a common theme. In the above example, everyone might agree that Jen wants, and needs, more responsibilities.

Communication Techniques for Talking in Groups

Pass the Ball

3 years and up

Only the person holding a ball may speak

Denise learned this talking-and-listening technique through her work with deaf children. Because deaf people who sign cannot communicate unless their listeners are watching, a conversation involving many people can fall apart if everyone isn't looking at the talker. In these large groups, a ball was passed around and only the person holding the ball was allowed to talk. If someone wanted to speak, they had to ask for the ball. Try this in your family, especially during family council (see page 57).

The Peace Circle

4 years and up

Encourages peaceful communication

Pass the Ball borrows from an ancient custom of certain Native American tribes who passed a peace pipe. Everyone would sit in a circle and wait for the pipe before speaking. The pipe is still used in many Native American powwow ceremonies as a means toward peaceful communication. Encourage peaceful communication in your family with your own peace-pipe ceremony. If you're uncomfortable using a pipe, find another item to symbolize peace. One family we know passes a ceramic dove that says "shalom," which means "hello," "good-bye," and "peace" in Hebrew.

When your family has chosen its peace item, sit together in a circle and take turns holding it. Only the person holding the peace item is allowed to talk, and diplomatically, at that. It defeats the whole purpose of the peace circle if the talker uses his time to hurt or blame someone else.

Spider Weave

A lighthearted way to stimulate conversation   4 years and up

Everyone sits in a circle. The person who starts off a conversation holds a ball of yarn. When someone else wants to speak, the first person holds on to the end of the yarn, but passes along the ball. As the conversation progresses from person to person, the ball of yarn will unravel in a sort of spider web, tracing the flow of talk among the group.

The web has to reach everyone, meaning even reluctant talkers must participate in the conversation. The more people talk, the more outrageous this activity becomes as the web becomes hopelessly tangled and people are clinging to so many parts of the yarn. For a real challenge, try to untangle the web by passing the yarn ball back to the beginning of the conversation.

> When dolphins are in danger, they drive away their predators and refuse to abandon their injured brethren. A group of children in St. Louis have applied the dolphins' compassion and sense of responsibility to their world.
>
> The Dolphin Defenders—hundreds of nine- to twelve-year-olds in St. Louis's highest crime- and drug-use area—are on an ongoing mission to clean up their neighborhoods. They use the money they collect from recycling glass, paper, and cans to create wildlife habitats on empty lots. Birds, raccoons, opossums, and red foxes have moved in. Other proceeds from the group are donated to such organizations as the Wilderness Society, the National Wildlife Federation, the Nature Conservancy, and of course, the Dolphin Alliance.

This is a great activity for creative storytelling. Instead of holding a simple conversation while passing the yarn ball, tell and "weave" a story. Each person tells a part of a story and then passes the yarn ball to another person while still holding on to a piece. Tell another story to untangle the last story.

Communication in Different Cultures

Introduce your child to other cultures   4 years and up

Expose your children to other cultures by attending ethnic celebrations and eating in restaurants run by people from different countries. Explore with your child the different ways people communicate. Pay attention to body language and customs. Does everyone around the world shake hands upon greeting? Can Americans accept the communication styles of other cultures? Japanese people bow when they greet each other. Would your child bow if she met a Japanese person in America? Would she bow if she were in Japan?

Borrow language tapes from your library and learn a few new words and phrases from several different countries. Point out to your child words that sound similar to, or very different from, their English counterparts. Explore a language from your own family history. If you're lucky enough to have older relatives who know a few words from the old country, ask them to teach these to your child. You can take this activity to its fullest by making a family commitment to learn another language. We know a Vermont family who both taught Spanish at a university and taught the language to their preschoolers. When the youngest turned seven, the whole family went to Mexico for a summer. By then, the children spoke fluent Spanish and made friends with Mexican children. During the school year, the family invited exchange students from Mexico to their home. The kids respect and appreciate language, and enjoy being bilingual communicators.

Activities That Encourage Positive Social Skills

First-Start Social Skills

All ages   *Teaching social skills*

We started our children on social-skill training before their first birthdays. Social skills don't come naturally, they're learned. The best time to teach a child how to act around others is as soon as they become aware others exist.

When our children could hardly speak themselves, we would model statements to other children, such as, "Hello, my name is Emily. What is yours?" and "I love to play in the sandbox, would you like to play with me?" By the time the kids started to formulate sentences, they knew just what to do. Still, both our children are on the shy side and tend to hang back when they meet another child for the first time. But after we start them off with a few cues, such as, "I bet that little girl is wondering what your name is," or, "You brought your crayons, I wonder if that boy likes to color?" they're socializing in no time. Instead of making the initial contact, we prod our children gently enough so they want to do it on their own.

101 Ways to Start a Conversation

Practice different ways of conversing with a variety of people

4 years and up

With your family, think of 101 (or as many as possible) ways to start a conversation. Imagine different conversational partners, such as a person you don't know, someone you've known for a long time, someone you had a big fight with the day before, a deaf person, a person who speaks a different language. Then dream up all sorts of creative ways to initiate the conversation.

After fully exploring ways to begin a conversation, see how many ideas your family has for ending one, or switching topics, or turning a negative conversation into a positive one.

Time Machine

Go back or forward in time to practice social behavior

Materials:
large box

4 to 10 years

Who hasn't wanted to go back in time to take back angry words or deliver that clever response you thought of an hour too late? And who wouldn't welcome the chance to zip into the future to practice for an upcoming social event?

Dream up a time machine with your child. Make it out of a cardboard box large enough for him to sit in. Equip it with play buttons, gears, gadgets, and levers. Remember to include a window for your child to peer out of.

Use the time machine to revisit situations in which your child either misbehaved or behaved appropriately. Go forward in time so your child can practice behaving at your cousin's wedding next week, or at school recess tomorrow. Spice up your play with a little humor. If you're brave enough, have your child take you back to your own childhood to examine those (very few) times when you were naughty. End your time travels by showing your child how you improved your behavior.

You can also use the time machine to help your child make friends. Bring the machine back to visit personal heroes or historical figures, such as Babe Ruth or Christopher Columbus or Amelia Earhart (played by you). Have your child get out of the machine and use his social skills to introduce himself and have a friendly, appropriate conversation. If you feel your child can handle advice, reframe a negative social skill with a positive one. The time machine knows no boundaries, so by all means fly it into the future to meet new friends. Give your child plenty of encouragement to try out his finest social skills on his future best friend.

Here are a few frequent time-machine destinations: back to a social conflict that your child did not resolve appropriately; to another country, planet, or universe; to a frightening place or situation so your child can practice mastering his apprehension; to an upcoming event where your child must behave at his best (a wedding or a party).

Let's Practice

2 to 10 years   *Practice makes perfect (or at least prepared)*

Practice with your child for an upcoming event, like a birthday party or a wedding. Use dress-up clothes and other props and act out the situation. For a wedding, dress up like the bride and groom and take turns being the guests. Show your child how to behave and show her what she can do to make the event fun. Use the same technique for ordinary events, like answering the phone. Use a play telephone to demonstrate the appropriate ways to answer and ask questions of the caller.

The Aquarium of Friends

Materials: *Use a pretend fish aquarium to practice social skills*
pictures of marine life

4 to 10 years   Turn your child's room into an aquarium by pasting pictures of fish, seaweed, water, and rocks on the walls. Be sure to have at least twelve removable fish in your aquarium, and give each a name.

Move the fish around to meet others. Pretend the fish are new in town and learning to be friends. Use the fish to act out different social situations, like inviting a new pal over to play, or resolving an argument. Playfully examine your child's social difficulties through the feelings of the fish.

Video or Book on How to Make and Keep Friends

4 to 12 years   *A project to reinforce ways to meet and keep a friend*

Have your child write a book or produce a video on making and keeping friends. Go through the steps of friendship making with your child. Start the project with social introductions and end it with your child and the new friend.

Teatime

3 to 8 years   *Play the boor to your child's make-believe play*

Next time your child is playing make-believe restaurant or tea party, crash the party and leave your manners at the door. It's up to the host to demonstrate proper behavior. Have her point out when you forget to say "please" and "thank you," and encourage her to model the correct way to hold cups and silverware. Believe us, your child will be happy to set you straight.

Pen Pals

Meeting new friends from afar

Having a pen pal gives children practice putting thoughts into words and building relationships. Depending on how far away the pen pal lives, it can also be a personalized way to learn about a different culture. Consult your local library or your child's teacher for information on locating a pen pal.

Welcoming Committee

Welcome new neighbors

Remember the welcome wagon? They still exist in some communities, but they're rare. Bring back the tradition of reaching out to newcomers by turning your family into a welcoming committee.

   With your child, establish a ritual for greeting families new to the neighborhood. Introduce yourselves with cookies and other goodies (believe us, any family in the midst of a move will appreciate a gift of food). There's a family in Massachusetts who lives in a growing neighborhood where new people are moving in all the time. The family gives each a care package that includes a map of the community, a local telephone book, and a homemade list of all the good shops, restaurants, and parks in the neighborhood. Including your child is a terrific way to explore new social relationships while emphasizing the need to care about others who are unfamiliar with their new surroundings.

Activities That Teach Teamwork and Cooperation

Sheet-and-Balls Game

A fun way to illustrate the importance of cooperation and teamwork

Materials:

a large bedsheet and a dozen or so Ping-Pong balls

3 years and up

Participants hold the sheet taut at arm level and put the Ping-Pong balls in the center. The goal is to get as many of the balls bouncing as possible, but the only one allowed to move is the designated Ping-Pong shaker. Start by choosing one Ping-Pong shaker from the group. It's essential that everyone else remain still. How many balls bounced? Not many. Choose a second shaker and keep adding more shakers until everyone is working together. The balls should really be moving now.

   Success was not possible with only one person working toward the goal. But with everyone trying, the team was able to meet its goal. In fact, it probably met its goal a little too well. With everyone shaking the sheet, the Ping-

Pong balls probably bounced right off the sheet. Set a new goal to keep the bouncing balls on the sheet. Figure out as a team how to accomplish this.

Hula Hoop Pass

Materials:
Hula Hoop

3 years and up

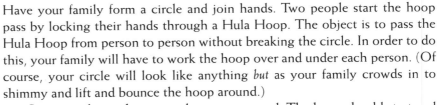

A game of cooperation

Have your family form a circle and join hands. Two people start the hoop pass by locking their hands through a Hula Hoop. The object is to pass the Hula Hoop from person to person without breaking the circle. In order to do this, your family will have to work the hoop over and under each person. (Of course, your circle will look like anything *but* as your family crowds in to shimmy and lift and bounce the hoop around.)

Set a time limit, then try to beat your record. The hoop should start and finish with the same two people.

Roll Play

Materials:
basketball

3 years and up

Team learning experience

Sit in a tight circle with your family, close enough so everyone is touching their neighbors. You'll find it helpful to extend your feet into the center of the circle. The object of the game is to move the ball from lap to lap as quickly as possible, without using hands. Time yourselves and try to beat your last time. Then add a few twists, such as yelling "Reverse," which means whoever has the ball has to send it in the opposite direction. You can also add more balls, different sizes if you like. Roll play is a game that not only teaches cooperation, but it gets everyone laughing, too.

Cooperative Picture Drawing

3 years and up

Draw a picture together

Younger children seem to especially like this activity. Decide with your family on a scene to draw. Then figure out who will be responsible for each component. For instance, your daughter may be particularly good at drawing the sun, so have her put that in. Dad's specialty may be clouds, so he gets to draw those, and so on. Draw your scene, one person at a time. Older children will find this more challenging if you do it in the dark. Sit at a table in a completely dark room, then take turns drawing your scene. In order for this to work, each artist must describe what they're drawing and where. Turn on the light. How does it look? Keep trying until you have figured out the best way to draw a picture in the dark cooperatively.

Our refrigerator door is covered with cooperative drawings, and we all take pride in the finished product.

One-Handed Tinker Toys

Teaches cooperation and teamwork

3 years and up

Challenge your children to assemble a sculpture using Tinker Toys, but using only one hand each and by working together. They should decide beforehand what they will make and how to go about it.

Finding Differences and Similarities

Shows that the best teams are made up of people with varying abilities

4 years and up

Sports teams know how the different strengths of players compensate for individual weaknesses. The following activity will help you apply this understanding to business or family "teams" by identifying members' strengths and weaknesses.

To start, everyone takes a turn discussing their personal skills and capabilities while a designated team secretary writes these down. Review the list for similarities and differences among members. Mark an *X* next to each strength that two or more people share, and an *O* beside each strength that only one person in the group has. Now try a problem. When you tackle a problem, think of your group as a sports team. Use similarities to gain momentum. When you reach a glitch, call upon the appropriate expert. This activity is a great way to prepare individuals to work together as a group. It increases productivity by encouraging collaboration and clarifying individual strengths and weaknesses.

While their classmates were worrying about cars and dates, a group of sophomores and freshmen at South San Antonio High School spent their spare time improving the environment.

Patricia Arambula, Jefferey Jimenez, Michael Reyes, Louis Rubio, and Iris Ybarra led their school's science club on a variety of recycling drives. They recycled everything from phone books to overcoats to tin and aluminum. They also raised money and planted more than one hundred drought-resistant plants and trees on school grounds and founded a local Trees for Life group, planting fruit and nut trees for the needy to supplement their diets.

Their actions have inspired the community to help find solutions to the environmental problems of their region.

The Story of Light

3 to 10 years *A story of teamwork and problem solving*

This story, written and illustrated by Susan L. Roth, is based on a Cherokee myth about a group of animals who work together to bring sunlight to the world. The animals keep bumping into each other in the darkness until they work out a plan to snatch a bit of the sun for themselves. Children will especially like the fact that the smallest of voices, a spider, plays a major role in resolving the problem. This story will remind you and your children to share talents to solve a problem.

Activities That Enhance Cooperation Between Siblings

"How can I get my kids to get along?" is one of the questions we hear most frequently from parents. There are dozens of activities for fostering children's appreciation and respect for each other, but the most educational are those that teach them how to think and act like a team. Getting along means teaming up. Teams don't have to be big; two people can make a team.

The following activities drive home the point that a sibling team will achieve so much more by working together than they will by working against each other. The following team-building exercises are fun. They'll get your kids laughing together, putting them in touch with the lighter side of their relationship.

Red and Green Circle Game

Materials:
a small box, circles of red and green construction paper

4 to 10 years

A weeklong game that teaches children to focus on the positive aspects of their relationship, and redirect their tendencies to argue

Each time you catch your children fighting, put a red circle into the box. Slip a green circle into the box when they are getting along. Sometimes all you have to do is reach for the red circle, and that's all the message your children need to call a truce. On those occasions, don't forget to give them a green circle for their effort to stop a fight. Encourage your children to recognize their green times themselves. At the end of the week, count up your circles. If there are more green than red, your family can do something special together, preferably something that your children previously decided on.

Banana Jam

Two children work as a single person to eat a banana

4 years and up

If you don't have a video camera, beg or borrow one for this activity. With a coffee table as your "stage," have one child kneel behind the coffee table, and the other child kneel behind her. Slip a large T-shirt over the first child's head, leaving her arms inside the shirt so the second child can put her arms in the T-shirt's arm holes. Bunch up the shirt and outfit the first child's arms with a pair of shorts, shoes, and socks, so it looks like you have one oddly proportioned kid sitting on the coffee table. That sight alone is funny enough, but wait until you give your "composite kid" a banana to eat. That fruit is going to wind up everywhere on that child's face before it reaches her mouth, unless the mouth tells the hands where to go. Eventually, they'll learn that through talking and listening, they can work together to accomplish a goal.

Have your kids take turns being the hands and the mouth. If you dare, try trickier foods, like spaghetti or ice cream. We know a family who puts on a show every Thanksgiving in which a sibling team makes and eats a banana split. It's a family tradition that the kids take very seriously, practicing for weeks before the big day, so that by the time the holiday comes around, they have their act down pat. Now, that's teamwork!

Double Walk

Learn the art of walking together

4 years and up

The way this activity is done is that one person stands very close behind the other, and they walk together. With a little practice and good communication, this pair will be able to walk briskly, turn right and left, and stop and start smoothly. Try adding more family members and work in a group of three or four. This is a real test of communication and cooperation.

Self-Awareness

Personal Insight

Feelings Management

Intuition

For Arielle's fifth birthday, we hosted a party at a local gymnastics center. One of the guests was two-year-old Aviva, who stood quietly by and watched, wide-eyed, as the other girls tumbled, flipped, and turned cartwheels on the soft, padded mats.

After the party and back in the familiar environment of her own home, Aviva climbed up on her parents' bed and announced that she wanted to do a somersault.

After a quick lesson, Aviva had partially mastered the forward somersault, but needed her mother's help going backward. Still, she was eager to demonstrate her new skill when her father walked in the room.

Proudly, Aviva did her front tumble to a great round of applause. Then she got in position and her mom flipped her over backward. Dad's face fell and he immediately closed down the gymnastics exhibition to warn his wife that the backward somersault placed too much weight on the toddler's neck. While Aviva watched from the sidelines, her parents discussed the possible danger of the move, father describing life-threatening injuries, and mother mostly rolling her eyes, but finally agreeing to retire the backward somersault until Aviva could do it on her own.

By all outward appearances, Aviva was oblivious to the debate. It seems, however, that she was actually paying close attention, because three nights later she brought it up.

It started in the bathtub when Aviva stood up and refused to sit back down again.

"You're making me nervous," her mother said, then explained that "nervous" means being afraid something bad will happen. Aviva considered that for a moment, then sat down.

After the bath, Aviva climbed up on the bed and requested help doing somersaults. "Backward!" she shouted, then paused. The expression that crossed her face mirrored the one of concern her father had worn three days earlier. She knitted her brows and said in a grave tone, "No, no, makes Daddy nervous," paused again, and without any further discussion happily bent over to do another forward somersault.

Like most children, Aviva pays close attention to her parents, learning from what they say and do. When the backflip event occurred, she observed and absorbed her father's look and expression of concern over the harm that the somersault might cause; second, she witnessed her mother's nervous reaction to her standing in the tub; third, she listened as her mother explained the word that would label the feeling; and fourth, Aviva applied this new knowledge to a feeling she herself had, and used it to help guide her actions. Having developed an understanding of this newly labeled feeling, she will now add it to her growing repertoire of information and call it up again.

Only two years old and already a child has begun developing self-awareness—insight and knowledge about herself and the world around her. Most dramatically, she is using that information to regulate her behavior. Aviva's story portrays the process of how children learn about themselves through observation, practice, and experience, and how they use this information to regulate their decisions and actions. In this chapter, we will discuss the skills of self-awareness: personal insight, feelings management, and intuition.

Personal Insight

Keeping pace with Aviva's growing knowledge about the world around her is her growing knowledge about the world within herself. Personal insight is the knowledge that children have about their desires and urges, feelings and moods, thoughts and beliefs, and a working understanding of the words that label them. Without this kind of intelligence, all of the knowledge in the world is useless. With personal insight, children also begin to connect their feelings, their thoughts, and their actions as in Aviva's story. The result over time is that the child's actions are not solely driven by the most immediate feeling or urge, but incorporate the possible consequences, alternative solutions, and hypothetical outcomes.

Being able to integrate these three different spheres of experience provides children with the ability to measure themselves against others, against their own values, and against their own goals, thus helping them reach a realistic (not overly critical or inflated) sense of self-worth.

As portrayed in Aviva's story, personal insight begins to grow as children absorb information about themselves through the eyes, ears, actions, and words of significant others. From these first observations, they begin to assemble an inventory of information about themselves to which they add each new feeling as it is labeled and understood. The inventory of knowledge grows deeper and deeper. If the information fits together in a sensible way, a child will reach a point where her thoughts, feelings, and actions work in harmony, each giving clues and messages that help guide her actions.

Relevent information from the past and the future will help children react in ways that are self-fulfilling. In the beginning, caregivers and educators help children with reminders such as "Why don't you check to see if you have to go to the bathroom? I know you were upset about wetting the bed, and would feel better if that doesn't happen again." As children mature, with personal insight they begin to make those connections almost automatically, even during times of upset and heated emotions. For example, as eleven-year-old Brett slams his bedroom door after another infuriating encounter with his little sister, he then has a flash of the last time he felt as angry as he does at the moment, lost control, and broke one of his favorite model airplanes. He regretted it later, and still wishes he hadn't done it. This interrupting thought helps steer him away from the same self-defeating actions and instead he slumps onto his bed and sighs loudly enough for everyone to hear, and says loudly, "You make me *so* mad!"

Feelings Management

Words help articulate feelings, and give a way to organize and inventory emotions so that they are accessible when we need them to communicate. Without the words, children instinctively defer to actions to express themselves, just as infants do to let a parent know they are wet or hungry. By assigning words to feelings, we give children a means for talking with themselves to soothe their anger, ease their hurt, and clear up confusion that powerful feelings bring on. This process gives them time to consider their choices and the consequences associated with each one.

The second time Brett experienced the same degree of anger he didn't break a model. An understanding of his feeling, and an association with a negative outcome in the past helped him regulate or manage his reaction better this time. Best of all, he was able to use words to express his angry feelings rather than out-of-control behavior. Feelings management is the part of our emotional intelligence that helps children keep themselves in charge of their feelings, especially under stressful circumstances.

Intuition

The path of personal self-discovery and the growth of self-knowledge leads to confidence in oneself and one's capabilities. Even when a child's actions are mistaken or inconsistent with a desired outcome, a nonjudgmental review and assessment will yield information useful to him. The information gradually becomes intuitive; the child begins to know what to do without consciously thinking through each step.

We worked with many children who, exposed to repeated abuse, develop a sixth sense that alerted them to impending danger. While this ability seemed almost mystical, upon closer inspection, it became clear that the child's warning system was actually a heightened awareness to details that would normally go overlooked, which developed over time due to repeated abuse. Intuition used with care is a wonderful self-awareness skill that can help guide us in a direction of unmatched opportunity and self-preservation. To use their intuitive skills safely, children need to draw upon the rational mind as well so that they can consider risk versus opportunity. Intuition plays a role in problem solving and crisis-management skills covered in the chapter on "Resolution."

Evaluating If a Child Has Difficulties with Self-Awareness

Review the "Over the Years Guidelines" to be sure that your expectations are in line with your child's age and developmental capabilities. Use the "Questions to Ask Yourself" as a checkpoint and a way of evaluating the child's strengths and weaknesses. If you answer yes to any of these questions, it will be beneficial to the child to develop these skills further.

Questions to Ask Yourself

Is the child prone to moodiness? Is the child easily frustrated and overly sensitive? (She cannot control the way she feels nor can she tell you why she is upset or what is troubling her because she seems not to understand either.)

Over the Years
Guidelines for the Development of Character Skills

Note: This guide is meant to serve as a general orientation to what you can expect and when to expect it. While there are no absolute norms or limitations regarding how and when characteristics within a developmental period appear, and every child is unique, there is a range of similar and expectable periods of development, each marked by patterns of behavior and capabilities. Keep in mind that the nature of personality development is dynamic and repetitive, meaning that it is ever-changing and traits and/or skills seem to appear, disappear, and then reappear throughout development.

Self-awareness—Personal Insight, Feelings Management, and Intuition

Stage 1 Infancy: Birth to 24 months
The stage of life from newborn through toddlerhood

Foundation period in which many behavior patterns, attitudes, and patterns of emotional expression are being established. Much of the first 12 months of this period are affected by instinctual drives for nurturing, food, and basic care.

Expect baby between 12–24 months to: first exhibit signs of self-awareness through sensory exploration of her body (mouthing objects, looking in a mirror, talking baby talk to hear own voice, sucking a finger or toe); first exhibit signs of self-identity by identifying herself by name, her clothing, bedroom, toys, and association with family and caregivers.

Do not expect baby to: show signs of insight or emotional management until the end of the early childhood stage.

Stage II Early Childhood—The Preschool Years: Ages 2 to 6
The stage of life from toddlerhood through kindergarten

This is often called the play age because it is the peak period of interest in play and toys, marked by exploration, discovery play, creativity, magical thinking, fierce strivings for independence, and acquisition of social skills. This is a time of preparation for learning the foundations of social behavior needed for the school years to come.

Between ages 2–4, expect children to: experience most of the emotions known to adults; exhibit emotional (loving, anger, fear, excitement) and behavioral (tantrums, silliness, hyperactivity, crying) extremes; show interest in learning the words and means for communicating their feelings.

Do not expect children to: understand the cause or precipitants to these emotional highs and lows, or how to control them; learn about these feelings on their own.

Between ages 4–6, expect children to: use their growing awareness of social rules of approval and disapproval to regulate how they act; begin to show more mature forms of emotional expression (sulking, whining, and brooding); be better able to articulate a feeling when asked ("I'm mad at my sister because she . . ."); attempt to understand their own and others' behavior ("I think she quit because she didn't know the answer and felt embarrassed").

Do not expect children to: participate in long discussions about feelings and thoughts; exhibit these newly acquired behaviors consistently or on demand; totally let go of immature ways of handling their emotions.

Stage III Late Childhood—The School Years: Ages 6 to 11
This stage of life begins with entrance into first grade and extends into the beginning of adolescence

This period is marked by major interest and concern for social involvement with peers, participation in rule-based group play, and increased motivation to learn, acquire technical knowledge, information, and achieve academic success. This stage is very important for establishing attitudes and habits about learning, work, and personal potential.

Expect children to: have few periods of heightened emotionality (moodiness) and be generally pleasant to live with; control external expressions of their emotions that they believe are socially unacceptable (i.e., crying, tantrums, fear) and as a result become tense, or irritable; discover ways to feel better and release emotional energy while still conforming to social expectations (i.e., laughing or playing strenuously, speaking to a friend, crying in private); work harder at understanding and managing their emotions outside of the home than they do inside.

Do not expect children to: adapt to social pressures without some amount of turmoil; on their own realize how their changing moods affect others in the family.

Stage IV Early Adolescence: Ages 11 to 15
This stage of life begins around the time a child finishes elementary school and concludes by the time he graduates middle school (junior high school) and enters the world of high school

This period is marked by change and turmoil, the onset of puberty, growth spurts, increased interest in peer relationships and the opposite sex, and fierce strivings for self-identity and independence.

Expect young adolescents to: experience heightened emotionality, moodiness, exaggerated reactions to events, confusion about how they feel, and ambivalence about their newfound independence; become most upset when treated "like a child"; express anger by brooding, refusing to speak, stomping away from the scene and into the sanctity of their bedroom to listen to music, or loudly voicing criticism; begin to be more aware of their good and bad traits and the role these have in social relationships; be so preoccupied with themselves that they forget about others; be ultrasensitive to criticism about appearance, style of dress, and perceived attractiveness; feel omnipotent and unrealistic about their abilities and limitations.

Do not expect young adolescents: engaged in self-defeating and/or self-destructive behaviors (promiscuous and unprotected sexual behavior, drug and alcohol use, school truancy) to recognize that these actions will not help them reach their goals or feel happier.

Does the child have difficulty answering questions about how he feels, why he did something, or what he is thinking? (He answers these questions with "I don't know," or says nothing at all.)

Does the child have frequent temper tantrums, emotional outbursts, and aggressive behaviors? (She reaches a point where she is out of control and unwilling to listen to reason or even speak to you. She won't talk about the problem, puts her hands over her ears, and promises to be good the next time.)

Does the child repeat the same behaviors for which she was in trouble previously? (This child seems not to learn from punishments, lost privileges, and other negative consequences.)

How to Build Self-Awareness in Your Child

1. One of the most common frustrations parents report about their own childhoods is that feelings weren't spoken about or taken seriously. Make feelings and the words that define them a regular part of your family's vocabularly and culture. Respect and honor feelings: yours, your child's, and those of other people with whom you and your child come in contact.

2. Make a conscious effort to teach a "feeling vocabulary" as they come up in conversation over the natural course of the day (or in an organized way—one word a day starting with the same letter of the day of the week). Think about the match between your child's age and the word, but don't shy away from one that is too difficult to pronounce or complicated to explain, for when it comes up again, the child will have heard it at least once before.

3. Share your feelings, thoughts, and experiences, positive and negative, to establish an atmosphere of openness. Children need to know and see that you have all sorts of feelings, just as they do, including: excitement, confusion, grouchiness, silliness, anger, worry, and so on. Seeing and hearing their parent own up to these feelings will give them inspiration to do the same, including the feelings they may not want. It also makes a parent or teacher human and fallible—someone real whom they can relate to and realistically aspire to be like.

4. Figuring out what and how to share can be confusing, particularly if your own parents never spoke about these subjects. Don't let this stop you. It is

better to try but make a few mistakes than it is to close this line of communication and modeling. Children are a very forgiving audience, and are more interested in the process of sharing than the content. Before sharing something, consider how the child will interpret it, and how you or another adult will feel with this information revealed. Take editorial license (it was in the package with the birth certificate and free diapers that came with your baby) and alter, cut, or enhance the story to make it comfortable, interesting, and fitting.

5. Do not confuse sensitive parenting with permissiveness. By acknowledging a child's thoughts and emotions and articulating these along with your own, your actions will make more sense to the child. Setting limits this way will communicate clear and unambiguous messages, teach more, and set a precedent of respect and understanding that will be returned to you.

6. Children attempting to master the language of self-awareness can be ultra-sensitive. It is normal and inevitable that they will express feelings that are disagreeable to adults, such as "I hate my sister." Be careful not to mock, criticize, or too quickly correct such statements; children benefit the most when they reach a new understanding on their own. When your child is sharing her thoughts, as much as you may feel the urge to finish a sentence, tell her the answer, or advise her what she is thinking, refrain from any of these responses. Instead, think of what you could say to lead her toward understanding her own feelings and solving the puzzle herself.

7. If your child manages to catch you off guard with an insight about you or your behavior, try not to become defensive. Take a deep breath and remember that she is not attempting to usurp your authority, and only doing what you've taught her. This is a sure sign of her growing self-awareness and insight, because she is now applying what she has learned about herself to others.

Activities That Enhance Personal Insight, Intuition, and Feelings Management

Feelings Cards

Gives your child the vocabulary to express feelings

Materials:
three-by-five index cards

3 to 10 years

Write each of the feelings listed below on a separate index card. Draw a picture of the feeling on the back, or paste a photograph of your child expressing that feeling. This will make it easier for your child to connect the feeling with its word. Now you have a deck of feelings cards for games and other uses.

Here are some of the most common feelings (a younger child will need only a few of these): mad, sad, glad, happy, angry, frustrated, warm, proud, quiet, shy, nervous, scared, bad, lucky, joyful, small, safe, upset, hassled, silly, alive, hopeful, creative, stubborn, loved, strange, funny, cool, beautiful, encouraged, uncomfortable, excited, confused, afraid, weird, stupid, worried, insecure, rotten, selfish, grouchy, put down, used, sick, awkward, furious, crazy, embarrassed, talkative, curious, clever, strange, loved, unloved, free, sensitive, ugly, successful, disappointed, likable, good, strong, left out, energetic, hateful, unimportant, important, hurt, sorry, rejected, bashful, smothered, calm, great, cheerful, fresh, brave, gross, inferior, worthless, worthwhile, depressed, troubled, hopeless, skillful, capable, confident, smart, tearful, accepting, jealous, judged, secretive, positive, wonderful.

Here are some games to play with your feelings cards:

Feelings Charades Play charades by having members in your family take turns acting out a feeling from a card. Other family members try to guess the feeling.

Flash-Card Feelings Use the deck like flash cards. Show your child the picture and ask him to guess the feeling, or show your child the word and have him express it.

Feelings Mix and Match Duplicate your cards for a mix-and-match game. Put both decks on the floor, one of them word side up, the other picture side up. Match the expressions with the words.

Right and Wrong Select a card and have family members take turns showing the right way and the wrong way to express the feeling.

When playing the games, reinforce to your child what the feeling *feels* like, what can bring it on, and how to express it appropriately. Use the feelings cards throughout your daily routine. When your child becomes moody, have her go through the deck and choose a card or two that indicates her emotions. Model for your child when you have a specific feeling by selecting a card for yourself.

Mime Your Moods

Express feeling without words

Use face paint to turn you and your child into mimes. Stand together in front of a mirror and practice expressing different emotions. Notice how different your face looks when you are angry and when you are happy. While still in makeup, put on skits featuring different feelings. Stage a Three-Penny-Feelings Opera, pretending to be sad, happy, mad, and frustrated while singing a song. Try singing the alphabet in a mournful tone, or jubilantly. This is good practice for identifying feelings.

Growth Chart

A concrete way to measure emotional growth

Small children have a hard time controlling anger and moodiness. This becomes easier only with time and maturity. Help your child chart her emotional growth by labeling the steps toward expressing feelings appropriately. These include: identifying feelings, choosing how feelings should be expressed, and expressing these feelings appropriately. Write these on a standard growth chart. Each time your child expresses herself appropriately, mark off another inch. When your child grows to a desired height, reward her for this emotional growth. Try to relate the reward to maturity.

Feelings Chart

Help your child identify his own feelings

Materials:
large piece of white felt, colored felt circle, Velcro

Make the feelings chart by writing "Today I feel . . ." at the top of the white felt. Hang it on your child's wall or door. Draw different facial expressions on the felt circles and attach Velcro to the back of each. When appropriate, ask your child to choose the face that represents his feelings and stick it on the chart.

Slow Motion

Helps child express herself during times of excitement

When your child gets overly excited and can't appropriately express herself, suggest she speak in slow motion. Show your child how to drop your speaking speed in order to calm her emotions. For example, "I am . . . very, very . . . angry . . . that you . . . did not . . . pick up . . . your toys." This is a good reminder for everyone in your family to take control of their feelings in order to speak about them.

Feelings Journal

5 years and up

Express thoughts in writing with a diary

Contrary to popular belief, diaries are not the sole domain of dreamy young girls who write in looping script and dot their *i*'s with tiny hearts. Some of our most influential leaders and greatest artists recorded their thoughts in a daily journal.

Encourage this habit in your child. Buy a special book for recording thoughts and reporting on daily activities. To the diarist, the blank book is a friend, a therapist, and most importantly, a window into one's own thoughts. Set the right example by keeping a journal yourself, if you don't already. And remember, the journal is a sacred document. Never violate your child's trust by reading his. By introducing your child to the joys of journal writing, you will be introducing him to a lifelong friend.

Here are a few feelings journals to get your kids started. These give children space to write or draw, and guide them through feelings explorations: *I Am Special* and *Marvelous Me Workbooks*, by Linda Schwartz (The Learning Works, 1978–9); *Feeling Good about Yourself*, by Debbie Pincus (Good Apple Inc., 1990), for three- to eight-year-olds; and *My Life*, by Delia Ephron (Running Press, 1991).

The Feelings Box

Materials:
cardboard box, magazine pictures of people expressing emotions

3 to 9 years

A large container filled with items that help people express their feelings

The feelings box provides a structured way to manage one's feelings. Family members should mine the feelings box when they're struggling to communicate an emotion. Write the words "Feelings Box" on a box and decorate it with pictures of people who are mad, happy, sad, and so on. Fill the box with the following:

> *feelings cards:* Put in a deck of feelings cards as described on page 139.
>
> *the mad-and-angry pillow:* To make a mad-and-angry pillow, draw pictures and write the names of angry feelings on an old pillowcase (frustrated, furious, upset, feel like popping my cork, etc.). Stuff the pillowcase with something soft and punchable.
>
> *the magic wand:* A stick covered with glitter
>
> *I-want-attention hat:* A hat with a message. Label an old hat with the words I Want Attention.

feelings masks: On paper plates, draw faces depicting a feeling, cut holes for the eyes, and glue on popsicle-stick handles. Make enough to cover a range of feelings.

mirror, tissue, a few puppets and dolls, and skill cards: (see page 84)

Here are examples of how to use each item.

The Mad-and-Angry Pillow If your child needs a physical outlet for anger, tell her to get the mad/angry pillow out of the box and tell her to hit it or use it for a pillow fight with a willing family member. Once she gets her aggressions out, ask your child to find the word for her feeling on the pillowcase. Now discuss the anger and ways to express it appropriately.

Magic Wand Use the magic wand to help your child deal with disappointment. Tell him to wave the wand and verbalize his wish for how things might have been.

I-Want-Attention Hat Anytime your child tries to get your attention by whining, crying, or throwing a tantrum, tell him to get out the I-want-attention hat. Let your child know that whoever wears it is telling you that you are needed. When your child puts on the hat, immediately praise him for getting your attention the right way. Either give him the attention he needs at that moment, or agree on a time to be together later.

Puppets, Dolls, and Feelings Masks Use the puppets, dolls, and feelings masks to playact real-life challenges. The toys will help your child practice handling her emotions and prepare her for potentially distressing events, such as going to a toy store to purchase a birthday present for another child.

Feelings Cards These will help your child pinpoint her feelings.

Mirror Have your child look in the mirror and describe what she sees (an angry face, a sad face, a happy face).

Skill Cards If your child has already expressed a feeling inappropriately, ask him to look through his skill cards for hints on how to do better next time.

Tissue The tissue is there for crying—an acceptable way to express feelings.

Whenever the child begins to fly off the handle, tell him he can either use the feelings box or accept the consequences. Join your child on his trips to the feelings box whenever you can, encourage appropriate use of items, and model the correct way to express feelings. If nothing else, the feelings box tells your child that you take his feelings seriously.

Feelings Safari Hunt

3 to 10 years

Your child looks for expressions of emotions in books and magazines

You and your child embark on a great adventure when you go on a feelings safari. Your quest: to find a range of human emotions. To start, you need a hefty stack of magazines, newspapers, books, and pictures (photograph books are good). You announce a feeling, and your child has to hunt through the periodicals for a picture of somebody expressing it. To play the game with several people, select a feelings card from the deck (activity on page 139). The first one who finds that feeling in the books or magazines wins. The winner keeps the feeling card. The game winner is the one who winds up with the most cards.

Expression Through Art

3 years and up

Child gets in touch with feelings through art

Simply put, art is self-expression. When children mold lumps of clay, or adults dab paint on canvas, they are giving the world a glimpse into their innermost selves. When you introduce your child to the arts, you are giving him a new way of communicating.

Art is anything your child creates. Consider the possibilities: painting, drawing, clay, knitting, weaving, needlepoint, photography, dance, drama, writing, singing, music, and so on. Learn about your child's chosen art and make sure he sees you involved with your own art or craft. Perhaps you will have similar interests and can broaden your art experiences together.

Feelings Collage

Materials:
poster board, magazines

4 years and up

Assemble a collage from pictures of people expressing emotions

Give your child a pile of old magazines and ask him to cut out pictures of people displaying a range of emotions. Arrange these into a collage on the poster board, with each feeling labeled.

Hang the feelings collage where your child can see it. When your child is feeling *something* intensely, but isn't sure what to call it, go to the collage together and see if he can select a picture that best represents his emotion.

Ten-Ways-to-Show-a-Feeling Game

This game helps children recognize different ways to express a single feeling

4 to 10 years

Use your feelings cards or write down a list of different feelings. Each participant selects one and shows through body language, words, and actions all the ways to express it. For example, anger may be shown by screaming and shouting, but it can also be expressed through a clenched fist and a red face, by muttering under one's breath, or by remaining stone silent.

Feelings + Positive Actions = Positive Results

An equation for managing emotions

Materials:
poster board

6 years and up

Have you ever felt so angry that you thought you would explode? How did you handle it? Did you explode and make matters worse? Or did you find a way to dissipate your anger?

Emotions are what make us human in the best, *and* in the worst, sense of the word. Intense feelings can make us feel elated—larger than life itself! But they can also flatten us—so we feel lower than low.

Working through our emotions is one of life's ongoing challenges. And if you think it's difficult for you to deal with anger, frustration, or jealousy, think of how hard this is for your child who has far less experience than you. This activity will help your children examine their emotions with a neutral eye.

Discuss with your child the positive and negative ways people resolve their feelings. For instance, a positive reaction to anger could be cooling off during a long walk or calmly discussing your feelings. A negative reaction might involve yelling at or hitting the person you're angry with.

Give each participant a large sheet of poster board labeled on one side "Feeling + Positive Action = (blank)" and on the other side, "Feeling + Negative Action = (blank)."

> Kanesha Sonee Johnson's bravery and insight helped her see beyond skin color when she started fifth grade in Hawthorne, California. An African-American, Kanesha was dismayed to see that the black children did not mingle with their Vietnamese classmates.
>
> She began making friends with Vietnamese kids who couldn't speak English, helping them with their homework, teaching them the ropes, and protecting them from the taunts of other children.
>
> "I just decided to, because I know how it feels when people laugh at you," Kanesha explained. "That old poem says, 'Sticks and stones may break my bones but names can never hurt me,' but some words do hurt."
>
> Kanesha was called a lot of names herself, but she held her ground, eventually ending de facto segregation on her playground.

On each side of the poster, list a range of emotions under the "feeling" part of the equation. Ask participants to discuss the ways they typically express each one. It will be helpful to recall actual incidents of high emotion. Next, have each participant think of the positive and the negative ways they tried to resolve each emotion. Write those under the "positive" or "negative" portions of the equation. On Mom's poster, for example, she may list under "sad" her reactions to news of her friend's divorce. On the positive side might be, "Mom talked over her sad feelings with her friend," "Mom cried with her friend," and "Mom read a book about divorce to help understand her feelings better." Her negative behaviors may include, "Mom turned sad feelings into angry feelings and got mad at her friend for letting the marriage fail," or "Mom cried by herself for a long time without telling anyone that her friend's divorce made her sad."

Of course, there will be situations where the actions were neither clearly negative nor clearly positive. This is where the = part of the equation helps. When you add a person's feeling to his accompanying reaction, you will get an outcome.

Using the sad Mom example, if Mom isn't sure whether getting angry at her friend is a negative or positive reaction, examine the equation: Sad + Angry with Friend = Friend Stopped Talking to Mom because she felt blamed for the divorce. Double-check the equation to see if there was anything helpful about Mom turning her sad feeling into an angry one. Most likely not. Therefore you can categorize it as a negative behavior.

When you are finished exploring feelings and accompanying behaviors, add up each equation. Write down each result. For example: Being Angry + Taking a Walk = Calming Down and being able to talk about what's bothering me.

Now your children have a guide map to their emotions. When a child is feeling a certain way, ask him to consult the chart. The likely outcomes of a positive and a negative reaction will be right there in black and white either to help him make a decision or to help him understand why his choice was wrong.

This chart will probably never be complete, as you will keep adding to it as situations change and as your child matures. However, by starting now, you are helping your child establish a productive pattern to fall back on whenever he feels overcome by a strong emotion. As he grows, he will internalize these guidelines so they can be called upon when he needs help traversing life's emotional minefields.

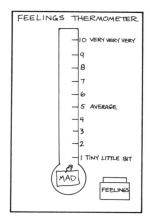

Feelings Thermometer

Helps family members gauge the intensity of one anothers' feelings

Materials:
poster board

3 to 8 years

Draw a thermometer on a poster board and mark it off 1 to 10 from bottom to top. Next to the number 10, write "Very, Very, Very." Next to the 1, write "Tiny Little Bit." Next to the 5, write "Average." Then have each person recall a specific incident and use the thermometer to point out the degree of their emotions at the time.

Feelings Favors

Recognize how to handle emotions

4 to 12 years

The most precious insight a person can possess is the ability to recognize her feelings *and* understand how to handle them. A feelings favor is like asking yourself, "How may I help you?"

For adults the activity is simple. Write down at least twenty different ways you felt during the past week. Next to each feeling, indicate what you did or could have done to make that feeling more productive and less destructive to your daily living. For example, you felt exasperated with your son because he slept through his alarm three days in a row. Your first tendency might be to correct the behavior: your son's lateness. And yes, this problem does need to be addressed (our first book, *Playful Parenting,* or this book in the chapter on Resourcefulness might help you there). But that doesn't address your exasperation. What can you do to soothe yourself? Maybe take a long, hot shower, or perhaps flip on your favorite music to listen to on the way to work. Our point is that you must take care of yourself so the feeling doesn't ruin the rest of your day (and make things worse between you and your son).

To do this activity with children, you need to help them discover their best ways to soothe a feeling. Give examples of your own feelings favors. Have them look through magazines and storybooks to see how others work through feelings.

Mark knows of a family that took the idea of feelings favors literally. They gave each of their children a half dozen party favors. On each favor, the children wrote a way to deal with a strong emotion. Each time they needed to deal with the feeling, they looked at their "favors" and selected the one they thought would work best. One child decided that she would use a real party favor for happy feelings, and just blow into it until her cheeks hurt!

Drama Walks

4 to 10 years   *Shows children how well our bodies can express feelings*

Sit or stand in a circle and choose an emotion such as anger, joy, sadness, happiness, disappointment, or excitement. Have one person walk across the circle displaying this feeling. Don't use words, only body language to display the feeling while walking across the circle. You can have several people walk at one time or have everyone walk at once. Talk about what you observed.

Activities That Teach Anger Management

Anger is one of the most difficult feelings for a person to manage. The following activities can help both you and your child work through this very powerful emotion.

TAP (Think and Prevent)

4 years and up   *A method for managing rage*

TAP is based on a technique called "self-talk"—the internal voice that narrates our days. A parent would use TAP to stop spiraling negative feelings and find productive ways to express anger. This technique suggests that you actually tap yourself on the leg or arm when you start to feel anger. The tap concretely structures your thinking so that you're able to contain unplanned words and angry reactions. To control anger, it's helpful to think of literally turning it off. The light tap on the leg is the "off" switch. It gives you the chance to take time out to think about alternative ways to express your feelings. This helps you break the cycle of events that usually follows when you lose control and lash out at those around you.

TAP works best if you delve into your history of previously successful bouts with anger. Develop a vocabulary for angry feelings and help your child develop one as well. You can rely on these words to replace an irrational explosion.

Here are three simple steps for using TAP: 1) When you feel the first signs of a meltdown, give yourself a tap and disengage from the situation. 2) Once you are disengaged from the challenge, plug into your own self-talk methods of controlling your anger by saying to yourself, "I can be calm," or "Becoming overly angry is a waste of my energy!" 3) Return to the situation with a renewed charge of self-control, then calmly express your feelings.

The Think Chair
A thoughtful "time out"

Material:
a chair

2 to 10 years

The think chair is another name for a well-known behavioral technique called "time out." However, the think chair reminds children to consider their behavior.

Take your child to the think chair when she loses control. It has the dual benefit of giving you both a concrete procedure to follow as well as a place to cool off. The think chair is most effective in correcting persistent behaviors that are impulsive, hostile, aggressive, and overly emotional. These are some of the most difficult emotions for your child to control, and probably the most upsetting to parents. For these times, the think chair is an invaluable way to avoid a power struggle and rein in runaway emotions. Here are a few suggestions for using the think chair:

1. Place it in a quiet area in your home, away from toys and the television.

2. When explaining to your child what the think chair is, spell out the behaviors that warrant a visit to it.

3. When the time comes to use the think chair, tell your child briefly why he is going there and what to think about while sitting in it. Remember, keep the explanation succinct. A lengthy description of his misdeed will only invite your child to bargain his way out.

4. Always indicate how long your child must stay in the think chair. A good rule to follow is one minute for each year of age (four years equals four minutes).

5. Use a timer with a bell so your child has no reason to keep asking you if the time is up yet. Give your child some control over the situation by putting him in charge of the timer.

6. When the bell rings, ask your child to explain his thoughts. If he expresses adequate and age-appropriate understanding of his misbehavior, he can leave the think chair; if not he may need to sit through another session of thinking.

7. Don't speak when your child is in the think chair. This is the time for him to think for himself.

The short-term goal of this technique is to interrupt and bring an immediate end to a specific misbehavior; the long-term goal is to teach your child thinking skills and encourage self-control.

The TNT Corner (Tantrums 'n' Tirades Corner)

2 to 8 years *A safe area of your home for tantrums*

Give your child permission to have a tantrum, but only in the designated area. Show her the TNT corner, and maybe even post a sign nearby indicating Tantrums Only! Anytime your child begins a tantrum, guide her (or carry her, if necessary) to the TNT corner. Ignore her while she's there. (You may need to TAP yourself to keep from getting pulled in.) She may leave the area when the tantrum is over. Ask her what happened, how she could have prevented the tantrum, and what other ways she could have expressed her feelings. Offer suggestions such as using STAR (Stop, Think, Act Right, page 195).

Combine this activity with others that will help your child think of alternatives to the tantrum corner. Reward, compliment, and praise your child when she goes to the tantrum corner herself or solves her problem another way. Distract her; there is nothing that squelches a tantrum more successfully than a child thinking there is something better to do. Model for her how you sort out your own feelings. Use the TNT corner yourself when you lose your temper. Bring the sign for your TNT corner with you when you travel, and try to plan, prepare, and prevent all the vulnerable situations for your child. (For example, overtired and overstimulated children do not fare well at a supermarket.)

Feelings Gears

A concrete way to switch negative behavior to positive behavior

It is amazing how a football player can muster every ounce of aggression in his body to plow into an opponent, then calmly step away a second later. When we watch a football game, Mark points out the great plays and Denise points out the player who smashes his opponent to the ground, then helps him back on his feet. With intense training, football players learn to switch gears from a rush of aggression to apparent calm. It follows that if they can do this, the rest of us can, too.

In this activity you show your child how to put the brakes on negative behavior and switch gears to express feelings productively. On a piece of paper draw two circles, one red, one green. Label the red circle "stop," the green one "go." Draw and cut out a gearshift (like the lever used to operate a manual transmission) from poster board and tape it in the middle of the paper. Pretend that we all have little buttons in our head to stop or start a feeling behavior and a shift to change a feeling. With your child come up with situations when he acted correctly. Apply the buttons and gears metaphor. For example, "The last time your sister called you a name, I know you felt angry, but you must have pressed the stop button because you didn't call her a name back or hit her. Instead you shifted gears and walked away." Give your child as many examples as possible. Then show how your child pressed the wrong button by giving examples of negative reactions to feelings. Once your child understands how the buttons and gearshifts work, use the stop and go buttons to practice situations she might encounter in the future. For example, being called names by a neighbor friend, not being able to get what she wants at the supermarket, or losing something in the house and not being able to find it for hours. Practice this activity from time to time. Eventually, she will see the feeling gears in her head and automatically press and shift the correct metaphorical buttons and gears when confronted with a challenging situation.

Magic Cream

A magical way to rub away tantrums

Wouldn't it be great if there were a magic cream that turned churlish children angelic? Well, magic cream is available. We have stockpiled quite a supply of this amazing mixture! Our three-year-old has an awful case of twilight tantrums, the kind that appear right around dinnertime and are so volatile that they can be ignited simply by pouring her milk into the wrong cup. As soon

as she throws her head back and begins contorting her face into prescream position, one of us will grab the magic cream (ordinary hand lotion with a little glitter mixed in) and say, "Oh, no, looks like you need a little magic cream. It will make your crankies go away." Almost without fail, she breaks out of her tantrum mode to accept a helping of the magic concoction. She regains her composure within seconds, or occasionally minutes, and dinner continues. Instead of spending the entire dinner in a battle of wills, we are all talking about "how angry Emily felt when she got the Winnie the Pooh cup instead of the one with the dalmatians," and "how proud she feels now that she pulled herself out of a tantrum."

Magic cream is very versatile. Just a little dab will stop your preschoolers from fighting, get them moving in the morning, and change a whine into a voice that is much more pleasing to the ears.

You're Bugging Me

A lighthearted way to point out annoying behavior

Materials: yarn and a small container

3 to 12 years

Make dozens of little fuzzy bugs out of yarn about one inch in length. Tie tightly in the middle with another piece of yarn and spread out the pieces so that they are shaped like balls. Fill a bowl in the kitchen with the "bugs," and keep it handy for anytime someone in the family irritates another person. Give this person a "bug" and tell him "You're bugging me!" Encourage your child to stifle aggression toward someone who's bothering him, and give out a bug instead.

Stomp Your Feet

Stomp away anger

Materials: plastic bubble wrap

3 years and up

Bubble wrap is ideal for protecting breakables—from angry children. You know the stuff. It's that plastic sheeting with pockets of air in it that you use for packing fragile items.

Keep a supply handy for when your child needs an outlet for aggressive energy. Give him a few sheets and have him stomp out bubbles until he has stomped out his anger. Your priceless Waterford will thank you.

Scott's Idea

5 years and up

Express feelings nonverbally

Take a peek at the story written by Scott Nadel, age eleven, on page 200, in which he explains how he problem solved and came up with this great idea for expressing anger with control. Tell your child to write his feelings down when angry. Instead of yelling at the person he is angry with, he should show them what he wrote. This separates the emotion from the message and keeps tempers in check.

Calm-Down Button

Feelings management   **2 to 8 years**

Pretend there's a volume switch on your child's neck that allows you to lower a loud voice, turn up a shy one, or turn off a whine. This is a gentle reminder to your child to control her tone of voice.

Chapter 9

Happiness

Joy

Humor

Playfulness

Stress Management

Alex is a bright and witty five-year-old who attends our daughters' school. At a recent event there, Alex's mother, Mary, and Denise did what parents most want to do, and began swapping you-know-what-my-kid-said stories. This is Mary's story: Alex was among a group of children who gathered in a circle at a party to listen to a storyteller. The storyteller began by asking questions, including that old standard, "What do you want to be when you grow up?" The children took turns answering. One wanted to be a firefighter, another an airline pilot, one a teacher, and so on. Alex was the last to give his answer.

"I want to be funny!" he announced with conviction. Everyone laughed—except Alex, who thought his answer made perfect sense, given his good-humored disposition and lighthearted outlook.

It seems her son spends a lot of time being funny. He's known as the class clown and he requests joke books for birthday presents. Denise and Mary joked whether Jerry Seinfeld, Roseanne, or Tim Allen think "being funny" is a serious business to get into.

Someday we might be able to say that "we knew Alex when he was just a cute, funny kid . . . now he's a famous comedian with a prime-time show and three best-selling books." The point and value of Alex loving to make people laugh almost as much as he loves to laugh himself isn't lost on us. People spend their whole lives engaged in serious pursuits: school, work, family responsibilities. On top of that they are inundated every day with bad news from the media. Alex's gift of humor touches all of those who know him for he helps them smile, something that we do not do enough of. Not only can Alex's parents feel proud about their son's knack for humor, they can also feel comfortable knowing that he is well on his way to developing happiness skills.

At first, you might think there is no such thing as happiness skills. Most of us know what happiness means: joy, bliss, pleasure, contentment, delight, optimism, the list goes on. But do you know how to teach happiness or where to find it when someone needs it? The fact is, happiness is a character skill that is elusive and complicated. It is something we know instinctively very early on in life, and need to keep with us, at the ready, every day we live.

Happiness can only be experienced on a day-to-day basis when a person's joy and stress-management system is fully working. This "system" calms and controls the pressures and strains of one's lifestyle through the use of humor, playfulness, body and mind exercises, relaxation techniques, and time away from it all. Stress management is a set of methods, skills, and "exercises" that help us manage the real pressures that impact our lives. Effective management means that despite these detrimental influences, we are able to care for our body and mind, reducing the proven deadly physiological effects of stress (heart disease, weakened immunity, emotional disorders, anxiety, and depression).

Stress management is so important to our lives, and so difficult to learn and sustain, that an entire industry has emerged to serve the needs of individuals, corporations, married couples, and even families. All over the world, people are learning to deal with stressful living at exercise centers, spas, health clinics, vacation destinations, and educational institutes.

This specialized industry is a great step in the right direction, but still there is not enough attention spent on joy and happiness "skills." The good news is that these skills are simple and fun to learn. But before we can teach these skills to our children, we must acknowledge the need to build them for ourselves. If we want our children to enjoy life, develop a sense of humor, find pleasure and happiness in most things they do, and pass these feelings on to others, we must as parents, educators, and caregivers embark on this course of living.

We see so many people who forget to be happy about the most obvious things—that they are alive, that the sun is shining—or to appreciate something as common and simple as the sound of a bird chirping. Staying connected to these simple pleasures enriches everyday living. Humor and playfulness help us find the joy even in life's downside.

Joy

To know joy is to be happy. A child brought up in a family that laughs, jokes, and smiles develops a deep understanding and awareness of joyful living. This child will seek the humor and happiness available in his life. He'll know how to laugh, joke, and smile, and odd as it may sound, this is something many people have not learned to do.

Humor

Being able to see the humor in a situation helps restore a realistic perspective and acts as a stabilizer, helping people avoid unhealthy highs and painful lows. Life isn't all joy and happiness, for sadness and disappointment are also part of living, but when these happen we draw upon our reserve of joy and love of life to help get us through. For example, a child who wins a school-wide spelling bee one day and gets a low grade on his classroom spelling test the next will benefit from a sense of humor when trying to maintain balance handling the two opposing situations.

A sense of humor helps diffuse tension that is normal in daily living and growing. Children sometimes take too seriously their mistakes, failings, and errors. Becoming well-grounded and happy people requires that they develop an acceptance for human imperfection—their own.

Playfulness

Having fun and being playful or silly are powerfully potent cures to what is ailing us; not only do they enrich our day-to-day experience, but they feed the human spirit and provide a relief from life's pressures and stresses. These stressors have been correlated with hypertension, high blood pressure, and other physical ailments; conversely, laughing and humor have been proven to strengthen the will to live and fight potentially life-threatening illnesses. Play and fun provide a respite from the rigors, demands, and occasional monotony of life.

Stress Management

Stress comes in many forms but it undoubtedly comes into parents' and children's lives much more often than it used to. Stress also invades our children's lives at earlier ages. Research has proven that children are growing up faster and dealing with adult issues at very young ages. Children experience pressures and demands of doing too much and being overscheduled, they have so much more to learn in order to handle such a complicated world, and their parents are feeling clearly more stressed out.

Evaluating If Your Child Has Strong Levels of Joy, Humor, Playfulness, or Stress Management

Review the "Over the Years Guidelines" to be sure that your expectations are in line with your child's age and developmental capabilities. Use the "Questions to Ask Yourself" as a checkpoint and a way of evaluating the child's strengths and weaknesses. If you answer yes to any of these questions, it will be beneficial to the child to develop these skills further.

Questions to Ask Yourself

Does the child have a difficult time expressing glee, delight, satisfaction? (She rarely laughs from her belly and giggles with delight. She very seldom reaches a state of satisfaction in each day and each moment, and seems to require more than the average effort to be happy.)

Is the child's playfulness short-lived, held in check, or guarded? (She seems to be missing a playful spirit, or is uncomfortable with the feelings it brings on or the image it conveys to others.)

Is the child unable to appreciate the simple things in life such as a caterpillar's transformation into a butterfly or the sound her feet make running in her favorite shoes?

Does the child have a hard time laughing out loud or loudly? Do her eyes rarely twinkle with excitement?

Does your child dwell upon what isn't there, what he doesn't have or didn't accomplish? (Things he has or has accomplished are minimized or invisible to him.)

Does the child find it difficult to express his sense of humor or silliness comfortably? (Silliness is a trademark behavior of the carefree child who knows deep down that life is a wonderful thing.)

Does the child seem to search out the negative or bad in every situation, and struggle to identify with and appreciate the good that exists in the world, in everyday life, and in himself? (A

Note: This guide is meant to serve as a general orientation to what you can expect and when to expect it. While there are no absolute norms or limitations regarding how and when characteristics within a developmental period appear, and every child is unique, there is a range of similar and expectable periods of development, each marked by patterns of behavior and capabilities. Keep in mind that the nature of personality development is dynamic and repetitive, meaning that it is ever-changing and traits and/or skills seem to appear, disappear, and then reappear throughout development.

Happiness—Joy, Humor, Playfulness, and Stress Management

Stage I Infancy: Birth to 24 months
The stage of life from newborn through toddlerhood

Foundation period in which many behavior patterns, attitudes, and patterns of emotional expression are being established. Much of the first 12 months of this period are affected by instinctual drives for nurturing, food, and basic care.

From birth–12 months, expect baby to: have periods of joyful contentment (dry diaper, bottle, being held) alternating with periods of distress (digestive discomfort, hunger, teething) in direct relation to her physical condition and basic needs being met. Between 6–9 months, expect baby to: show signs of joy when physical and visual stimulation elicit smiles, coos, and gurgles. Between 12–18 months, expect baby to: show signs of unhappiness and frustration when told "no" or not catered to (efforts to reach for an object are thwarted, left in playpen). Between 20–24 months, expect baby to: exhibit signs of a developing sense of humor with her realization that her actions can elicit a smile or laugh from others.

Do not expect baby to: develop an understanding of what frustrates him, or any means for coping with it (other than crying, tantrums, hitting, or biting) until age three.

Stage II Early Childhood—The Preschool Years: Ages 2 to 6
The stage of life from toddlerhood through kindergarten

This is often called the play age because it is the peak period of interest in play and toys, marked by exploration, discovery play, creativity, magical thinking, fierce strivings for independence, and acquisition of social skills. This is a time of preparation for learning the foundations of social behavior needed for the school years to come.

Between ages 2–4, expect children to: express joy in acting silly, giggling loudly; take delight in making messes, and doing favorite activities over and over; react to stress and intense emotions with negative behavior (demanding, opposition, tantrums); without warning becoming cranky, uncooperative, or antagonistic due to lack of sleep, fatigue, and hunger.

Do not expect children to: understand what brings them joy and happiness, or know what to do to combat negative feelings and other stresses.

Between ages 4–6, expect children to: realize their ability to make others smile and laugh; imitate behavior that elicits peer approval and laughs (act silly, clown, retell a story of something he found funny); take special delight in sounds and words that describe body parts, functions, and sounds (butt, poopy, pee-pee, BM, fart, burp); begin to understand what causes them stress; be mostly happy and carefree, delighted with themselves, the world around them, and their ability to understand humor.

Do not expect children to: know when enough is enough (i.e., telling a joke or making a face that was funny once again and again until others feel irritated); cease reacting to stress with heightened emotions and inappropriate behavior.

Stage III Late Childhood—The School Years: Ages 6 to 11
This stage of life begins with entrance into first grade and extends into the beginning of adolescence

This period is marked by major interest and concern for social involvement with peers, participation in rule-based group play, and increased motivation to learn, acquire technical knowledge, information, and achieve academic success. This stage is very important for establishing attitudes and habits about learning, work, and personal potential.

Expect children to: be relatively happy, humorous, and stress free; express happiness and humor through actions immature by adult standards (i.e., uproarious laughter, giggling, practical jokes, talk of sex and sexual organs, rolling on the floor, keeping secrets with a close friend); unwind by talking with friends, playing sports, fantasizing; be happier if their school experience is a positive one; enjoy involvement in extracurricular activities and group sports, but be unhappy and stressed if they are overscheduled with after-school interests, sports, homework, and family commitments.

Do not expect children to: be as responsive to being cheered up with tickles and simple distraction; understand adult dislike of silly and gross behaviors; show happiness or stress-management skills in an environment of family discord, dramatic change, or other problems.

Stage IV Early Adolescence: Ages 11 to 15
This stage of life begins around the time a child finishes elementary school and concludes by the time he graduates middle school (junior high school) and enters the world of high school

This period is marked by change and turmoil, the onset of puberty, growth spurts, increased interest in peer relationships and the opposite sex, and fierce strivings for self-identity and independence.

Expect young adolescents to: experience emotional distress and unhappiness as they struggle with a multitude of social, physiological, and psychological adjustments characteristic of the first stage of adolescence; be more unhappy if they are poorly prepared, immature, socially rejected, or have been making poor adjustments since childhood; find happiness if they are able to solve the problems they face with reasonable success and maintain positive and supportive relationships with parents and close friends; seek relief in humor and pleasurable pursuits with friends (sports, shopping, eating, listening to music).

Do not expect young adolescents to: communicate their feelings of sadness or ask for support as openly as they did when they were younger; find happiness without opportunities for independence and the struggles of adjustment necessary for growth.

child who, after struggling to put together a puzzle, model, or building blocks, soon destroys it because it wasn't good enough, which is not to be confused with the child who takes equal delight in building a sand castle and smashing it to the ground—both arts of enjoyment.)

Does the child scorn others' attempts at happiness and play? Does she sabotage another person's project because she doesn't tolerate others' happiness? (She is unable to rejoice in others' success, and does not experience a part of it vicariously.)

Does the child see only competition in play? Is her happiness dependent upon the approval of others, upon winning, upon achievement?

Does the child find it hard to laugh at herself without tearing herself down? (When she safely slips and falls she cannot laugh at how silly it must have looked without feeling shame or painful embarrassment.)

Does the child seldom enjoy and savor her own accomplishments, and reject praise, recognition, and congratulations?

How to Enhance Joy, Humor, Playfulness, and Stress Management in Your Child

1. Not having grown up in a happy environment, having been hurt by ridicule or mean-spirited humor, having had one's spirit for living squashed, or simply never having had models for happy living are factors that make it difficult for parents, teachers, and other caregivers to offer children encouragement to a path to happy living. We can find in our child's, our student's, or even our grandchild's happiness that which we did not have. Please give yourself permission to relish a child's natural desire for happiness. Support it and allow it to grow; for this is one of the most precious gifts we can give our children. And when we as parents, educators, and caretakers give it, everyone benefits—our society benefits.

2. If you find yourself feeling pressured to take this special gift away, stop and ponder your reasons. Listen closely to yourself rationalize, and see if it makes sense. Whose voice do you hear; is it truly your own?

3. A very talented public speaker, owner of a company called The Humor Potential, and a dear friend, Loretta LaRoche, often ends her seminars with a

powerful message that says it all about this chapter: "Life isn't a dress rehearsal, this is it." Loretta talks with tremendous warmth and humor about the unhappiness that people inflict upon themselves by not focusing on the positive, and makes a compelling point for striving for enjoyment and infusing our lives with humor. As far as we know, we have a limited amount of time in this life, we should do all that we can to live it to its fullest, to find the humor even in the darkest corners, to savor happiness and cling to it tightly.

4. By accepting a child unequivocally and loving her unconditionally we give her a helping hand toward self-love and self-respect. Making light of mistakes and life's little failings (not trivializing or making fun of them) helps a child take a more sympathetic look at her own human nature. Laughing at ourselves without tearing ourselves down is a sanity keeper. This child will naturally realize that one's mistakes are not life threatening and should not become a powerfully negative force. Through this understanding she'll be inspired to get up from a fall, dust herself off, and try again rather than fall prey to negative thinking and self-criticism.

5. If you are not entirely convinced, look at it this way. A happy and joyful child will be better behaved, a more motivated learner, a more enjoyable person to spend time with. This is possibly the best reason for leaving behind your own issues that interfere with giving the gift of happiness to children in your life. Set your mind on the future and make a commitment to bringing joy and humor into your life and your child's.

Activities That Teach Joy and Humor

Joy Jig

Spontaneous explosion of joy   All ages

You know exactly what a joy jig is . . . that comical little dance a child does upon hearing great news or witnessing something hilarious. Adults do it, too, but most often in private, or in front of their closest friends or relatives—and it usually requires something huge to set it off—like a job promotion or winning the lottery.

The demise of the joy jig is one of the saddest consequences of maturity. Think back to when you were a child and how free you were to express pure, unadulterated joy. Think back to second grade and the final bell before summer vacation. You probably jumped up from your school desk, cheered with delight, clapped your hands, danced around, jiggled and gyrated and waved your arms. Wouldn't you like to do that again? And wouldn't you hate to see your child grow out of that sort of spontaneous display of pure happiness?

Joy jigs are essential for the total well-being of a child. Adrenaline flows, the body is energized, and the spirit is lifted, igniting a rush of positive feelings.

For this activity, reclaim your personal joy jig, and in the process, help your children retain theirs. To start, everyone should define their joy jig. What do they do when they're even just a little bit happy? What does their face look like, what do they say? Take the time to notice and describe one anothers' actions. Practice in front of one another. Finally, put your personal joy jig into action. Choreograph a family joy jig, where everyone spontaneously breaks out into their own dance whenever one of you is happy. We guarantee it will lift your spirits higher than you thought possible.

Lots to Be Happy About

3 years and up *List everything that makes you happy*

Take time to enjoy life. There would be a lot more happy people running around if we only allowed ourselves more private celebrations of everyday joys. Sit down with your child and come up with your own list of things that make you and your family happy. Include the very big as well as the very small, and be sure you let them jig a little joy into your lives.

Goofy Goggles

3 years and up *Helps change a negative outlook*

We have several pairs of glasses lying around the house. They help us see—the lighter side of life. These are gag glasses, the kind with a nose attached or tiny windshield wipers on the lenses, or googly eyes that pop out on springs. They remind us to lighten up when we get too gloomy.

When your child is feeling negative, have her slip on a pair of goofy goggles and look in the mirror. Don't make fun, but have fun. Put on the glasses yourself when you're feeling a little low, and give in to your silly side. Often, it's your best side.

Silly Human Tricks

Entertain one another and yourselves   3 years and up

This is one of our favorite family activities. Everyone has a unique talent. The best ones are highly impressive, but outrageously silly. Denise can play her face (nose, mouth, and cheeks) to the National Anthem. Mark makes his eyebrows dance (one at a time) to virtually any musical score. Arielle can touch her tongue to her nose, then stretch it down to touch her chest (putting her chin to her chest, of course!). Emily can do splits so well that it looks as if she is going to split in half. What's your special trick? What about the rest of your family's? Practice them regularly to keep yourself performance ready. Then amaze and astound friends and relatives (and one another) with impromptu talent shows.

Get-You-Going Songs

A pick-me-up song   3 years and up

Music is a wonderful motivator—to get the house cleaned, to garden, to run a mile, even to get up in the morning. Most of us have a specific song that gets our adrenaline flowing. Ask each family member to reveal their personal get-you-going song, then make sure there's a copy of it in the house to flip on whenever someone needs a little pick-me-up. See if you can come up with a family get-you-going song to be used during Saturday morning cleanup, or weekend yard work, or simply when the family needs to be shifted out of gloom gear.

Play Day/Night

Play together   All ages

Every home needs to set aside a day, evening, or at the very least, an hour, to simply play together. It can be structured play, such as cards, a sport, or a board game, or it can be a free-for-all (our favorites are fashioning tents out of blankets, playing rough-and-tumble on the floor, and engaging in good old-fashioned pillow fights). The activity you choose is less important than your commitment to get down and play with your kids.

Goofy-Getups and Silly-Stuff Box

Materials:
a dress-up box filled with costumes, silly hats, and crazy body wear for the family to share

All ages

A simple but effective way to add joy to family life

We find ourselves dipping frequently into our goofy-getups box to change the flow of mood at our house. We have an assortment of hats, king and queen costumes, crowns, capes, devil horns, a halo, magic paraphernalia, face masks, and the most bizarre assortment of sunglasses on the face of this earth. The idea grew from our children's dress-up box. We kept finding ourselves borrowing from it to make a point or get a laugh from our kids. We started adding more things that fit our adult-sized frames as well as our own brand of comic relief. For example, we have a detective outfit in the box that we wear when the kids are caught in a recognizable lie that needs a "thorough investigation." When one of our daughters is having a bad day, the fairy costume comes in handy. (Mark is especially attractive in this fluffy pink getup.) Sometimes we use the box simply to help us get into a better mood. And of course, the kids use it just for play.

Take the time to build your own collection of silly stuff. The props and goofy getups in your box should reflect your family's unique sense of humor. You will be amazed at how often you find yourself digging through your goofy-getups box for just the right getup to match your day. Recently our daughter was hit with a bad case of the chicken pox. She was miserable and itchy. Mark dressed up like a foolish artist complete with beret and long, furry mustache. He took a paint brush and a "palette" of calamine lotion and painted a masterpiece directly on Arielle. His outrageous accent alone was enough to keep her laughing.

Greatest Goof Award

All ages *Reward the funniest family member*

It seems there's a clown in every family, classroom, and workplace. These are the people who aren't afraid to act goofy because they love to make people laugh. Everyone wants to make people laugh but most of us restrain our silly tendencies because we're afraid of being thought foolish.

Let your lighter side come out and play, and encourage your kids to do the same. To help family members feel comfortable doing this, establish a Greatest Goof Award. A simple blue ribbon will do. The person who got the best laughs during the week wins the award. All family members should consider themselves contenders. At the end of the week, review the goofy things everyone said or did, then vote together for the funniest. Write down in a book each week's Greatest Goof Award winner along with what he or she did to get this prestigious honor. This book of goofy acts will become a wonderful family keepsake.

Just-Because . . . Celebrations

Celebrate a nonoccasion

All ages

Who says we need more reasons to celebrate? In fact, who needs a reason to celebrate? Try holding a just-because celebration at least four times a year. Choose your days far ahead of time and be sure they're not connected to a birthday, holiday, anniversary, or any other traditional reason to celebrate. The message here is that life is reason enough to rejoice.

Plan your day together. Perhaps you'll throw a party with presents, cook a special dinner, or spend the day having a cookout in the park. Mark these days down on the calendar and be sure to keep up with them every year.

Joy Jar

Pick a joy

Materials:
container and paper

All ages

Have your family think of at least twenty-five places, things, or activities that make everyone happy, for instance a trip to the park, pepperoni pizza, taking a holiday from work and school and just hanging out with each other. Write these down on separate pieces of paper and fill a jar with them. Whenever your family needs a dose of joy, pick one out of the jar, and follow its prescription. This activity does two things for families: It teaches you to change a bad day into a good one, and it makes life a little more spontaneous and free.

Nutty News

Make your own newspaper

Materials:
newspaper and tape

5 years and up

A mother we know was reading the newspaper when she saw an article about a child who had been severely hurt. The story was so depressing that the mother broke down in tears. She went on to the next story, about a hit-and-run drunk driver, and became infuriated. Her daughter, who saw this, asked her mother why she read the newspaper if it made her feel so awful. The mother tried to come up with a good answer, but was eventually forced to acknowledge that the newspaper can be a pretty dreary place. Her solution: to create her own newspaper, one whose aim is to lift the reader's spirit.

She and her family patch together "nutty news" from real newspaper headlines and articles that they clip out and reassemble into nonsensical phrases and stories. They try to keep the subject matter light by mining their material from the lifestyles, food, horoscope, and sports sections. The result is a nutty version of their regular newspaper—news that, for once, makes them smile.

Lunch-Box Surprise

2 to 12 years   *Pack a light (hearted) lunch for your child*

Give your child a midday lift with an inspired lunch. Tie the meal to a holiday by decorating the food. For Halloween, we turned the girls' lunch boxes into spooky graveyards with pretend cobwebs and plastic spiders. We wrapped the sandwiches like tombstones and wrote on them "Here Lies Foney Baloney." On birthdays, the girls find streamers and confetti inside their lunch boxes. But you don't have to wait for a special occasion to do this. Turn lunch into something special whenever your child could use a little levity. It's a wonderful pick-me-up in the middle of the day.

Character Class

All ages   *Build character by being a character*

Run a clown school in your home. Pool your skills, such as juggling, doing magic tricks, tumbling, and making balloon animals, and teach them to one another. Create your own clown faces and costumes, then put on a skit. This is an ideal activity for family gatherings.

Goofy Family Picture

A visual record of your family's silly side

All ages

In addition to your annual family portrait, take a goofy family picture. Denise's family did this when she was growing up. One year everyone posed for a formal portrait wearing Groucho Marx glasses. Another time they balanced spoons on their noses. Another year, the whole group dressed in their most elegant outfits except for Denise's father, who wore his Shriners' clown costume.

These studio sessions confirm for your family (and friends and relatives) that you are well attuned to the lighter side of life.

Activities That Teach Stress Management

Dream Starters

A simple story to take your child on a peaceful journey via her imagination

Materials:
magazines, paper, and yarn

2 years and up

Search through magazines and books with your child for pictures of places she would like to visit. For each one, make up an adventure featuring your child. Have your child look at the picture, then close her eyes and imagine she is in it. In a soothing voice, and away from outside interference such as television, tell your child your made-up story. After doing this a few times, your child can use a dream starter to launch her own private pleasure trip whenever she needs time out from a stressful day. Because this is such a nice experience to share with your child, you should continue from time to time to take her on the adventures yourself even after she has learned to go on her own.

A nice twist is to reverse roles and have your child take you on a trip with a dream starter that you have selected.

Give-It-a-Rest Drawer

2 to 12 years *Pack away your child's worries*

If your child's worries interfere with sleep, have him write about or illustrate them, then put them in a special drawer where they will stay all night. Help him understand that he deserves a good night's sleep and you will tend to the worries the next day.

Pillow Play for Stress Relief

1 year and up *A physical outlet for stress*

We all know how stressed out we get, but kids need ways to relieve their stress, too. The relaxation techniques we've described in this chapter help, but sometimes kids need nothing more than to burn off excess energy.

Customize a physical outlet for your child. Perhaps her thing is whacking a softball around or shooting baskets until she's dizzy. Our kids' favorite stress reliever is an all-out pillow fight. Pillow fights are fun, they release pent-up energy and get the family laughing. Our other family favorite is to go to the park and run around like crazy. We may bring a ball, and sometimes the dog, but when we go back home, we always leave our stress behind.

Do Not Disturb

3 years and up *Accustom your child to being alone with his thoughts*

We all need time to defuse at the end of the day. Sometimes it helps just to sit quietly without television, music, or computers. Teaching children to be quietly alone with their thoughts takes patience. Kids are so used to outside stimuli that they feel empty without it. Designate at least fifteen minutes of do-not-disturb time each day for you and your child. You may have to wean your child from diversions, so in the beginning let him read or listen to soothing music. Eventually, however, this time should be emptied of all distraction so your child can experience the benefits of being alone each day with his thoughts.

Calming Corner
A quiet place   All ages

Choose a corner of a room where your child will not become distracted or overstimulated. Try to use an actual corner, so your child's visual field is limited. Furnish the corner with a small table and a chair facing the wall, a tape recorder to play soft music, and a supply of books, games, and crafts that encourage quiet and concentration.

Breathing Techniques
Make a game out of breathing deeply   3 years and up

Breathing deeply is essential to relaxation, but has little fun potential. The following ideas do:

1. Use bubble stuff. Have your child take deep breaths and breathe slowly into the wand. Challenge him to blow the world's largest bubble.

2. Tape a strip of crepe paper to the bridge of a pair of child-size sunglasses. The paper should be about four inches long and hang directly in front of the nose down to the chin. The object is to keep the paper off the face and floating for an increasing amount of time by blowing slowly on it.

3. Have your child choose a short song to sing or hum in one breath. This requires a deep breath in order to sing the song while slowly exhaling. Have your child keep trying until she masters an entire verse or short song in one breath.

4. Have your child inhale and exhale into a harmonica to your cues. See how long he can keep the harmonica going.

When your child has become a master at breathing games, remind him he can use these new skills to ease stress.

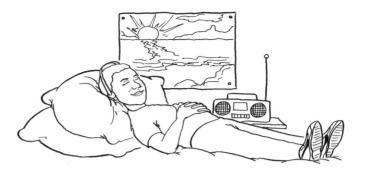

Music Relaxation Center

Materials:

a soft mat to lie on,
a stereo with headphones,
soothing music

2 years and up

Make a music relaxation center for your child

Use the music relaxation center to teach your child how to soothe himself through visualization and fantasy. Use magazine picture of peaceful environments to set the scene for the visualization. Make up a story that places your child in that peaceful setting and play related music. For example, if you are using a picture of the ocean, play whale songs and have your child pretend to be a graceful whale under the sea. Encourage your child to visualize these stories, eyes closed, while listening to the music in the relaxation center.

Play-Doh Tension

Relieve tension

Who needs high-tech stress relievers when we've got Play-Doh? When you or your child is feeling wound-up, go straight to that famous yellow can and squeeze, squish, pummel, and pound. Just remember: Don't throw it. Don't eat it.

Relax-to-the-Max Bath Kit

Materials:

bubble bath for children,
night light, battery-operated
tape recorder

5 years and up

Take a soothing bath

Adults use hot, bubbly, and candlelit baths to calm jangled nerves and relax overstressed bodies. Children can find similar pleasures in a soothing bath. Make this bath special by creating a relax-to-the-max bath kit that includes bubbles, soft music (from a battery-operated tape recorder), and a night light. Show your child how to lie motionless in the bubbly water while listening to soothing music in the glow of the night light. If you plan on sitting with your child while he is relaxing in the tub and your child is modest, let him wear his bathing suit. After all, relaxation is secondary to cleanliness in the relax-to-the-max bath.

Relaxation Tape

Make your child her own personalized relaxation tape

Listen to several relaxation tapes available through your library or at a bookstore to understand how they're done. Use the concepts and techniques described in the tapes to invent a relaxation method for your child. Record it, using your child's name throughout. For example, "Samantha feels relaxed and light as a feather." You may want to play some tranquil music in the background. Give your child the tape when she needs to unwind—perhaps while she's in her relaxation center, or taking a nice, long soak in the tub.

Materials:
tape recorder and cassette

5 years and up

The Car Wash

A relaxing arm massage

3 to 10 years

We all know how comforting a loving touch can be. Here's an idea that incorporates this soothing sensation with imaginative play. While your child lies on his back with eyes closed, hold his arm and pretend it's a car going through a car wash. First comes the rinse—lightly run your fingers from shoulder to fingers. Then the wash—gently massage his arm. Next comes the rag wash—tickle his arm with a soft rag or cloth. Now, another rinse—run your fingers up and down his arm again. And finally, then blow dry—blow on his arm lightly.

This feels marvelous and it is very relaxing. The car wash can be as short as a minute or as long as half an hour, depending on your child's age, attention span, and level of interest. This isn't for every child all the time, so remember to be respectful and consider your child's right to refuse to be touched.

Totally Losing It

Permission to run wild

All ages

Plan time in the week (or day) when your child has permission to lose it totally. This is carte blanche to run, jump, swing, yell, holler, or even yodel if the spirit grabs him. For this you'll probably need a large open field, a park, or an indoor gym. Remind your child to wait it out at restaurants, school, or socially structured situations until lose-it time. And don't just be a bystander. Model for your child when you need to lose it. Take yourself to the park and let it all out.

Fun Ways to Discipline with Humor

Caution: Tantrum in Progress

2 to 5 years

A lighthearted way to deal with public tantrums

This was a favorite of ours back when our children's tantrums would erupt with more force than Mt. Vesuvius. We made a five-by-seven-inch sign that read Caution—Tantrum in Progress and carried it with us, so whenever one of the kids fell to pieces in the supermarket, mall, or other public place, we would stick this sign next to them and stand by quietly. The people nearby were amused, not exactly the reaction the child hoped for. We only had to pull out the sign a couple of times, but our kids knew we had it with us, and that was all they needed to hold their tempers.

Eric Love was accustomed to conflict. As a student leader at Boise State University, Eric had always taken a strong stand for human rights. An African-American, he led protests against skinhead rallies in Idaho, home of the Aryan Nation movement. He also pressed for campus recognition of Martin Luther King Day and helped to make it a state holiday. But he was unprepared for the hostility that greeted his speech at a gay and lesbian rally. His support for gay rights cost him some of his black support on campus, but Eric didn't back down. As one of the speakers at his graduation, Eric declined to give the traditional congratulatory address. Instead, he stirred up still more controversy by challenging his fellow graduates to take on injustice rather than accept the status quo.

Magic Memo and Fragile Funnies

Materials:
fragile stickers and sticky notes

4 years and up

Gentle ways to get your point across

Keep nagging to a minimum by letting the note be your messenger. Jot down reminders for your child on sticky-backed pieces of paper, and put them in unexpected places, like your child's pillow or inside her shoes. Also, keep a supply of "fragile" mailing stickers handy. When you feel your frustrations getting the best of you, slap a fragile sticker on your forehead and announce what you need to keep from cracking.

Big Ears

Materials:
cardboard

4 years and up

A fun way to point out that your child is not listening to you

Make a large pair of ears out of cardboard to stick on your child whenever she tunes you out. Give her permission to stick them on you, too. It will get you both thinking about how often you don't listen to each other.

CHAPTER

10

Sensibility

Our friends the Knotts family have four children under the age of six. Jake, their oldest, was just five years old when he learned a lasting lesson of morality and tolerance. Here is how Jake's father, Timothy, tells it:

Moral Awareness

Independent Thinking

Responsibility and Self-Discipline

Jake came home from kindergarten near tears one day early in September. A classmate named Andrew had shoved him to the ground. This was the first time my wife, Bethelena, and I had to deal with this behavior as parents, but it seemed we could respond in one of three ways: We could teach our son to fight back, teach him to defend himself, or do nothing. We chose the last option, hoping the incident was an isolated one.

However, the next day, Andrew pushed our son to the ground again and gestured obscenely, as we learned at dinnertime when Jake presented his middle finger to us and asked, "What does this mean?" I nearly choked on my mashed potatoes. Not only was this Andrew bullying my son, he was corrupting him!

We told Jake that the middle finger represented an ugly word and asked him not to make the gesture again. Then we began to plan our strategy for dealing with the situation to turn it into a learning experience, one that would solve Jake's dilemma while conveying a lesson about tolerance and morality.

My wife and I believe that intolerance is often at the root of immoral behavior. So we encouraged Jake to take the high moral ground and be tolerant of Andrew. We told Jake that Andrew was probably a frightened little boy who needed to frighten others in order to feel more powerful. We suggested that by ignoring Andrew's aggressive behavior, Jake might strip the bully of this power. We pretended to bestow Jake with his own magical power—the power not to react to Andrew's bullying.

◆ 173

The next day at school, Jake walked away when he saw Andrew approaching on the playground. Later that day, Jake averted his gaze when Andrew caught his eye in class. Andrew stopped bothering our son.

Later that week, Jake asked Andrew to be his friend. It wasn't until weeks later at parents night that we discovered just how successful our son's overture was. Andrew's mother sought us out to tell us how much Andrew talked at home about his new best friend, Jake.

Both Jake and Andrew learned valuable lessons that September, including the fact that by acting morally responsible, less aggressively, and more tolerant, you open yourself up to new experiences and newfound happiness.

Bethelena and Timothy's story typifies what parents must do to equip their children with the tools to make the decisions that yield rewarding outcomes. There were many things Jake's parents could have advised their son: to stand his ground, to fight back, to get the bully before he got him, to stop complaining, to tell the teacher, to stare the bully down. All familiar statements, some of which you may have heard yourself while growing up. But none of these would have made sense to Timothy and Bethelena, given their moral code and their desire to pass that down to their children.

We call this chapter "Sensibility" because the decisions that children make must make sense to them. Not common sense, but moral sense, which comes from the values and beliefs taught and demonstrated by a child's entire environment including parents, family, extended family, caregivers, religious organizations, and teachers. Jake's parents viewed the problem as a learning opportunity and decided what to do with that in mind. They gave their son a way to understand the bully's behavior, a suggestion for what to do (with an understanding grounded in the family's beliefs), and a little bit of magic strength. They gave him a way of responding that fit all his sensibilities: to be strong, to be fair, to be tolerant, to handle the problem independently. This chapter is about the three things that help children make sense of their world and the decisions they must make: moral awareness, independent thinking, and self-discipline.

Moral Awareness

All people want to feel good about themselves. To feel this way, they need to know that they are doing the right thing—acting in ways that are good and just, and bring them positive regard. Moral awareness is knowledge, feelings, and judgment that help a child do this. These parts work together to alert the child to the existence of moral dilemma, enable him to interpret accurately and judge the issue against a system of values and codes of conduct that he has learned. For example, imagine two children walking home from school, and one child says to the other, "Let's cut through this yard, it's faster and everybody does it." The early warning system of the child who was offered the challenge would be cued. If this system is adequately developed, he will have a feeling that communicates "something is wrong here." His reasoning mind will organize questions for him to hear such as: Should we do this? Is there some issue here that goes against what I know to be right or wrong? Am I breaking a rule by cutting through this yard? Does everybody doing it make it okay? In a matter of seconds the child will draw on his moral knowledge base to address these questions and make a decision about how to react and respond.

Children acquire the moral knowledge needed to complete the process described above in many ways. The data that make up the knowledge bank come from many sources and in many forms, including real-life lessons (such as Jake's), parents' rules, society's laws, the spiritual guidance of a mentor, teacher, or religious person. The learning takes place at home, in school, in houses of worship, in front of the television, and even on the playground. Given some of the potential sources, parents and educators should be as concerned with the data picked up on television, video games, and playgrounds as they are with the information offered at home.

Moral knowledge force-fed or bought with bribes will not mean much to children. To become capable of moral action, a child must be morally intelligent. To do this, moral teachings must be integrated with his experience and feelings. He needs to experience and identify the feelings associated with events and situations he is in, feelings such as goodness, fairness, virtuousness, honesty, responsibility, and pride. These feelings are compelling and cause the child to feel good about herself and therefore seek to act in these ways again. Experiencing feelings also makes morals and values make sense. For instance, children are taught by parents, teachers, and religious Scripture that it is wrong to lie, but it is not until they are caught in a lie that they experience the dread and anxiety that define the negative associations with lying and make the lesson make sense.

Adults seeking to teach children moral awareness should utilize real-life situations as the best opportunities for learning. Children, particularly during the preschool and early elementary years, will seek the advice of trusted adults; however, as they reach preadolescence, children will be more likely to take these challenges on for themselves, apart from their parent influence. It is especially then that they will need moral knowledge and sound decision-making skills.

Independent Thinking

Moral awareness equips children with the capability to make good decisions and form opinions independent of negative influences and pressures. This kind of thinking will come about when a child combines her moral awareness with a review of the choices before her and the consequences attached to each choice. The child must then weigh each choice and the attached consequences to form her independent opinion or decision. Having done this, she will feel confident with her decision and stick with it even against adversity.

The skill to think independently is critical to the development of children with healthy character and emotional intelligence. It is essential for helping children develop self-worth, learn to solve problems, and survive the perils of adolescence by taking charge of their destiny, challenging negative influences, abstaining from premature sexual activity, as well as saying no to drug and alcohol use.

Children need to see that moral and conscientious thinking pays off both intangibly (positive feelings, praise, and self-respect) and tangibly (a paycheck, a good report card, a hug, or a reward). As children mature, responsibility naturally shifts from parents to them. To develop the ability to handle increasing responsibility, children need a balance of parental limits and opportunities to make autonomous decisions. The more the young child realizes that responsibility will bring him the reward of choice, and ultimately what he wants, the more he will embrace it.

Responsibility and Self-Discipline

This skill is an internal force that drives children to meet their goals and follow through on promises, not for fear of punishment or wrath of a parent, but because the child's emotional intelligence tells him he must. It is an accountability to himself, his goals, and his promises to the people to whom he is responsible: his parents (I will clean my room), his environment (I won't litter), his teacher (I will finish my homework), and his friends and siblings (I will think of your feelings).

Self-discipline is a prized commodity; once learned, it can stay intact throughout a person's life. It makes everything in life work more smoothly, things such as finishing homework, completing chores, getting to places on time, and caring for one's health and body. Anything that the individual sets as a goal is more likely to be realized if the person has self-discipline. Self-discipline is the evidence that all three spheres of the child are working in harmony: her thoughts, feelings, and actions.

Evaluating If a Child Has Difficulties with Moral Awareness, Independent Thinking, Responsibility and Self-Discipline

Review the "Over the Years Guidelines" to be sure that your expectations are in line with the child's age and developmental capabilities. Use the "Questions to Ask Yourself" as a way of evaluating the child's strengths and weaknesses. If you answer yes to any of these questions, it will be beneficial to help the child develop these skills further.

Questions to Ask Yourself

Does the child focus on getting caught and the severity of the consequences as the major factor in decision making and as the main deterrent to bad behavior? (He doesn't seem to have a conscience or a compelling force inside him rewarding him for good behavior and making him uncomfortable with bad behavior.)

Does the child often turn to dishonesty, sneaky behavior, deceit, or trickery to satisfy her needs and wants? (She seems focused upon immediate gratification and unaware of the long-term consequences.)

Is the child unable to make up her own mind, opinions, likes and dislikes? (She always seems to mimic another whose approval she seeks, conforming to that person's behavior, style of dress, speaking style, or stance.)

Does the child need constant reminders to accomplish even the simplest task such as personal hygiene? (He doesn't brush his teeth, clean his room, or make plans until reminded three or four times or finally threatened with punishment.)

Does the child seem to be in trouble more often than not and doesn't understand why that is happening? (He doesn't seem to understand how his thinking and decisions land him in the predicaments in which he finds himself.)

Is the child confused about right and wrong, good and bad? (He seems to want to be good, he appears to try hard, but nevertheless continues to have trouble.)

Do the child's moral awareness and thinking abilities seem fixed or frozen, not keeping pace with physical and other intellectual growth? (She does not seem to have mature, moral thinking which is generally expected at her age.)

Note: This guide is meant to serve as a general orientation to what you can expect and when to expect it. While there are no absolute norms or limitations regarding how and when characteristics within a developmental period appear, and every child is unique, there is a range of similar and expectable periods of development, each marked by patterns of behavior and capabilities. Keep in mind that the nature of personality development is dynamic and repetitive, meaning that it is ever-changing and traits and/or skills seem to appear, disappear, and then reappear throughout development.

Sensibility—Moral Awareness, Independent Thinking, Responsibility, and Self-discipline

Stage I Infancy: Birth to 24 months
The stage of life from newborn through toddlerhood

Foundation period in which many behavior patterns, attitudes, and patterns of emotional expression are being established. Much of the first 12 months of this period are affected by instinctual drives for nurturing, food, and basic care.

Expect baby to: show no signs of these skills before 12 months. *Between 12–18 months expect baby to:* be neither moral nor immoral because he has acquired no scale of values, no sense of conscience, and acts in accordance with instinctual needs and wants. *Between 18–24 months, expect baby to:* begin to make independent decisions and take more control of his behavior in terms of the pleasure or punishment the action may bring (is allowed to keep the candy, is put in time-out, is slapped on the hand).

Do not expect baby to: show signs of self-discipline or self-initiated responsibility until the end of the preschool stage.

Stage II Early Childhood—The Preschool Years: Ages 2 to 6
The stage of life from toddlerhood through kindergarten

This is often called the play age because it is the peak period of interest in play and toys, marked by exploration, discovery play, creativity, magical thinking, fierce strivings for independence, and acquisition of social skills. This is a time of preparation for learning the foundations of social behavior needed for the school years to come.

Between ages 2–4, expect children to: learn the difference between appropriate and inappropriate actions, conform to rules to win approval of others; judge acts as right or wrong in terms of their consequences rather than in terms of the motivation behind them; forget what they were told and repeatedly make the same mistake or misbehavior over and over.

Do not expect children to: analyze their own behavior or to generalize lessons learned from one situation to the next; understand or explain their behavior in terms of abstract principles of right and wrong.

Between ages 4–6, expect children to: embrace social rules and expectations in hopes of gaining rewards (i.e., waiting their turn in line, cleaning up after themselves, telling the truth); need frequent external cues and reminders to complete tasks and responsibilities and take pride in attacking them with purpose and ownership, and begin grasping and applying abstract concepts of right and wrong.

Do not expect children to: ignore or overcome temptations to take something that isn't theirs, or consistently apply new understandings and principles without cues and reminders from caregivers and educators.

Stage III Late Childhood—The School Years: Ages 6 to 11
This stage of life begins with entrance into first grade and extends into the beginning of adolescence

This period is marked by major interest and concern for social involvement with peers, participation in rule-based group play, and increased motivation to learn, acquire technical knowledge, information, and achieve academic success. This stage is very important for establishing attitudes and habits about learning, work, and personal potential.

Expect children to: adjust and expand the rigid and narrow moral concepts they used to direct their behavior in early childhood; realize that judging right from wrong is a relative concept that takes into account the circumstances surrounding the moral violation (i.e., lying to protect a friend from getting beaten up by a bully is different from lying to a teacher about homework); modify their moral code to incorporate the standards of their peer group; be reluctant to make independent decisions that conspicuously identify them as different.

Do not expect children to: apply these newly acquired understandings and heartfelt principles consistently or when under peer pressure to conform; practice independence without considerable support and cues from caregivers.

Stage IV Early Adolescence: Ages 11 to 15
This stage of life begins around the time a child finishes elementary school and concludes by the time he graduates middle school (junior high school) and enters the world of high school

This period is marked by change and turmoil, the onset of puberty, growth spurts, increased interest in peer relationships and the opposite sex, and fierce strivings for self-identity and independence.

Expect young adolescents to: no longer accept without question the moral code handed down to them by parents, teachers, or even their contemporaries; show a passion for developing and announcing their own opinions and beliefs, often opposite from their parents' (i.e., about religion, politics, sex, world issues); begin incorporating these moral values into decisions about how to act, how to choose friends, how to spend free time; take on tasks and projects more independently; begin to exhibit a higher sense of responsibility about chores, family, and school obligations.

Do not expect young adolescents to: automatically apply these new insights to their own behavior (they may be scornful and mean to younger siblings, defiant and disrespectful toward parents and educators).

Does the child manipulate situations by saying all the morally correct things, but does not seem to deeply feel the moral statements? (She is quick to say "I'm sorry" and "thank you" but doesn't seem to mean it.)

How To Build Your Child's Sensibility

1. To become the best possible teacher of these skills, begin by taking inventory of your own values, beliefs, and practices. Are these what you aim to teach your children? Parenthood and the pressure to raise moral children provides an excellent opportunity to evaluate our own skills and habits, and become better role models in the process.

2. Remember that moral development is a gradual process that takes years to happen. It is best to step back and look for patterns of behavior rather than spend time focusing on any individual issue or incident. Be patient, fair, and realistic with your child and yourself.

3. If your child seems to be lagging in one area of independent thinking, she probably feels as concerned and frustrated as you are. Remember, it is no fun for a child to feel she has no self-control, or can't figure things out. Simplify things by defining some manageable goals and focus on little areas in which she has already shown some competence.

4. The best place to begin developing these skills is through the practice of choices. Instead of giving straight-out commands, present your child with options from which to choose. Keep these simple and with predictable outcomes that you are prepared to follow through. (Don't make one choice leaving a restaurant in the middle of dinner if you are not prepared to get up and leave.) Limit the choices to two for a preschooler. And remember, when you give your child the opportunity to make decisions, you are not giving up your parental rights, but rather, you are setting parameters.

5. Parents, even those who are apprehensive about losing control, are often surprised by the number of small but significant decision-making opportunities that exist for their children. There are ways to offer risk-free developmentally appropriate opportunities to children no matter what their age or skill level.

6. Of course, giving your child opportunities to build his independence may try your patience. Things won't get done as quickly or as efficiently as you're used to but this is a small inconvenience when compared to the benefits of rearing an independent child.

7. Encouragement will go a long way toward helping a child progress. When you recognize signs of growth, share what you see with your child. By doing this, you are confirming for her that you care about right and wrong and want her to also, and she will feel good about her efforts (remember, it is often more difficult to do the right thing).

Activities That Teach Moral Awareness

Moral of the Week

Helps children apply the highly conceptual notion of moral behavior to their everyday lives

2 years and up

Examine your moral beliefs and choose one to become your family's "moral of the week." For example, "Our family believes in giving to others." Post this on the refrigerator and have each family member describe what the moral means to them. Find examples of when family members followed the moral. Ask everyone to think up activities that require that particular moral behavior. Do the activities throughout the week.

Bumper-to-Bumper Morals

Make a bumper sticker reflecting a moral belief

Materials:
a sheet of sticker paper

5 years and up

A child who lived in a residential foster-care facility for three years before being adopted often said, "Family is good, so be good to your family." The staff was so taken by these words that they put them on a bumper sticker.

You and your children can do the same. Summarize one of your moral beliefs and, using permanent marker or a computer program, write it on a three-by-eight-inch strip of peel-and-stick paper. You can buy the paper at an office supply store, and cut it to the right size.

Materials:
solid-color wallpaper border

4 years and up

Good-Ways Room Border
Wall border decorated with moral beliefs

Discuss your moral beliefs with your child, then write these on a roll of paper long enough to wrap around the walls of your child's room. Have your child illustrate each statement and title your border "Good Ways to Live." At night before tucking your child into bed, review these morals and promise each other that you will try your best always to live this "good way."

4 years and up

Moral Laws
Child comes up with own Ten Commandments

Have your child come up with ten moral laws to live by that reflect her beliefs as well as her family's. Help your child make them succinct enough to fit on one page. Post these laws in your child's bedroom or have them engraved onto a plaque.

3 to 12 years

Right-On Song
Compose and perform a song that conveys your beliefs

People have always used song to express their spirituality. Your child can do the same. Begin by writing down your child's morals, values, and personal laws. Any of the above activities will help you come up with a substantial list. Weave these into a rhyming song. Rhymes tend to stick in our heads, so they're a good way to help a child remember something. Set the song to an existing melody or make one up. It can be sung in the style of rap, pop, blues, or even a nursery rhyme. Just remember, it doesn't have to be a Grammy award winner. Here's one that a six-year-old wrote, called "The Right Way" (sung to the tune of "Twinkle, Twinkle, Little Star").

> *Annie had one way to live,*
> *to care and love and always give*
> *her very best at living right*
> *by being honest and to never fight.*
> *Annie says to one and all,*
> *"Live like this and you'll stand tall."*

Right-from-Wrong Finger Puppets
Play devil and angel to help your child figure right from wrong

Imagine how helpful it would be if every time we faced a moral dilemma, a tiny angel and a tiny devil popped up and battled it out for us. We don't live in cartoon-land, but that doesn't mean we can't visit there every once in a while for some moral guidance. We bring out the good conscience and the bad conscience whenever our girls are having trouble choosing between right and wrong. We do this by painting one index finger white, with a tiny smiling face (the good guy) and the other red, with a frown (the bad guy). Sometimes we complete the look with a pipe cleaner halo for the good guy and horns for the bad.

We put our little guys to work by standing behind a child and placing the little angel on one shoulder, the little devil on the other. Then we offer a dilemma, such as, "A friend tells you to take a candy bar from a store without paying for it. What should you do?" We let the child answer. Usually, it's what we want to hear, but then the fingers jump in. The bad guy says in a creepy voice, "She's your very best friend and maybe she won't like you anymore if you don't do it." The good guy says in a nice voice, "That's stealing, and you know that's wrong!" The bad guy continues, "Don't listen to that guy, the store has lots of candy bars, no one will even notice one missing." And so on.

Our kids laugh, but they really listen to this "internal conflict." That's no small feat when you consider the power of outside influences. This technique is also helpful to use in a pinch. Our children are so used to our good guy–bad guy dramas that it's not always necessary to costume our fingers. The voices alone are enough to get our kids listening to their inner voices.

We did this recently after noticing an off-limits porcelain doll had mysteriously moved from its proper place. The two fingers came out and rested on the shoulders of one of our daughters. "Hey! Your mom found the special 'don't touch' doll in a different place," the bad guy said. "Tell her you have no idea how it got there and lie so you won't get in trouble." Before Mom could get the good guy to talk, our other daughter put one finger on her sister's shoulder and said, in the nice voice, "Quick, tell the truth before the bad guy says another word!"

Materials:
washable markers, pipe cleaners

4 years and up

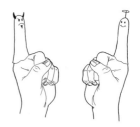

The High Road and the Low Road

An effective way to teach groups of children about making the right choices in the presence of bad influences

Draw two roads on the paper and mark the top one "The High Road," the bottom "The Low Road." Pave the high road with righteous statements, such as "honesty," "caring for others," "think before acting," "listen and learn," and "always try your best." Pave the low road with statements that show poor judgment and wrongdoing, including, "lie," "care only about yourself," and "don't share."

Materials:
a large piece of butcher paper, about four by four feet, or several smaller pieces taped together

5 to 12 years

Post your roads on the wall and refer to them whenever your child is faced with a moral decision.

Two Sides of the Coin

Teaches children to see the wrong and right sides of an issue

Materials:
index cards, a coin

4 to 12 years

When we teach our children morality, we tend to focus on good moral behavior and neglect to mention bad. But in order for a child to grasp the full implications of a moral dilemma, it's essential to examine both sides equally.

Write a moral dilemma on each index card, using situations your child has experienced, situations from your own childhood, and possible challenges your child will face in the future. Try to have at least twenty different situations.

To play, a player picks one moral-dilemma card, then tosses the coin. If the coin lands on heads, the player solves the dilemma in a morally correct way. If it's tails, the resolution should be as nasty, immoral, or just plain wrong as the player can imagine. You may be surprised at how good, and bad, your children's answers are.

Ashley Black enjoys video games as much as the next kid, but in April 1991 she was horrified to learn that some European manufacturers were releasing Nazi-theme computer games. Manufacturers in Austria and Germany were making games with names like Aryan Test, in which the player would earn points for gassing or hanging death-camp prisoners. The prisoners were often identified as Jews or "Polacks." The graphics featured swastikas and likenesses of Hitler.

Ashley reacted by starting a petition campaign to ban the games in New Jersey, where she lived. Within two months, she had collected more than two thousand signatures. She enlisted other children in her cause and mobilized her community, local media, and the New Jersey state legislature.

The bill was passed, and Ashley's efforts led to an even larger victory: the publicity she generated resulted in an international agreement stating that Austria and Germany would not export any of these computer games to the United States.

Thinking Out Loud

Let your child listen in on your decision-making process

All ages

When you have a decision to make or an issue to resolve, voice it. Let your child hear your internal debate. This will help your child understand how to look at various sides of an issue, and how to weigh the different points.

Pick and Ponder

This activity will not only liven up your dinner table conversation, it will boost your child's moral development

Materials:
index cards

4 years and up

Come up with interesting, morally challenging situations for your child to ponder and resolve. To get you started we have listed a few below. Write these on index cards. Keep your deck of cards on the dinner table. Pick one to discuss each evening. If your child is old enough, ask her to add her own statements to the deck. This will give you some insight into her moral development and will give her a chance to see how you would work through her issues. Ponder questions:

- You've been saving all summer for a new pair of roller skates. Summer's almost over and you're still thirty dollars short. You find a wallet on the sidewalk with thirty dollars in it. Do you keep the money or try to find the rightful owner?

- You buy a single report cover from the stationery store. Neither you nor the cashier notices that there's a second cover stuck to the first. You discover this when you get home. Do you return the second cover or keep it for your next school report?

- You're taking a math test when your best friend whispers from the seat next to you for the answer to question 5. If you don't answer, she will be angry with you. What should you do?

- Your neighbors are going to an amusement park and have invited you along. But the night before you are to leave, your grandmother becomes sick. The rest of your family plans to pay her a visit the next day to cheer her up. Do you go, too, or do you go ahead with your plans to go to the amusement park?

- There's a new girl in your class who wears braces on her legs to walk. She's very shy. At recess, you're running toward the slide when you notice her sitting alone. Do you go ahead and play on the slide or should you see if there's something you and she can do together?

At-Peace Barometer

Teaches child to respond to his gut reactions about moral dilemmas

3 years and up

Imagine we all have an "at-peace barometer" inside us, which monitors our level of comfort with personal decisions. When we make a morally correct choice, our barometer registers a high degree of comfort. When we do something we know is wrong, the barometer plummets and our transgression gnaws at us for days. Then when we finally think we're over it, the memory pops back up and we're edgy and upset all over again.

This activity teaches your child how to use this internal barometer to

> After working four summers as a lifeguard with the City of Atlanta Parks Department, Linjalynn Grier realized that the program was failing to reach many of the city's poor children. She started using her off-hours to recruit children for her own free water-safety classes. When no public pool was available, she took them to her aunt's private pool.
>
> Linjalynn became a well-known student leader and one of the Exodus Players, a group that gives performances and workshops based on problems confronting inner city youth. Her message to children is, "Don't ever give up. No matter how hard it gets, don't ever give up."

help navigate moral choices. Start by deciding what an at-peace barometer looks like, then draw a picture of it. Talk with your child about moral and immoral reactions to situations and decide together where each would fall on the peace barometer. Once your barometer is calibrated, you can use it to gauge future dilemmas.

When you make a decision that reflects some degree of moral thinking, describe to your child how your choice would rate on the barometer. Depending on your child's developmental capacity to understand that you are capable of making mistakes, point out the wrong decisions you made in the past and where they fell on the peace barometer.

Activities That Teach Honesty

Lie-Detector Machine

Draw attention to fibs in a humorous manner

Materials:
small box, wires, buttons, markers, adding-machine paper

3 to 12 years

Explain to your child how a lie detector works and make one together. When someone in your family appears to be shirking the truth, hook him up to the lie detector and make humorous beeping sounds to indicate a lie is in progress. Be sure to hook yourself up whenever you find yourself being less than truthful to your family.

Tell the Truth, the Whole Truth

3 years and up

A simple but straight-to-the-heart way of getting to the truth of the matter

Ask your child to raise her left hand, and place her right one over her heart and repeat after you: "Tell the truth, the whole truth, and nothing but the truth!" Often our children will answer truthfully, or retract a lie because they're uncomfortable with the notion of lying to their heart—their truest judge.

The Fairy Tale Book

A gentle way to point out those grandiose stories and outrageous lies your child is bound to tell from time to time

Next time you catch your child weaving a wild story, write it down in a notebook as if it were a fairy tale and ask her to illustrate it. After that, anytime your child gets carried away with a lie, take out the notebook and claim, "That's a good one, let's write it in the Fairy Tale Book."

Materials:
paper and markers

2 to 8 years

Activities That Teach Responsibility

A word about rewards . . . As with every other parenting practice, the notion of rewarding children for desired behavior has both its believers and its detractors, each camp believing passionately that it is right and the other is wrong. Proponents will reel off a long list of benefits and argue that rewards are an effective motivational tool because they validate a child's sense of self-worth while recognizing immediate achievements. Detractors will insist with equal conviction that rewards corrupt children's fledgling internal frame of reference by robbing them of the personal satisfaction of doing a job well. They will insist that rewards for good behavior are contrived and artificial and predict that rewarding children will ruin their lives by turning them into praise junkies, always hungry and searching for the next ego boost.

Rather than getting all tangled up in this controversy, we'd like to offer a compromise: Humans are driven by a combination of external and internal motivators. We work to make money (external motivator) as well as to feel valuable and to reach goals (internal motivator). Similarly, we exercise to feel better (internal motivator) and to appear more attractive and fit (external motivator). Unfortunately, humans are not born with incentive glands that spontaneously release internal motivation to do the right thing. Sometimes we need a little push—a reward, if you will—which, after all, is simply a benefit associated with a task. Our motivation to do something that is not intrinsically appealing often starts with some benefit outside of ourselves. Chores, for instance, are generally not fun. But with a little incentive and encouragement, they become palatable, then maybe even enjoyable as we develop an inner pride in doing a job well. Hopefully, the satisfaction a child feels when finishing a chore will continue to motivate him long after the external rewards are forgotten.

Your ultimate parenting goal in using rewards is to encourage your child to go from feeling good about getting a reward to feeling good about simply reaching a goal. Eventually, your child will move from an external motivator (reward) to an internal one (self-praise, enhanced feelings of self-worth and self-confidence). Rewards and motivation programs should be used to teach, communicate, and model the behavior(s) you expect from your child. Additionally, rewards should be used to ignite, not fuel, motivation.

One benefit of reward programs may be even more instrumental in bringing about success than the actual rewards themselves—they establish a structure for both parent and child. This structure helps the parent stick to a plan and focus on the goal. Finally, the most sensible rewards are those that make sense to your child. Therefore, be sure to include her in the process of setting goals and the rewards for reaching those goals.

Contracts

A formal, mutual agreement between you and your child regarding a specific behavior

5 years and up

Together, agree on what behavior(s) you want your child (and perhaps yourself) to adhere to. Write it down, using legal language. For example, "I, Justin B. Black, promise to get in my bed every night at 8:30, and I, Daddy, promise to read a book at 8:35 every evening, once Justin is in bed. Signed, _____." Keep your contract on file in case you disagree on its terms.

It was early one football season at Marsing High School, when Ernesto "Neto" Villareal decided he'd had enough. The fans were hurling racist taunts at the team's Hispanic players, so the star fullback and linebacker organized a boycott of football practice. Neto and the team's ten other Hispanic players talked with their coach, and that same night, Neto brought the team's complaint to the school board.

The board passed a resolution to have anyone making racist comments at a game escorted out. The next day the student council unanimously approved a letter to be read out loud at the next game to inform fans of the new policy. Encouraged by the school's support, the team ended the boycott. There hasn't been a racist insult since.

You may be tempted to give a reward for sticking to the contract, but contracts should be honored strictly because they're contracts. This is true in the real world, and by honoring a contract at home, you're teaching your child the ethical responsibility of following through with something that he has already signed on to.

The Privilege Program and Responsibility License

6 to 12 years

A program that gives your child an increasing number of liberties in exchange for meeting responsibilities

This method requires your child to work toward earning a responsibility license in the same way a teenager who wants to drive must earn a driver's license.

Review the privilege program charts 1 and 2 below, which require your child to collect a specific number of points to graduate from one level to the next. The program moves from the basic responsibilities and related privileges of level one to the more sophisticated responsibilities and privileges of level four.

Be sure to seek your child's counsel in setting down the responsibilities and rewards for each level (remember, a way to ensure success is by engaging your child in the activity). Make sure the required number of points is within your child's grasp. Start each level with zero points. Set a minimum number of points that must be maintained or risk demotion to the next level down. When your child reaches level four, he will have earned his responsibility license. He can keep his license and all the privileges that come with it as long as he lives up to his responsibilities.

Chart 1

LEVEL PROGRAM

Name:

	Responsiblity	Privilege	
Level 4 need ____ pts	Help Mom cook Wash Dad's car Walk dog Do chores In bed on time	Time w/Mom Time w/Dad 1 dollar You decide time You decide time	Must have ____ pts a week to stay in level 4 Total Pts ____
Level 3 need ____ pts	Wash Dad's car Do chores In bed on time	Special time w/Dad By bedtime 9:30 bedtime	Week(s) Total Pts ____
Level 2 need ____ pts	Walk dog Do chores In bed on time	Earn 50 cents Done by 6:00 8:45 bedtime	Week(s) Total pts ____
Level 1	Do chores In bed on time	Done by 4:00 8:30 bedtime	Week(s) Total Pts ____

Chart 2							
Level Program Chart							
Points Earned for One Week on Level Program							
Good Behavior (and possible points):	S	M	T	W	T	F	S
Do chores							
In bed on time							
Walk dog							

Red, Yellow, and Green Responsibilities

Categorize your child's responsibilities

Materials:
red, yellow, and green circle stickers

4 to 12 years

This is a helpful activity for a young child who is negotiating his ever-evolving independence, but quite frankly, this one is as much for you. Parents are often unsure about how much responsibility they should give their children. Therefore, they tend to be inconsistent, letting the child try something one day, and forbidding it the next. Parents need to teach responsibility gradually and in conjunction with a child's developing sense of independence.

Categorize your child's responsibilities as those she can do on her own (brush teeth, wake up in time for school), ones for which she must seek permission (go out to see a friend, watch a PG-rated TV show), and those you forbid (going into the liquor cabinet, going into your drawers). Use the "Over the Years" section on pages 178–79 to familiarize yourself with the basic developmental issues regarding independence and responsibility. Decide how these stages apply to your child and family. Go through your home and put green stickers (green light!) on items to which your child has restricted access; yellow ones (use caution before proceeding) on things she has to ask permission to use; and red ones (stop!) on things that are strictly off-limits. For instance, a seven-year-old might have the green light to choose her own clothes, to eat any vegetables in the refrigerator, and to play with certain toys, so green stickers would be on her closet, the vegetable bin, and on the toy box. However, she may need permission to turn on the television, eat cookies, ride her bicycle, and use the telephone. These items would be marked with yellow. Red stickers would be on things like the stove, cleaning products, and power tools.

Have your child help you categorize. Periodically review your choices and decide whether to make changes. For example, if she has shown good

judgment with yellow responsibilities by remembering to ask permission, you may want to reward her by turning one or more into green privileges. If, however, she does not ask permission, turn some yellows into reds. This is one of the clearest forms of logical consequences that your child can experience. When a yellow turns into a red, your child is getting a strong example of how her behavior robbed her of some independence.

> Norvell Smith lived in a South Side Chicago neighborhood so dangerous that every year kids she knew were killed in gang crossfire. She was in the eighth grade when a ricocheting bullet struck and killed her best friend.
>
> At twelve, Norvell was pressured by high school girls to join their gang. Despite their threats and the twin temptations of protection and drug-selling money, Norvell refused.
>
> Soon after, Norvell won a speech-writing contest at her school. The subject of her speech was gangs. She went on stage before almost one thousand students, many of them wearing gang colors. Mustering all of her courage, she looked directly into the faces of gang members and talked about her outrage and sorrow.
>
> Despite threats to Norvell and her family, she spoke again and again about gangs, at her own school and at others in the city. She hopes that her words will keep someone from joining a gang, or persuade a member to leave.

The Point and Catalog Program
Earn points that can be redeemed for items from a reward catalog

Materials:
construction paper or a notebook, magazine pictures

4 to 10 years

Make the catalog with your child by binding paper into a booklet or decorating the cover of a notebook. Fill it with drawings or pictures from magazines or store circulars, as well as activities and privileges that your child can earn. Negotiate the price of each item in points, and list this next to its picture.

If your child's problem is keeping her room clean, issue points throughout the week each day she cleans her room. At the end of the week, add the points and have your child choose a reward from the catalog. Once she spends her points, she must earn more to continue purchasing items from the reward catalog.

When making your catalog, include rewards that are easy to buy (ice cream cone equals ten points) as well as more expensive items that require more time and commitment (new sneakers equals two hundred points). Keep a "balance sheet" in the back of the catalog so you and your child can keep track of points earned and spent.

The Family Reward Catalog Make a catalog for the entire family. Fill it with rewards all members will enjoy.

The Parent Reward Catalog Just deserts aren't just for kids! This child-rearing business is hard work and you deserve a few rewards yourself. Make a special parent catalog of rewards that you desire, such as a morning to yourself or a night out with your spouse. Give yourself points for reaching goals. Let your child witness you rewarding yourself for a change.

Lazy Lizards and Do-It Dinosaurs

Materials:
poster board and a picture of a lizard and a dinosaur

4 to 7 years

This activity gives your child a concrete picture of both procrastination and promptness as well as the excitement of a race

Draw or find pictures of a lizard and a dinosaur. Laminate or glue each to stiff cardboard and cut them into five to ten pieces, like a jigsaw puzzle. Every time your child acts lazy or procrastinates, add a piece to the lazy lizard puzzle. Each time your child does what he is told or acts responsibly, add a piece to the do-it dinosaur. If the dinosaur is completed before the lizard, then your child gets a reward.

The Pet Project

5 years and up

Teach responsibility through animal care

Children who lack motivation to take care of themselves often do wonderfully caring for an animal. Feeding, exercising, and grooming a pet or cleaning its cage teaches your child to complete tasks and meet expectations. Let your child choose a pet, but make sure she's capable of caring for it. A five-year-old may want a horse, but a goldfish may be more within her range of responsibility.

Read up on your choice of pet before you bring it home. Discuss its needs and what it will require of your child. When you feel your child is ready, it's time to welcome the new critter into your home. Keep in mind that pet care is a process of trial and error that reinforces the importance of following through on responsibilities. (Cleaning up a dog's "accident" teaches children the natural consequence of not letting a dog out—having a mess to scrub out of the living room carpet.) As your child becomes more proficient in caring for her pet, she will become more self-sufficient. Be sure to point this out to her.

There is a caution with this activity: Your child may not be successful with her new pet. Keep this in mind when you choose it, because it may be you that ends up with the extra responsibility.

Let's Make a Deal
Give your child a job

Materials:
classified section of the newspaper

5 to 12 years

As much as we dislike the idea of paying children to be responsible, we all know that money talks. This activity can be a useful way to teach children the realities of responsibility. Show your child how people search the classified ad section of the newspaper to find a job, and tell her she has a job: to fulfill responsibilities to herself and her family.

Write a classified ad containing a job description and salary for different tasks. Post these on your family bulletin board or refrigerator. Hire your child for the job, and at the end of the week (assuming she does the work to your satisfaction) give her a paycheck.

Birthday Privileges
Reward your child on each birthday

All ages

Rewards don't always have to be contingent on desired behavior. Sometimes your children deserve a new privilege simply for *being*. We think of this as a sort of cost-of-living raise, and the most obvious time to award one is on our children's birthdays.

We started doing this when our kids turned three. We explained that they grow older, wiser, and more skilled each year and because of this, they deserve greater privileges. We made a growth chart showing the new liberties our children would receive that year, including later bedtimes and the right to choose certain things for themselves. Our kids understand they will earn these privileges regardless of how their year went. This may sound contradictory to our contention that responsibility begets privilege. But keep in mind that acting irresponsible is part of learning. We make mistakes and when we learn from them, we grow wiser.

Fortunately for thousands of needy people, Elana Michelle Erdstein's grandmother is a collector. When Elana was twelve, she noticed a basket of soaps, lotions, and shampoos that her grandmother had brought home from hotels. Elana realized that her grandmother probably wasn't alone in this practice. She figured there were hundreds of these little bottles and packages in people's homes. Maybe people actually used them from time to time, but Elana knew they could be put to better use.

In less than two years, Elana collected over fifty thousand miniature toiletries and distributed them to people in shelters for the homeless, for battered women, for troubled teens, and for the elderly.

Elana has given speeches to dozen of audiences appealing for donations. She has written hundreds of letters seeking collection sites, distribution points, and potential donors. She has made, delivered, and maintained collection boxes and has written how-to kits so other people can replicate the system she has created.

Treat each birthday as a time to reflect on the accomplishments and setbacks of the past year, because with these come personal growth. By rewarding our children with new privileges on their birthdays, we are rewarding them for crossing through another year.

We had an unexpected outcome from doing this every year. Our kids know ahead of time what their birthday privilege will be, so in their minds they feel they have to live up to their new responsibility—almost as if it's a privilege to get the privilege. They view their birthday reward as something to honor and cherish.

Activities That Teach Independent Thinking

Bubble Heads

Materials:
magazines, picture books, or family photos

4 to 12 years

Helps your child think through a decision by helping her to sound out the internal decision-making process

We named this activity bubble heads after those thought balloons that float over the heads of comic book characters. Make a stack of thought bubbles by cutting circles from paper. Flip through the photographs and pictures with your child, stopping at ones that suggest some form of thinking is going on. Look for pictures that could help your child relate to an issue in her life. For instance, if she's trying to save up her allowance for a new set of oil paints, but finds herself blowing it on candy each week, select a picture of a child in a store, or in front of a piggy bank. Ask your child to imagine what is going on in the mind of this child. Write her answer in the thought balloon and stick it over the character's head. Now, turn these thoughts into a decision that has to be made.

Here's how this might work. Picture: A child is grocery shopping with her parent. The bubble over her head says, "That candy over there looks really good. I have a whole dollar in my pocket, so I can buy some. But if I do that, I'll *never* save up enough to buy that new baseball glove. The candy will taste good, but the glove will last longer. I guess I'll save the dollar instead."

Thought bubbles don't have to be limited to the printed page. Use them anywhere to help your child "eavesdrop" on a person's decision-making process. Whether it's something happening on a TV sitcom or in the head of that man gazing at the chocolate eclairs in the bakery case, use your thought bubble technique to discuss (quietly in public, of course) what you imagine someone is thinking.

Independence Day
Celebrate your child's independence   6 years and up

What child doesn't love the Fourth of July, with its parades and fireworks! Make sure your child understands that we celebrate this holiday to commemorate the day our country declared itself independent of its mother country, Great Britain. Explain that children become independent, too, and motivate him to take on more responsibilities. Perhaps you think it's time he made his own bed or cleaned up after himself at dinner. Make a list of your expectations, and when he demonstrates that he has accepted these new responsibilities, throw him an Independence Day party. Celebrate his newfound independence with a barbecue and sparklers. And remind your child that independence takes a lot of hard work—just as it did for our country more than two hundred years ago.

My Independence Bag
A bag of items a child can play with alone   3 to 7 years

Fill a bag with games, books, and toys that your child can use without help. When you leave your child for a period of time, suggest he get his independence bag and remind him of how well he does things by himself. The items in the bag will surely distract him during your separation.

STAR (Stop, Think, and Act Right)
A self-talk technique that teaches children self-appraisal and self-control   3 to 10 years

Children do not come equipped with an automatic braking program that stops them from acting incorrectly. For a child to control emotional outbursts and thoughtless conduct, he needs to tune in to his inner voice and listen as it talks him through a more productive course of action.

Teach your child the STAR method by showing him how to 1) STOP. This means shutting off his arms and legs and turning on his brain. 2) THINK about what he's doing. Consider whether his behavior will get him what he wants, weigh his options, and decide how to proceed. 3) ACT RIGHT. Test his decision and find out for himself whether it got him what he wanted. For example, your child has trouble controlling his anger and sometimes hits others. Teach him this technique and next time he begins to lose his temper, remind him to be a STAR and stop and think before striking out. Eventually, the word alone will remind your child how to behave. You may even want to use STAR in a playful way by pasting star-shaped stickers on your child every time he turns a negative behavior into a positive one. By the end of the day, he could be covered with stars for his good work.

You can also turn this technique around and encourage your child to evaluate a situation in which he made an inappropriate decision. STAR spelled backwards is RATS: Review Actions and Try Solving. This catchy and lighthearted expression will give both you and your child a simple structure to follow in examining a problem behavior. When you tell your child "RATS!" you'll be breaking the tension of the moment at the same time you're signaling him to review his behavior and explore alternatives.

In the Know
3 years and up   *A gentle way of questioning your child's preparedness*

Before your child sets out to complete a new task or responsibility, ask, "Are you in the know?" This is your child's cue to ask for clarification on any areas that he or she may be uncertain about. For instance, your child leaves for a friend's house with instructions to be home by five P.M. When you ask, "Are you in the know?" your child understands this to mean, "Do you know what time you are expected home? Do you know what time to leave your friend's house in order to get home on time? Do you know how you will get home?"

When Bad Choices Are Made . . . What to Do

Excuse List
3 years and up   *Keep an accounting of everyone's excuses for poor behavior*

Anyone who has ever made a poor excuse for a mistake should do this activity (in other words, your kids probably won't be the only ones doing it). We all have a personalized excuse list that we use to justify our wrongdoing.

Have each family member write down their favorite and most-used excuses. Help each other think of what theirs might be, but don't be punishing about it. Rather, lighten up and find humor in everyone's worn-out and overused attempts to exonerate themselves. When finished, post these lists in a convenient place. Whenever someone tries to ditch responsibility by making an excuse, check that person's list. Chances are it's there. In that case, you can literally point out that it's an "old excuse." If it's not on the list, add it. Pretty soon, there won't be any new excuses left.

Flag on the Play

A quick and lighthearted way to let your child know when he is about to foul out

4 years and up

Keep several handkerchiefs around so you can grab one at a moment's notice and wave it in front of your child just as a football referee uses a flag to signal players who foul. Let your child guess what the foul was. If he refuses to (because 99 percent of the time, he knows what he was doing wrong but won't admit it), tell him yourself. It will be easier to accept if you state the foul in a referee's voice, "Inappropriate yelling and disrespectful behavior! Two yards back into the room until improvement is seen!" Your child is allowed to throw the flag as well if he catches you fouling out.

Parental Veto Power

Acknowledges that, although a child has the right to flex her independent will, the parent remains the boss

6 years and up

A child is reassured by knowing the parent is in charge. It means there will always be someone looking out for her. As a parent with veto power, you have the right to assess a prior decision and, if necessary, veto it. Here's an example: You and your child decided that she is mature enough to pick her own bedtime each night. However, lately she has been staying up so late that she's tired and cranky the next day. You veto the decision to let your child go to bed on her own, and reinstate a specific bedtime.

Instant Replay

Model for your child how to apologize after losing your temper

3 years and up

We all lose control with our children, and it's a pretty awful feeling. Children also regret losing their tempers (believe it or not), and good modeling can show them what to do when they wish they had handled a situation differently. Unfortunately, you can't take back something that was already said, but you can resay it. Apologize for your behavior, then say what you wish you had said. You may even want to add a little humor to your instant replay by freezing a frame and rewinding to the moment before you blew up. When Denise loses her cool and screams at the kids, she forces herself to stop in her tracks, then hits the "rewind button" and yells backward until she gets to the point where she was before she blew her top. This certainly eases a tense moment and helps everyone lighten up and get a fresh start.

Restitution and Repair

3 years and up   *Teaches the consequences of bad behavior*

When a child does something bad, a parent's first instinct is usually to lecture. There's nothing wrong with a good hard-hitting lecture every now and then, but a far more effective way to help your child see the error of his ways is to have him make amends. The restitution exercise teaches your child the consequences of bad behavior, and to make the idea a little easier for your child to swallow, we devised the following activities with a little playfulness.

The Fund-Raiser (for destroying property) Explain to your child that he has to compensate the owner of the property he destroyed. Find out how much money it will take to replace or fix the broken property and suggest your child raise the cash through a fund-raiser. He can wash cars, collect cans and bottles for their deposits, or even put on a talent show and charge a small fee. Even a walk-a-thon is appropriate. Have your child collect pledges from relatives for every block he walks. Whatever the event, be sure to label its true purpose: to raise funds to make restitution for destroyed property.

After your child collects the money for his hard work, have him ceremoniously give it to the victim of his behavior. Be sure to encourage your child to express how he felt when he was being destructive and how he feels now that he is being constructive.

Lets Make a Deal, Don't Steal If your child has stolen something from a store, have her apologize and return the item and then do something to benefit the store owner. She can volunteer time to the store owner or manager or donate a homemade poster encouraging other children not to steal. Be sure to ask your child how it felt to give of herself.

The Formal Apology If your child has hurt another person, have him make an apology card or letter to the injured party. If you can, ask the parents of the child who was hurt to suggest something your child can do to make amends. Older children may enjoy taking out a small ad in the local newspaper to announce their apology to the hurt child. One child we know went as far as decorating the teased child's locker at school with his formal apology.

What's the Natural? What's the Logical?

This activity uses the idea of natural and logical consequences to teach inner discipline   All ages

A natural consequence of leaving your bicycle in the driveway after being told to put it away is that it is mistakenly broken when a car backs over it. A logical consequence for not putting a bike away is for Mom or Dad to take it away for a period of time. When you illustrate these two types of consequences to your child, you are laying out the cause-and-effect relationship between inappropriate behavior and your responses to that behavior. The value of both natural and logical consequences is that your child will learn self-discipline through personal experience.

To use this technique apply this basic rule: When your child misbehaves, let the logical and natural consequences be the punishment. For example, if your child has not been turning his homework in on time, the natural consequence would be a lower grade, while the logical consequence would be to rearrange her schedule so there's more homework time and less play. This approach holds him responsible for his poor grades, forces him to be accountable for his decisions, and affords him the opportunity to learn from a series of events rather than complying with the authoritative demands of others.

In order for this technique to teach your child self-regulation you will need to be consistent and to follow through with the consequences you provide. You can implement logical and natural consequences for misbehavior by following these four guidelines: 1) When your child misbehaves, tell him the consequence. 2) Try your best to issue the consequence without being angry or smug. 3) As you follow through with the consequence, reassure your child that he will have an opportunity to try again and solve the problem. 4) If the behavior is repeated, either apply the same consequence or come up with another one.

Try not to get into a struggle over the consequence itself, and avoid having hidden motives of controlling your child. This defeats the purpose of letting your child struggle with his own dilemma.

Be patient! It takes time for a child to understand and experience the effects of either logical or natural consequences. If one of your parenting goals is to teach children to become responsible for their own behavior, then it makes sense to hold children accountable for their actions. When you respond to children's misbehavior with natural and logical consequences, they will come to learn that it is their decisions and choices that shape their future.

CHAPTER 11

Resourcefulness and Resolution Skills

**Problem Solving and
Conflict Resolution**

Creativity

**Self-Preservation and
Crisis Management**

Hi. My name is Scott Daniel Nadel. I am eleven years old and in the fifth grade. Something happened recently that taught me a lot about solving problems and getting along better with people. I am an only child living with my mom. My parents got divorced when I was eight, but I'm a pretty lucky kid because my father sees me often. I have a step-brother who is really cool and fun to be with who lives in Florida.

My mom is a great mom. She helps me, is nice to my friends, and allows me to have a lot of pets. We have three European ferrets, a green iguana, two white tree frogs (one is from Australia and one is from Indonesia), and a ball python.

Ever since I was little, I used to fight with my mom when I wouldn't get my way. Even when I was a toddler, I never wanted to listen. This always upset people a lot, especially my parents. I'm sure that part of the reason is my ADD, which is attention deficit disorder, and the other part is that I am very intelligent and competitive. I have never liked anyone telling me what to do, and I know that this is a big part of the problem.

One night recently, my mom and I got into one of our usual arguments because I was being stubborn and wasn't listening to her. She was getting mad, so I called her a jerk, which got her even madder. Usually she is pretty nice and we work out these problems and get along really good, but this night we were both tired and went crazy. My mom got so angry that she was screaming at me, which made me angrier and caused me to scream even louder back. Mom was really upset and so was I.

After spending some time alone cooling off, I thought of a way to stop us from arguing. I knew we had to do something different so we wouldn't spend the rest of our lives fighting. I went to my mom and said, "I have a solution. Whenever we get mad at each other, instead of yelling and screaming angry things, we will write down our feelings about the problem on a piece of paper and show it to the other person at the end of the day. Each day we will start with a fresh piece of paper." My mom liked the idea a lot, and thanked me for thinking of it.

It didn't take long for us to get mad at each other. The very next morning while I was hurrying to get ready for school, Mom said something that made me mad. I was kind of cranky, so I told her to shut up. What happened next amazed me. I was being rude and mean, but my mom didn't yell or anything. Instead she sat down at the table and began to write. I couldn't wait until the end of the day to find out what she wrote, so I picked it up and read it. It said, "It hurts my feelings when you tell me to shut up. I feel so sad." Reading that made me really think about what I had said to her. I told her that I was sorry and gave her a kiss.

Since that day we have been writing down our feelings and thoughts when we get mad and then showing them to each other. We stopped yelling at each other and don't get mad as much as we used to. My solution really works! My mom and I get along much better now.

Scott's true story exemplifies how much children need skills in problem solving and conflict resolution. The situation between him and his mother is very common and very damaging. Rather than continuing the pattern of arguing and hurtful name-calling or worse, Scott harnessed his motivation and skills to seek a better way of handling the problem. This happened because of several personal characteristics and skills that Scott had developed and was able to draw upon, including having enough insight and responsibility to recognize and accept his role in working the problem out; he valued his mother and their relationship enough to want to work at it; he had practiced creative problem solving and conflict resolution often enough to draw on that skill; he knew when to walk away from a heated conflict before it was too late; and lastly he had the ability to communicate with his mother, as a talker and a listener.

Scott's ability to play a pivotal role in improving the problem made them feel very proud and optimistic about his future and their future together. He combined skills written about in preceding chapters with those that we will discuss here. This chapter is about helping children develop the necessary skills and resources for managing crises, resolving conflict, and ensuring self-preservation, all skills that begin with and depend upon creative problem solving, the subject we will discuss first.

Problem Solving and Conflict Resolution

In contrast to the decision-making process that closely follows social rules and limits established by parents and other role models, the problem-solving process is sometimes about breaking all the rules in order to form new ideas and paradigms for doing things. Many of the problems that children encounter involve conflict between people: for attention, for a toy, for a friend, for status, for a good grade, or for many other things. For them to find their way through these problems, they'll need effective ways for handling these situations and finding solutions.

To resolve conflict, children need to take certain steps in a logical sequence; they have to keep the conflict from escalating, reach a temporary accord, gain enough distance from the problem to cool down, and form an accurate reading of the problem. Once these steps have been taken, the child can take the time and space needed to explore solutions. For children to learn how to solve problems and resolve conflict, they must learn to be organized, creative thinkers who have the ability to analyze accurately and create ideas that focus upon the problem.

We can learn a lot about problem solving by looking at the innocent behaviors of a newborn or an infant for whom the skill is purely instinctive—something the child is equipped with at birth and puts to use without consciously thinking about it. For example, a six-month-old who is trying to retrieve her rattle from inside its box will utilize all her resources to reach the goal—crawling or scooting to reach the rattle, picking it up to shake it out, mouthing it to gauge its dimensions and taste, crying or whining to alert others to her frustration and need for assistance. After each of these is tried she will search for new ideas until she has either reached her goal or exhausted her energy. This six-month-old is following a basic driving need of all human beings to overcome problems and feel powerful.

The simple problem-solving strategy used by the six-month-old is not unlike that used by the ten-year-old or for that matter the thirty-year-old. The basic formula that each would use is the same and is as follows:

- identifying the problem and a goal
- reviewing what is already known about the situation or similar situations
- tapping the skills and resources that will help address the problem and reach the goal
- deciding upon and initiating a course of action
- reviewing one's efforts/solutions

As with any of the skills in this book, temperament and personality affect how easily and intuitively these skills are learned; for some children, creative problem solving and conflict resolution will come almost magically, while for others it will need to be learned step by step through trial and error in an environment of trust and openness to risk taking and mistakes. Caregivers create the opportunities for learning these methods by allowing children independently to evaluate a situation before them, decide what they want to accomplish, and try whatever solutions they arrive at (their safety having been considered).

Creativity

Looking at life and its challenges from the point of view of a problem solver opens up doors of opportunity that are often hidden to others. The child with a deep understanding and belief in his potential to solve a problem will feel empowered to take on almost any new challenge. The power he holds is creativity—the ability to imagine, invent, and form new ideas.

Unfortunately, creativity has not until very recently received attention or support from the people who determine and develop the curriculum that is used to teach within our schools. The problem may be that it is difficult to quantify or score, that it does not exist in the polarity of right and wrong or good and bad, or possibly because it is a way to think rather than what to think. For whatever the reason, creativity as a subject has made people uncomfortable, and is conspicuously absent in many people.

Without creativity and ingenuity, efforts at resolving conflict and solving problems fall flat and cause feelings of frustration.

Self-Preservation and Crisis Management

We have grouped these two terms together because they are both critical skills our children must have for navigating the dangers they may face while growing up. They are included in this chapter because at the heart of both skills are problem solving and creative resolution (whatever works). In addition, they draw upon personal potential, self-esteem, morality, decision making, and intuition.

Child abduction, sexual molestation, getting lost, emergency situations, gang violence, drug and alcohol abuse, and natural disasters are very real dangers that threaten our children's safety and our peace of mind. Therefore it is logical and necessary that we prepare children with the skills to protect themselves from abuse and abduction, to find help safety when lost or involved in a medical emergency, to understand the problems of alcohol and drug abuse, and to know how to respond to natural disasters and fire emergencies.

However, there is a strong natural instinct to protect children by shielding them from such information; many parents and educators are reluctant to introduce some of this more upsetting subject matter to their children and students, fearing it will upset them too much, reinforce their fears, or make them feel hopeless or scared. Adults themselves are still struggling with and scared by growing violence in our society and as a result, children are often unprepared and uneducated about these problems and may misjudge critical situations or become paralyzed with fear when they encounter danger. What needs to be taught is not necessarily the subject but rather the skills that will prepare children to manage the advent of one of these problems.

Many times parents imagine their child to be safely shielded from sensitive issues only to find out that the child already learned about them from television (news shows, dramas, kids' TV), conversation with a friend, a relative, or another caregiver (day-care teacher, grandparent, baby-sitter), or from the parent herself (overhearing conversation, observing reactions to events, picking up on the parents' emotions and anxiety about an issue). The bottom line is that it is very difficult to shelter kids from information, and children often learn much more than their parents realize, or even in some cases know themselves.

Because a child's ability to understand these complicated issues varies with age, environmental factors, temperament, and how the information is explained to them, we have to take great care in exposing them to these subjects.

Furthermore, misinformation, and even good accurate information, can cause worry, concern, and anxiety. Fears left unattended can take on gigantic proportions developing into anxiety that takes over control and causes paralysis or failure to act in a way that is self-preserving. Anxiety can cause problems across every sphere of a child's life, from interfering with school performance, learning, concentration, and social relationships to physical manifestations such as headaches, stomach pains, and dizziness.

However, fear can become an asset rather than the problem. Fear is misunderstood as being only a negative emotion, when in reality it can be very useful, even lifesaving. Feelings of hesitation, apprehension, or caution are instinctive and learned elements of fear that your child can use to alert himself to an impending threat. Additionally, when frightened, a child's adrenal system alters his body chemistry and enhances physical strength—something that might enable a child to think more clearly, run faster, or yell louder. Fear can be a tool—an internal alert system that indicates to the child his best course of action.

The more practice a child has using this tool, the more effective and automatic her lifesaving abilities are. In any situation that presents a threat of harm, a child must be able to draw upon the same mix of problem-solving strategies (analysis and creativity) discussed in the previous section: she must be able to size up the circumstances and the elements that make up the danger, understand the nature of the threat, recognize what she must do and what she is equipped for and capable of doing, and come up with a plan of attack. All of these are essential for the child to remain focused and goal directed (I have to get away from this person and get help; I have to follow the safety plan we practiced; I have to get help for my mom—she's hurt real bad).

Knowledge and skillfulness help children become proactive and to be advocates for their own survival. These three points are helpful in remembering what is most important about teaching self-preservation and crisis management:

1. To be safe and secure does not mean one should be isolated from danger, it is the ability to think and react quickly in dangerous situations.
2. Children should be taught to be careful instead of fearful.
3. Children should be taught first how to live and act in such a way as to avert a crisis, and second, how to get out of one.

How to Determine If a Child Needs to Develop Better Skills in Problem Solving and Conflict Resolution, and Self-Preservation and Crisis Management

Review the "Over the Years Guidelines" to be sure that your expectations are in line with the child's age and developmental capabilities. Use the "Questions to Ask Yourself" as a way of evaluating the child's strengths and weaknesses. If you answer yes to any of these questions, it will be beneficial to help the child develop these skills further.

Questions to Ask Yourself

Does the child seem to find more than his share of trouble with peers, getting in the same kind of trouble over and over, never seeming to learn from what occurred? (A typical response is "I'm sorry, I won't do it again.")

Note: This guide is meant to serve as a general orientation to what you can expect and when to expect it. While there are no absolute norms or limitations regarding how and when characteristics within a developmental period appear, and every child is unique, there is a range of similar and expectable periods of development, each marked by patterns of behavior and capabilities. Keep in mind that the nature of personality development is dynamic and repetitive, meaning that it is ever-changing and traits and/or skills seem to appear, disappear, and then re-appear throughout development.

Resourcefulness and Resolution—Problem Solving, Crisis Management, Conflict Resolution, Creativity, Self-preservation

Stage I Infancy: Birth to 24 months
The stage of life from newborn through toddlerhood

Foundation period in which many behavior patterns, attitudes, and patterns of emotional expression are being established. Much of the first 12 months of this period are affected by instinctual drives for nurturing, food, and basic care.

Between 6–24 months, expect baby to: exhibit simple problem-solving activity such as figuring out how things work (pressing buttons on a remote control), how things fit together (shape sorting, inserting objects in the VCR), and how they come apart (emptying mother's purse); exhibit instinctual drives in self-preservation by crying when hungry, differentiating caregivers from strangers, and showing anxiety with strangers; react to conflict, crisis, or threat according to his inherent temperament (assertive child's response is heightened emotion and loss of control, passive child's reaction is withdrawal and regression).

Do not expect baby to: develop functional capabilities in conflict resolution, crisis management, or self-preservation until toward the end of the preschool years.

Stage II Early Childhood—The Preschool Years: Ages 2 to 6
The stage of life from toddlerhood through kindergarten

This is often called the play age because it is the peak period of interest in play and toys, marked by exploration, discovery play, creativity, magical thinking, fierce strivings for independence, and acquisition of social skills. This is a time of preparation for learning the foundations of social behavior needed for the school years to come.

Between ages 2–4, expect children to: enjoy repetition, be adventuresome and not be held back by fear of getting hurt, become involved in mischief, mess making, and misbehavior (i.e., taking things apart, wandering away, forgetting safety rules, experimenting with food preparation, sexual show-me play).

Do not expect children to: engage in any significant problem solving or learning through verbal dialogue, nor to learn more about self-preservation concepts other than basic safety routines and rules.

Between ages 4–6, expect children to: begin understanding more complex concepts related to these skills (who is a stranger, difference between good and bad touches, assertion vs. aggression, compromise vs. capitulation, obedience vs. self-protection); talk for short periods about a problem, a hypothetical situation (What would you do if?...), options (I guess I could've asked for help or...); feel most comfortable and learn most ably through hands-on activity or exercise.

Do not expect children to: reliably put these new understandings into practice situations; reach the safest or most appropriate conclusions or plans of action without the guidance of an adult caregiver; capably protect themselves without adult supervision.

Stage III Late Childhood—The School Years: Ages 6 to 11
This stage of life begins with entrance into first grade and extends into the beginning of adolescence

This period is marked by major interest and concern for social involvement with peers, participation in rule-based group play, and increased motivation to learn, acquire technical knowledge, information, and achieve academic success. This stage is very important for establishing attitudes and habits about learning, work, and personal potential.

Expect children to: hold increased powers of deductive reasoning and therefore relish problem-solving activities, puzzles, and games; be better at comprehending and evaluating events and situations; be open to seeking assistance from parents and other trusted persons; be preoccupied with problems relating to social relationships, interpersonal conflict with friends, and school; feel pressure from peers to conform rather than think creatively; gain status by offering creative leadership; leap forward in their ability to understand and learn to react to dangerous situations (i.e., abuse, violence, drug use).

Do not expect children to: overtly ask a caregiver for help even with a serious problem unless shown unconditional availability and nonjudgmental consideration; think creatively or always act in their own best interests when under pressure to conform.

Stage IV Early Adolescence: Ages 11 to 15
This stage of life begins around the time a child finishes elementary school and concludes by the time he graduates middle school (junior high school) and enters the world of high school

This period is marked by change and turmoil, the onset of puberty, growth spurts, increased interest in peer relationships and the opposite sex, and fierce strivings for self-identity and independence.

Expect adolescents to: know more effective, mature methods for resolving conflict and problems they face, but to regress to more immature ways of handling the same situations during times of heightened emotionality; feel increasingly capable of handling responsibilities such as baby-sitting, cooking, staying home alone; venture into new areas of creative exploration usually in music, clothing, and hairstyles, but also in art and literature; demand the right of coping with their own problems independently, rebuffing attempts from parents and teachers to help them, instead turning to peers.

Do not expect adolescents to: solve high-intensity problems (i.e., sexual activity, drug use, and peer violence) well without preparation and practice.

Does this same child have difficulty identifying the nature of the problem (being able to differentiate the things that precipitated it from the end result of getting caught or hit), and explaining or describing it in his own words and from his perspective? (When asked to discuss the matter, this child cannot tell more about what he will do to avoid it recurring in the future.)

Does the child have difficulty playing on his own without attention from an adult, or without extravagant toys? (A typical comment made is "I have nothing to do, I don't have anything to play with, pleeeeease play with me.")

Is the child uncomfortable playing without the structure of adult-led or rule-oriented play, making up new rules, adjusting a game to be used without a missing piece, or in a way other than its advertised use? (Typical comments are "you can't do it like that, it won't work, there are too many [few] people playing, let's do something else.")

Does the child shy away from or function poorly or uneasily when given open-ended questions, unstructured school projects or lessons, independent studies, or adventures without clearly defined goals or parameters for right and wrong, success and failure? (This child looks to adults to define where she is going [goals] and what steps she will take to get there [process].)

Does the child tend to look at things predominantly in terms of black and white, right and wrong, or good and bad? (He does not see the vast number of possibilities between these extremes, and is reluctant to ask questions, wonder why and what if, seek answers in nontraditional places, or experiment.)

Is the child the kind of learner who quickly becomes frustrated and pessimistic when something doesn't go smoothly, or shows a pattern of giving up when the first problem arises? (Typical comments are "I can't do this, it will never work, everything is wrong.")

Does the child's model for responding to problems rely upon emotions and reaction to the external stimuli? (Typical comments are "I couldn't help it, I got mad. She made me so upset I couldn't think of anything else to do.")

Is the child overtly friendly and spontaneous (without restraint and care) with strangers? (Your child might go with a stranger if promised something such as being able to play with a puppy, getting candy, etc.)

Does the child feel responsible for pleasing other people, or demonstrate a strong desire for approval? (Is he likely to assist a stranger who appeals for help, without considering the rules, the dangers, the possible outcomes?)

Does the child pay little or no attention to her surroundings, and to the presence or absence of adults or other children? (Her senses and intuition tell her little about her surroundings and environment. She doesn't know how to recognize a feeling and its meaning, how to listen to and respond to her inner alarm [intuition], tends to ignore or discount it, believing that she is imagining things.)

Does the child ignore or forget to follow established safety rules and plans in your presence and when she is alone? Is she so easily distracted by things she sees or what others are doing that she strays off course? (For example, a child who forgets to answer the phone without disclosing too much information.)

Is the child influenced by the opinions and actions of her peers and the pressure to conform? (Under these conditions, she tends to abandon commitments she has made to others, as well as her own principles and values.)

Does the child exhibit questionable and inconsistent judgment? (For example, children who routinely accept dares, and feel compelled never to back down from one.)

Does the child keep many things secret or private from her parents? (She has difficulty sharing things that trouble her, and is reluctant to reveal how she feels. She may feel overly sensitive to criticism.)

Does the child have difficulty engaging in hypothetical discussion about social issues and problems? (A typical comment is "I won't know until it happens.")

Does the child withdraw if she feels threatened, shy away from asserting her thoughts, opinions, or feelings, or quietly set aside what she wants if there is any opposition to it?

Does the child get stuck when faced with a problem, becoming frustrated without assistance from a trusted adult?

Do you question the child's ability to remember and use the most fundamental resources such as dialing 911, seeking out help from a store employee if lost, remembering fire safety steps and plans, his home phone number and address, his parents' first and last names?

Is the child's nature so quiet and shy that he would be reluctant to make a scene if necessary to alert an adult to his need for help? Is she afraid to say no to peers and trusted adults?

Is the child overly accepting or gullible by nature or because of learning problems? Does she often accept everything she is told as truth without applying her own analysis? (She has an above-average degree of trust in what others tell her, particularly adults, and might not recognize tricks that sex offenders and abductors use to confuse or gain trust and compliance.)

Does the child have an immature understanding about his rights to privacy and his own body? (He can't discern between physical contact that is positive and the kind that is inappropriate, doesn't know the names of his genitals or their function. He doesn't understand his own feelings about issues related to his body and sexuality.)

How to Build Your Child's Resourcefulness and Resolution Skills

1. For many parents, learning to think independently, finding new ways to resolve conflict, and looking out for their own interests goes against everything they were taught as children. You know what you did not like about how you were raised, what you want to do differently, but not how to go about it. View the process as being a parallel learning experience for you and your child; as you follow the directions to teach them, you will be opening doors to your own growth and learning.

2. If you do not feel that you are a creative person, do not assume that your children cannot be. Every child, and for that matter every adult, can learn to think expansively, and develop his creative self.

3. Teach a child to feel pride in her total accomplishment, not just the finished product. Remind her to look at the steps she took to develop and complete the project, how she overcame obstacles, her use of ingenuity and creativity. Many coaches and parents become so preoccupied with competition and performance that they overemphasize accomplishment and production and forget about the means to that end. This risks taking the joy and wonderment out of learning and creativity, and problem solving simply cannot be taught this way.

4. When asking a child to be creative or expansive, we must put away our criticism, rigidity, and judgment, and allow him to tell us what he created. This often means leaving it "wrong," "incomplete," or "messy."

5. Turn off the anxiety about being normal, average, or different. Give yourself and your child permission to break the rules. Read a book from back to front, paint a body or a piece of wood instead of a piece of paper. To become creative thinkers with courage to follow their instincts, children need to have freedom to create without the burden of performance and comparison.

6. To develop creativity a child needs to be exposed to opportunities to experience his surroundings through imagination and discovery. This happens not only during planned activities (art class, visit to discovery museum) but most significantly through unplanned spontaneous moments of solitary or group play (fixing a broken kite with makeshift parts, making a castle out of a plain box).

7. Teach problem solving, conflict resolution, and crisis management by poising questions and queries rather than by providing solutions or answers about how or what to do. Children will relish the experience of having figured it out and will passionately hold on to this new knowledge. And rest assured, your child will realize that your questions were what led him to find answers and realize his goals.

8. Make room for mistakes. Set a tone in your home that allows for the process of problem solving and learning by doing (trial and error). A supportive or encouraging response might inspire her to continue her pursuit of improvement and practice, while a harsh or overly critical one may lead her to become cautious about trying, sharing, satisfying her curiosity, or breaking new ground.

9. As much as children need to know about the real dangers that exist in their world, they need even more to know about themselves, their strengths and weaknesses, limits of ability, resources. A realistic appraisal of these will help your child avoid "getting in over his head," or following a dare or challenge to achieve social status and peer acceptance.

10. Rather than attempting to shelter your child from the risks and complications of your society, work to find a balance of enough but not too much information. Plan and share nonthreatening, practice-oriented learning experiences designed to develop your child's innate capability for self-reliance and effective response in dangerous situations.

11. Teach emotional intelligence by helping your child become acquainted with her full range of emotions, using methods for identifying and defining them with words and sensations. Teach her to rely upon these for controlling herself and her emotional responses to the situations she encounters. But most of all, teach about her intuitive sense—the brain's innate early warning system that alerts a child to danger and threat with cues such as a shudder, a strange feeling in the stomach, a visual cue that catches her attention, a feeling of foreboding.

12. Encourage self-sufficiency and independence in your children. These experiences convince them that they are not utterly helpless. Self-suffi-

ciency is vital and will empower a child to feel confident, in charge, and capable of handling both big and small crises.

13. In reviewing and reinforcing specific safety skills, start where your child seems confused and unclear. Review each safety skill periodically.

14. Each child learns personal safety skills differently. You will need to spend more time on some skills and less time on others depending on your child's strengths and weaknesses.

15. Teach how problem solving and carefully weighed risk taking can help you reach personal goals (family, career, friendships). Share with a school-aged child the responsible risks you've taken and how you thought them through. For example, leaving a secure but unsatisfying job to fulfill a dream of owning your own business.

Activities That Teach Problem Solving

In our first book, *Playful Parenting,* we introduced a problem-solving process to help parents and children approach sticky family issues in a methodical and clearheaded manner. Children can become fluent problem solvers by following this format and practicing on both big and little problems. We call this process getting into SHAPE, which is an acronym for each step of the process: 1) State and define the problem. 2) How will you solve it? 3) Agree on a goal. 4) Practice new skills. 5) Evaluate and recognize efforts.

Step One: State and Define the Problem In step one, each family member states the problem as he or she sees it. Everyone else listens quietly, which shows the speaker that everyone values his or her opinions. When everyone has taken a turn, integrate each viewpoint into a common family understanding of the problem. It should be defined clearly and without attaching blame to anyone.

Step Two: How Will You Solve It? The "skillution" is the method of using your child's skills and strengths to solve problems. It is a threefold process requiring that he 1) recall past accomplishments, 2) identify the personal skills and strengths he drew upon to achieve success, and 3) understand how those skills and strengths can help solve the new problem. While your short-term goal may be to solve a specific problem, this step will help your child develop skills and behaviors that will enable him to overcome obstacles throughout his life.

Step Three: Agree on a Goal Step three will help your family develop a formal solution. This solution is mutually agreed upon and phrased in such a way that it combines step one (the integrated definition of the problem) and step two (skillutions). For example, your son, Jake, has a problem getting to bed. In step one, you and Jake define the problem like this: "It takes Jake too long to get to bed after he's been told, and this results in a lot of yelling and crying." In step two you list the skills and strengths Jake already possesses to help with his problem. Combine the first two steps to create a goal: "Jake has agreed that his difficulty is going to bed when told. He is good at moving quickly, listening to his baseball coach, and telling time. His goal is to use his quickness, good listening skills, and time-telling expertise to get himself to bed on time."

Your family may find it helpful if you set up your goals in the form of a contract. The problem-solving worksheet included in the Appendix will help your entire family feel as though you are literally signing an agreement to solve the problem together. This also ensures that each member of the family understands the problem-solving process from start to finish.

Step Four: Practice New Skills Step four is defined as the work-it-out stage of the problem-solving process. It allows your child to experiment with new ways of behaving and use fun activities to overcome his difficulties. You may want to select one of the play activities to help him reach his goal.

Step Five: Evaluate and Recognize Efforts Step five is the most overlooked step in problem solving. It asks your family to integrate all you have accomplished and evaluate your progress toward reaching the goal. Families need to take the time to assess their achievements and acknowledge their successes. When you do this, focus on the achievements, improvements, intentions, and overall efforts of all family members. Remember this is not a time to criticize a child. It takes practice combining new behaviors to fix old problems. Step five also helps families recognize that they don't always meet their goals the first time. The important thing is to keep trying. When reviewing your efforts, look back at what worked and what didn't. Generally, when problem solving fails, it doesn't mean that a person has failed, but that there has been a breakdown in the process.

If your child has not been able to solve a problem, point out whatever small progress he has made. Reassess the problem, the skills used, and the goal he was trying to reach. Have him evaluate whether or not the goal is too difficult or if he needs to think of more skillutions to the problem. At this point, you might want to consider revisions and try again.

Ideally, your problem-solving technique worked the first time. If it did, don't stop there. Talk with your child about his accomplishment. Evaluate how the problem was solved and how each family member contributed to the solution. Above all, praise him liberally and nurture his confidence by letting him know that this proves he is capable of solving other problems.

You may want to select one of the following activities that addresses your problem and will help your child reach his goal.

New Frame of Reference

Materials: picture frame, stickers

4 years and up

Teach your child to look at an issue from a new perspective

One of the most common obstacles to the problem-solving process is a narrow frame of reference. When we're caught up in a problem it's hard to step outside to view it from a different angle.

Select a problem that your child is having difficulty resolving. Talk about the skills needed to consider all of the possible solutions to a problem. These include the ability to detect progress, no matter how small; an optimistic point of view; and an imaginative approach to considering solutions. Also talk about skills that your child is aware of but maybe hasn't tried, such as asking someone for help. Write each skill on a separate sticker and apply these to the frame. Next, have your child draw a picture of the problem (either what it looks like, or an abstract representation of how it feels). Make sure the picture will fit in the frame, then slip it in. This is your child's new frame of reference for viewing the problem. Use the frame whenever a family member feels stuck in a seemingly hopeless situation.

Solution of the Week

Materials: paper or premade certificates from an office supply store

4 years and up

Acknowledge the hard work it takes to solve a problem

Make a certificate to award the family member who came up with the best solution to a problem, or the one who solved a particularly sticky one. Present this award at least once a week and talk about what the recipient did to deserve it. Families need to take the time to recognize solutions rather than focus on the problems.

Solution Recipe Cards

Keep a card file of solutions to problems

Cooks use recipe cards to prepare their favorite dishes. Apply this idea to your favorite solutions. When your family hits upon a really great one, write it down on a recipe card and put it in a special container. Your recipe should include both the problem and an exact accounting of how it was solved. Keep records of both the big ones (reacting safely to an emergency) and small ones (resolving a fight with a friend or sibling).

Collect these throughout your children's growing years, being sure to add a few personal ones of your own. Pull out your recipe file whenever someone's confronted by a problem that somebody before them has resolved. Younger children can borrow solutions to problems that their older siblings already encountered, and parents can pass down their solutions whenever a similar problem pops

Materials:

three-by-five index cards and card file holder

4 years and up

"Dear Mr. President, Please will you do something to stop pollution? I want to keep on living till I am one-hundred years old."

Melissa Poe was only nine when she wrote that letter to George Bush in 1989. She expected a reply but what she got was a form letter urging her not to use drugs. This is where Melissa's youthful optimism kicked in. She turned what could have been her first lesson in the mindlessness of bureaucracy into a crusade to get the president's attention. After holding a yard sale to raise money, Melissa had her letter reprinted on a billboard in her city of Nashville. When that didn't get the president's attention, she rented billboards coast-to-coast, including one on Pennsylvania Avenue in Washington, D.C.

Her efforts landed her on the *Today Show*, and that's when the president finally wrote back. But Melissa didn't stop there. She founded Kids for a Clean Environment (Kids FACE), which has grown to two hundred thousand members with an annual budget of three hundred sixty thousand dollars.

In her effort to get the president's attention, Melissa set in motion the solution to a much greater problem—the earth's environmental health.

up in a child's life. By writing down the solutions to your problems, you are taking the time to "be there" for each other, even when you're not there in person.

Ready-Set-Go Skillutions

Materials:
skill cards, blank index cards

5 years and up

Teaches children to use strengths, skills, talents, attributes, and special abilities to solve problems and meet challenges

Each player needs a deck of skill cards (see activity on page 84). On blank index cards, write additional skills that each player uses for solving problems. For example, a child who plays a sport can use the listens-attentively-to-coach skill to help solve a problem that requires close listening. Once everybody's skill cards are complete, make "problem" cards by writing on index cards the possible dangers, challenges, difficulties, and crises that have or could come up in your family. Your problem cards should include the simple, such as "lost a game" or "misplaced favorite shoes," as well as the complex, such as "you are threatened by a bully at recess," and "you become lost at a store." Make up at least thirty problem cards. To play the game, players hold their skill cards, and the pile of "problem" cards (descriptions of problems facedown) is in the center of the players. Each player picks a problem card, reads the problem, and then searches through their skill cards to find a possible solution. Make the game more challenging by having each player find more than one solution using numerous skill cards. Continuously add to the deck as new problems arise. We know a family that has over 200 problem cards in their skillution game.

When Russell Essary was seven years old, he learned that chlorofluorocarbons like those in the family car's air conditioner were destroying the earth's ozone layer. Russell cried himself to sleep that night. The next day, he convinced twenty-three of his classmates to start a petition and letter-writing campaign to ban CFCs. Their commitment landed Russell and his friends on television when they were asked to speak for a citywide CFC ban before the New York City Council. They also testified at the UN Youth Conference on the Environment and were instrumental in getting then president George Bush to support their efforts.

With help from their parents, Russell and his younger sister Melanie organized KiDS STOP, a children's activist group that now has more than four hundred chapters and twelve thousand members.

Melanie used her KiDS STOP group to launch a letter-writing campaign urging South Korea to sign a treaty banning the import of illegally obtained African ivory. The effort was so successful that the president of South Korea, swamped with letters from children all over the United States, promised to support the ban.

Picture This

Teach children empathy and problem solving

Materials:
magazines and photos of your child and others in your family

2 years and up

This activity requires that you take the time to search for pictures in magazines and books. Look for scenes that show people in emotionally charged situations: being screamed at, threatened, persuaded to do something wrong. Take a picture of your child (and yourself and anyone else you want to include in the activity), and carefully trim it, so you can place it, like a paper doll, in the magazine or book scenes. Now that your child has been placed in this difficult situation, ask him to talk about how he feels and what he needs to do about it. For example, you stick your child's photo into a picture of teenagers drinking beer. His job is to describe how it feels to be persuaded to do something wrong and how he will get out of the situation. You may also want to place your child's photo right over the picture of someone who is displaying a strong emotion, such as sadness or fear, and ask your child what it feels like to be that person. Put your photo in the picture as well and let your child ask you questions about how you feel.

Blowing Off Steam

Lightens the moment and defuses tension

Materials:
feather

3 years and up

When your children are getting into an argument, announce that they must blow off some steam. Then challenge them to keep a feather afloat by blowing on it. The deep breathing this game requires will calm the children and the game of keeping the feather in the air will improve their moods.

Fight Right

Draft rules for family arguments

All ages

If you're going to fight, fight right. As a family, come up with five rules for fair fights, such as "No hitting, no calling people hurtful names, listen to others, react calmly, express your feelings, but not at the expense of other people's feelings."

Work It Out!

Leave petty arguments to your children to resolve

4 years and up

This is a family favorite of ours. Instead of putting ourselves in the middle of our children's petty fights, we make a simple statement: *"Work it out!"* This is the signal that we will have no part of "she started it; she called me a booger; he threw sand at me. . . . "

We already taught our children how to work out a disagreement and we have attached negative consequences to fights. If the kids haven't put their differences aside in five minutes, they have to stop what they're doing and go on to something else. This five-minute time limit has done more to hone our children's problem-solving skills than any other activity. It's amazing how quickly and calmly they can work out their problems. It also saves us from playing referee. In the beginning it took a solid minute or so to convince our children we meant it when we said we wouldn't get involved. And sure, we had to give them some pretty obvious hints about what they'd have to do to work it out on their own. But now our children have become so accustomed to us saying "Work it out" that we don't even have to say the words. We just give them a certain look, and they know what to do.

Peacemaker

3 years and up   *Turn your child into the family peacemaker, the person responsible for mediating solutions to family problems*

The peacemaker's job is to do her best to help resolve disagreements, even if she's not personally affected by them. She can do this by using SHAPE (see page 212) to work through a problem, or she can come up with another plan to restore peace. Other family members should consult with the peacemaker when they're in disagreement.

Rotate the job of peacemaker so everyone has a shot at acting the mediator. If the designated peacemaker is stuck in a problem of her own, she should ask someone else for help. The very best peacemakers recognize when a problem is too big to handle alone.

At the White House

7 years and up   *Elect your child president*

"When I grow up I want to be president of the United States." Does that sound familiar? Well, here's your child's chance. This will help your child understand American problems, politics, and presidential challenges. It also gives her a chance to offer her opinion about the way this country is run.

Design a pretend Oval Office in your home using a desk, chair, American flag, and a selection of presidential-looking decorations. After your child assumes office, have her hold a press conference and field questions from journalists (who just happen to be parents and siblings). Use real national problems that your child is aware of. You can make a list of questions in advance with your child's help and explore issues such as the environment, racism, and health care. Throw in silly questions as well, like, "We are tired of searching for our unmatched socks, what do you plan to do about this problem?" Select some of your child's best answers and send these to the president. Every little bit helps, after all.

If Only . . . Rewrite History

Gain insight into today's problems by looking at our past   5 years and up

This is an interesting exercise, especially if you're looking for some good conversation starters. History is filled with examples of problems that were dealt with incorrectly. Obviously, we can't correct past mistakes, but by examining them with a critical eye, we learn how to handle present-day challenges.

Choose a historic wrongdoing with your child: enslaving Africans, polluting our environment, ignoring crimes against humanity in other countries. Imagine together how the world would be different today if the issues that led to these errors in our ways were handled differently.

Encourage your child really to think it through. For example, the answer to pollution is more than simply saying don't pollute. It could have been avoided through foresight and smart, thoughtful action that would have allowed industry to grow without harming the earth. What could those actions have been? How would they have helped today? These are great questions to raise whenever a crisis is brought to your child's attention.

> Erica Hansen was a child herself when she saw a commercial for Save the Children and decided to do just that. At nine, Erica sold roadside snacks, walked dogs, and did the neighbors' recycling to raise the twenty dollars a month she would need to adopt a young Palestinian refugee in Amman, Jordan.

The best way to understand a national or global problem is to examine the history behind it. We are not suggesting that you dwell on the past. Rather, we want to teach children to respect the lessons of the past, and consider how a problem left unsolved can contaminate the future. Understanding our past mistakes can help children reconsider their actions of today.

Activities That Enhance Creativity

More Than You Think!

3 years and up   *Games that challenge creativity while extending play*

You could say our kids are pretty lucky because their parents happen to be in the play business. We get to test out a lot of toys, and guess who helps us? This is great fun for the kids, but it can also undermine their own developing creativity. Never have there been so many products that cater to the growing minds and bodies of children. However, we have some reservations about all this high-tech play. Some of these new-fangled toys and computer programs do *too* much. They give out all the answers and do all the work, leaving nothing for a child to figure out. We wonder what a steady diet of these products will do to a child's imagination and problem-solving abilities.

To counter the effects of handing over these shiny new solutions on a silver platter, we encourage parents to consider some back-to-basics play to ignite your child's imagination. One way to get the creative juices flowing is to challenge your child to create her own play from an ordinary item. For example, we give a nontoy item to our children and then challenge them to come up with at least ten ways to play with it. We played this with a pillowcase most recently. Here are the results from over a week of creative play (and problem solving):

Ten Great Things to Do with a Pillowcase

1. *The Mermaid Race* Pretend the pillowcase is a mermaid tail (you can draw one on the pillowcase). Children stand inside the pillowcase and walk around as though they're competing in a potato-sack race. Mermaids race to the finish line, hopping on their tails.

2. *The Caterpillar Crawl* You need two pillowcases for this one. Cut the sewn end open on one to allow the child to slip it over his torso. He sticks his legs into the other pillowcase, then lies on the floor and squirms like a caterpillar. The object is to race against the clock, or a second caterpillar, to get to the finish line (without the benefit of arms or legs).

3. *Pillow Pal Relay Race* Two kids and one pillowcase. One child sits on a pillowcase and the other holds the end and pulls. This

is fun as a relay race between teams of children (changing places when they get to one end) or as a race against time.

4. *Lava Leap* Give a child two pillowcases and tell her the floor has turned into hot lava. She has to use the pillowcases to get across the room, leaping from one to the other, picking them up and throwing them down as she goes along.

5. *Three-Legged Relay* Two kids, one pillowcase between them. Each kid puts one leg into the pillowcase and they walk together.

6. *Magic Carpet Shuffle* The pillowcase becomes a magic carpet that takes the child on a fantasy adventure. The child sits on the pillowcase on an uncarpeted floor and scoots around on it.

7. *Pillowcase Volley Ball* Great game for four players. One pillowcase per team. Teams of two stretch a pillowcase tight between them. The ball is placed in the center of one pillowcase and "served" to the other team, which catches it in their pillowcase. Fling the ball back and forth, see how long your volley can last.

8. *Pillow Knockoff* Two players each with pillow in pillowcase. Players stand on a line of wide masking tape stuck to the floor. The object is to bat your opponent off the line with your pillow without falling off yourself.

9. *Pillow Shmertz* One pillowcase and lots of room (outdoors). Place ball inside pillowcase and tie a string around pillowcase and tight around ball. (Ball now has pillowcase "tail.") Holding the tail, whip the ball around and set it flying in the air. Try and catch the tail of the pillowcase on the way down.

Of course . . .

10. *Pillow Fights* The very best way to work up a good sweat is to have an old-fashioned pillow fight!

P.S. Every holiday season, our children's generous grandparents lavish them with new toys. Guess which toys the kids play with the most? None of them! We're proud to say they're always drawn to the boxes the toys came in—especially the big ones! Don't throw away those boxes. You might find them to be the longest-lasting toys of the bunch!

Hands-on Television and Computers

2 years and up   *Reinforce lessons learned via video*

Challenge your child to take something she learned from television or a computer game and replicate it in real life. The idea is to make the flat world of the screen into a three-dimensional lesson that your child can see, touch, feel, and smell. Many of the CD-ROM games for young children can be adapted to real life. For example, what your child learns on the computer about nature can be enhanced and more importantly, made *real* when taken off screen and learned in a museum, zoo, park, or even a walk around the block. We are fond of how the media and computers can teach children to solve problems, but one thing they also do is make learning and problem solving one-dimensional.

Challenge yourself and your child to find ways to use the computer and television for igniting creative thinking that then launches him into the real world for the hands-on answers and solutions.

Thinking Out of the Box

3 years and up   *Encourage your child to move beyond normal thinking patterns by noticing and commenting on original thoughts*

We call creative or expansive thought "thinking out of the box." When you catch your child looking at something in a new way, call it a "TOB of an idea." Write down these ideas and store them in a special box. In the future when you have a challenge or a problem, go to the box for ideas or incentive to think up a creative solution.

Creative Brainstorming

4 years and up   *Work together to come up with creative ideas and solutions*

When you bring together many minds for a common purpose, the result can be a virtual blizzard of ideas, suggestions, questions, inspirations, notions, and solutions. But the climate has to be right in order for the words to roll. This means lifting restrictions on thoughts, prohibiting censorship of others, and saturating your group with enthusiasm.

Brainstorming happens when a group works toward a common goal by freely throwing around ideas, solutions, suggestions, and thoughts. Here are some ways to practice brainstorming with a group of people. Pose a problem to your group, then follow these phases:

Phase One, the Brain Flush: Open those storm clouds and flush out great ideas. Write them down.

Phase Two, Puddle Jumping: Take a while to splash around in your ideas, imagining the possibilities for each.

Phase Three, the Rainbow: Either one idea, or a combination of several, will emerge as the solution to your problem. Follow it to your pot of gold.

When you're ready to brainstorm, assemble your group. Explain the problem and encourage everyone to offer a solution, no matter how silly it seems. Write down each idea. Another way to do this is to cover the table with a paper tablecloth and have each person in your group jot their ideas onto it. Try to cover the table with as many words of wisdom as possible. Examine each idea and write down its possibilities. Finally, the brainstorming team decides on a solution.

> It bothered David Levitt's conscience to see all the food wasted each day in his school's cafeteria. But when the eleven-year-old asked about having it donated to the needy, he was told that several adults before him had tried but given up in disgust because of red tape. Undaunted, David took his request to the school board. The board agreed to donate food from all ninety-two schools in Pinellas County, Florida.
>
> But David didn't stop there. He persuaded restaurant owners and the hosts of private events to give unserved food to a feeding agency, got manufacturers to contribute containers to hold the food, and even helped transport donations from a local supermarket to the charity.
>
> At David's bar mitzvah, he asked guests to bring food in support of his project. Over five hundred pounds of food were donated.

Idea Cards

Another creative problem-solving activity   6 years and up

This is a popular method for problem solving and a process for generating ideas that is used by creative designers who work for Disney and Hasbro Toy Company. Write on a big piece of paper the specific challenge and/or problem facing your family or a family member. Tape this to a wall. Next, pass out at least ten index cards to each person in your family and ask them to write down any idea that might solve the challenge. Remember the rule, *no* idea is a bad idea . . . so encourage everyone to write whatever comes to their mind. Tape all the idea cards to the wall and read them aloud. Some of these ideas will seem to belong together, so push them together. Decide as a family which ideas seem to thread together and will give you direction toward solving a problem or coming up with a way of handling the challenge. Now you know how the talented people at Disney and Hasbro come up with their creative ideas!

Brainstorming Blanket or Sheet

Materials:
a king-sized white sheet or old blanket

3 years and up

A new way to brainstorm as a family

When you become overwhelmed with a challenge and need to break the tension it is time to bring out your brainstorming blanket or sheet. Spread it on the floor and have everyone write a solution directly onto it. Then wrap yourselves up in the blanket, or crawl underneath it and shout your ideas. The important thing is to have fun. Next time you have a problem, bring out the blanket, add more ideas, and review the old ones. You may find your solution is already there.

Only Half

2 to 12 years

Children imagine the end of a book or video

This is a simple but beneficial activity. When your child watches a new video or reads a new story, stop halfway. Turn off the video or close the book and ask your child to imagine its ending. Take the time to explore possible events and adventures leading up to the conclusion. Encourage your child to introduce new characters, situations, and challenges.

At first your child might find this frustrating. But after some time, this activity will become fun, and perhaps even preferred to the actual story.

We discovered this activity with our children when we would have to stop a new video to get them ready for bed. Because the story line was fresh in their minds, our kids took it to the bath with them and made up the rest of the story. It was fascinating. Now our children close books and turn off the video themselves so they can finish it their way.

Junk for Your Brain

3 to 12 years

Encourage your children to imagine possible answers to their questions

We're always on the lookout for something to spark our children's imaginations and encourage them to solve a problem freely, without directives. For example, while playing outside our children might find an object and ask us what it is. Before leaping to answer, we ask them what they think. We prompt them to consider all the possibilities by asking where they suppose it came from, and what they think it's used for. Our kids know that's their "cue" to unleash their imaginations and try to answer their own question.

Sometimes, we will save strange things we find just for this purpose. Believe us, we have created an entire novel of imaginative stories from the junk we find in our backyard alone!

Inventors, Inc.

An inventors club for kids

4 years and up

The single goal of the Inventors Inc. Club is to invent things to improve everyday living. We have seen this done in classrooms, and the results are amazing. One child invented special sponges to wear on his feet so he could wash the floors and dance to music at the same time. Another child created a goldfish alarm system to alert his family to fish-feeding time. You can create small versions of invention clubs in your home by taking time to come up with family inventions of your own. Try not to guide your child, however. Let him work out his inventions on his own. Give him a challenge like "How can we put a stop to losing socks?" Or "Can you come up with an invention that would make your bed for you?" Even if your child doesn't have the material to "make the invention," encourage her to think through and draw pictures of the possible inventions.

Eight-year-old Aaron Gordon decided to jolt a few officials in Dade County, Florida, after he was jolted from his seat in a near accident on a school bus. Aaron got four thousand people to sign a petition to install shoulder harnesses on school buses. He took his case to the school board, arguing that in the United States, more than six thousand children a year are injured in school bus accidents. Still, the board decided not to spend the money.

Aaron spent the next two years lobbying federal, state, and local officials. He even designed a shoulder harness based on the type airline flight attendants wear during takeoff and landing. In 1991, State Representative Daryl Jones got the Center for Urban Transportation Research to begin working on a new shoulder restraint with many design features based on Aaron's suggestions. The center approved the design, but the government is unwilling to spend the estimated forty million dollars to install harnesses in buses nationwide.

However, U.S. Representative Andy Jacobs, Jr. of Indiana sought Aaron's advice on legislation that would prohibit the manufacture and import of school buses without seat belts.

"I hope other kids get the message that if you follow through with something, lawmakers will listen," Aaron said.

Great Escape

Present your child with a challenging adventure in which he must use his own smarts to escape danger and make it to safety

4 years and up

Save this one for long car rides or while waiting in a restaurant. For younger children, keep the adventure fun and simple, such as: "You were skating down the street when all of a sudden a big, friendly dog came galloping up beside you. Then his leash wrapped around you and he ran off, taking you on a wild and crazy trip to . . . " Your child's job is to finish the story by figuring his way out of the predicament.

With an older child, you can make the adventure more exciting by adding some elements of danger, such as being caught in an earthquake, lost on a snowy mountain, or being chased by aliens from another planet. Make it even more complicated by adding a few tools that he must use in the story in order to accomplish his escape. Some of these can be quite useful, like ropes and nets. Others should be less obviously so, like a fork and a toothpick. This requires that your child stretch his creative mind in order to work the items into the story line.

Back-to-Basics Box

3 years and up

Fill a box with back-to-basics toys and crafts supplies and bring it out whenever you want to unglue your child from the computer or television set

We call this the "instead box" because it encourages children to do something instead of plugging themselves into a high-tech play device. Select a large box and decorate it in bold, bright colors. Write the words "Instead Box" in big letters on the front. Fill the box with fun, engaging play items such as Tinker Toys, Lincoln Logs, Play-Doh, puzzles, roller skates, a football, Nerf indoor play items, board games, and arts-and-crafts items. Add a few adult items for yourself so that your child can watch you do something other than sit in front of a screen. Place the instead box on top of your television set or near the computer to persuade your child to turn on his or her imagination rather than the electronic device. Occasionally add new and intriguing items to the box to keep it exciting and competitive with the high-tech items.

NIT-Picking

Materials:
index cards

A card game that requires players to choose three dissimilar statements from a homemade deck of cards and use them to invent a story, a contraption, or a solution to a made-up problem

7 years and up

We invented NIT-picking a few years ago to teach children how to get their creative juices flowing. Divide a pack of index cards into three piles of twenty. Mark one deck "Nonsense," the other "Incentive," and the last "Truth" (NIT). On the front of each nonsense card, write a statement that is completely absurd: "Hot ice cream"; "Cotton candy toilet paper"; "Ear factory." On the incentive cards, write statements combining purpose and action: "Study to pass a test"; "Clean your room because you just invited friends over to play"; "Feed the dog, he's hungry." On the truth cards, write truisms: "Apples grow on trees"; "Pollution hurts the environment"; "Fish need water."

To play the game, place the three decks facedown. Each player picks one card from each pile. Before a player looks at his cards, he has to decide whether he will invent a story, a thing, or a solution to a problem. Now he can look at his cards. The challenge is to combine the three statements to meet your goal. For example, you pick "Hot ice cream," "Flunking a test," and "Fish need water." You already established that you wanted to invent a story, therefore you have to create one using all three statements! Keep adding new statements to the deck as time goes on. The kids we have done this activity with absolutely love it. Not only does it give us all a good laugh, but some very good ideas have risen from this game. You might be amazed by what happens when you push your creative muscles to the extreme.

Newspaper Construction

This activity will help your child see the possibilities in even the most mundane of things

Materials:
piles of newspaper and tape

3 years and up

Save up your newspapers for this one, because you'll need a big stack. Show your child how to turn a single sheet of newspaper into a tight cylinder by rolling it into a thin log, then taping it in place. It's your child's task to build a piece of furniture of your choosing, using only the newspaper cylinders and masking tape. With careful design this newspaper construction can be built several feet tall. The last time we did this activity with a group of eight-year-olds, their newspaper construction was nearly eight feet tall.

The way Audrey Chase figures it, she will have saved more than $5.5 million in pollution control by the time she reaches old age if she meets her goal of planting a tree for every year of her life.

Audrey was in the fourth grade when a state forester visiting her school told the children that in the course of fifty years, a single tree recycles enough water and air to provide sixty-two thousand dollars of pollution control.

Audrey was so taken by the impact of a single tree that she helped form a group called Leaf It to Us, in Salt Lake City, where she lives. Its members convinced both her city and the state of Utah to help buy trees for planting. Utah now sets aside fifty thousand dollars each year for kid-run tree plantings.

Apple Stack

Build an apple tower

Materials:
apples

4 years and up

You'll need a few dozen apples and a group of children for this activity (to play, and to help you eat the apples, afterward). Each group of four to ten kids must try to build the tallest apple tower in the shortest amount of time. If the stack falls, the group has to start again from scratch.

Making Flying Objects

Materials:

sheets of paper

5 years and up

Creative challenges using paper flying objects

Try this challenge and then try it on your child, friends, and so on. Using a sheet of paper, make a paper airplane or flying object that can be thrown about thirty feet. You get only one sheet of paper, so work at it. Use your creative thinking to come up with a great design. Hint: We didn't say it has to *look* like a traditional paper airplane, so if you crumple it into a ball and give it a good toss you'll probably find it's your best design!

Creative Box

4 years and up

A box filled with household goodies for making things

Fill a cardboard box with household recyclables such as egg cartons, cereal boxes, ribbons, and other odds and ends. Add in some colored paper, glue, scissors, and whatever you feel will fuel your child's imagination. Give your child the box and let them create whatever their creative mind wants. Of course they can use the cardboard box!

Activities That Teach Self-Preservation and Crisis-Management Skills

Personal Alarm System

Materials:

twelve-inch square from a piece of poster board, construction paper, buttons

4 to 12 years

Redefines fear as a useful reaction to danger and rechannels the energy that generates panic into action that is strong and decisive

Build an alarm system and label each button and lever with the following: "Scream," "Run," "Call for help," "Check with parents," "Think fast," "Call police/911," "Fight," "Say *no!*" "Breathe deeply," "Remember escape plan." Connect the control panel of the alarm system to your child with pieces of yarn. Turn it on by describing a hypothetical situation that requires fast thinking and emergency action. Have your child press the button or pull the gadget that represents the best response. Ask her about her choices and suggest other ones you think would have been better. Switch roles and try out the panel yourself, asking your child to critique your choices. This exercise is a metaphor for how the brain works when faced with a frightening situation. By practicing this activity, you will be imprinting a visual image of the control panel in your child's mind where it will be readily available should she need it.

Family Fire-and-Emergency Plan

The goal of this activity is to help your family become more familiar with your home and prepare for what to do in the event of a fire or natural disaster

Materials:
poster board

2 years and up

On a large poster board write or draw instructions of what each family member should do in a fire or other emergency, such as an earthquake or hurricane. Include a floor plan of your house that illustrates escape routes as well as a safe place to meet outside. Children love to make maps and will get more out of the project if they help create this master plan.

Reinforce your message by equipping your home with emergency items including smoke alarms, emergency lights, fire extinguishers, and ladders for second-story windows. Practice your plan with periodic family fire/emergency drills. Be sure to make these fun and nonthreatening.

Safety Kid

Helps children overcome paralyzing fears and develop safety skills, self-esteem, and self-reliance through fun and play

Materials:
long piece of material or a towel

5 to 10 years

Turn your child into Safety Kid, Conqueror of Fears and Foes! Together create a superhero costume (even a bath-towel "cape" and safety pin will do). This is a great way to empower a child, and the practice will teach him how to act in a frightening situation and give him hours of fun.

Sit down with your costumed child and make a list of all his strengths, abilities, and skills that would help during a dangerous predicament. These include: fast, smart, strong, quick, creative, fast thinking, powerful, agile, proud, likes self, caring, capable, convincing, commanding, forceful, clever, resourceful, loud, good screamer, thinks before acts, noisy, apprehensive, cautious, contemplates, appraises, good memory, acts safely, alert, keen, dexterous, crafty, listens to own feelings, says no, inventive, thoughtful, energetic, mighty, works hard, doesn't give up, street-wise, calms self, asks for help, perceptive, observant, aware.

Remind him that he does not possess magical powers . . . he cannot fly, ray-beam criminals, or flatten bad guys with powerful punches. He is a regular kid with a lot of "smarts" and real skills.

Playact different threatening situations with your child in which he must think and act fast to protect himself. Pretend that you are a kidnapper or a drug dealer or make believe a hurricane is coming. When you are through playing, remind your child that even with his costume off, he still possesses all of the skills and abilities of Safety Kid. Children learn a great deal by becoming teachers themselves so ask your Safety Kid to share his "powers" with a younger sibling who can then in turn become Safety Kid.

What-If Games

4 to 12 years   *The goal of the scenario game is to help children develop insight as well as problem-solving and decision-making skills*

Write down potential dangers to your child and then turn this list into twenty-five to fifty questions. Begin each question with "What if? . . . " For example, "What if you saw a man staring at you at the park?" or "What if your friend fell down the stairs and there were no adults in the house?" Ask your child to answer each question thoughtfully. Encourage conversation about the scenarios. If you're concerned about your child's response to a question, try not to correct her. Instead ask what else she could do to handle the situation, or offer your own response and ask for her opinion.

This is a great game for long car rides, and can be used with one child or with groups of children. If your family enjoys drama, you might try role-playing these scenes with varying interventions and outcomes. Here are a few sample questions:

What if . . .

1. a kind-looking woman came up and asked for help finding her lost kitten?

2. a stranger knocked on the door and said he needed to use the phone?

3. you were sleeping and a fire alarm woke you up?

4. you got lost at a busy mall and couldn't find your parents?

5. a person drove up in a car and asked for directions, said he couldn't hear you, and asked you to come closer?

6. someone you know wanted to touch you in a private area of your body?

7. someone called your house when no adult was home and asked to speak to your mother?

8. someone, even someone you know, came to your school and told you that your mom wanted you to go with him?

9. someone grabbed you while you were walking on the sidewalk?

10. a friend fell off his bike and was bleeding?

11. you were walking home from school and a car was following you?

12. you were dropped off for an activity but it was the wrong day?

The Don't-Mess-with-Me Screaming Club

Encourage your child to act assertively

2 to 12 years

Welcome to the Smithtown Don't-Mess-with-Me Screaming Club. Leave your quiet voices at the door. Our goal is to scream, stomp, and make so much noise that the vibrations will set off car alarms for miles.

Once a month, invite a group of neighborhood children to your home for a little snack and a lot of screaming. Use statements like the one above to set the climate for the meeting. Too often children are told to keep their voices down. And it's true, yelling isn't a desirable way to communicate. But we have to remember that a good strong voice is a good strong defense weapon. Help your children fine-tune theirs by role-playing situations that require them to scream their loudest. Have monthly contests to break screaming records. Record their screams and play them back so your kids can hear just how powerful their voices are. Don't forget to wear earplugs and have fun!

Safety Kit

Prepare your family for a household emergency by assembling a customized safety kit

4 years and up

Brainstorm with your children all of the items to include in a household safety kit. Think of the different dangers that could strike. For instance, during a power failure you would need a flashlight, candles and matches, a battery-operated radio. In the event of a natural disaster that affects municipal services, you may want bottled water and freeze-dried food. Include a floor plan of your home in the kit as well as important telephone numbers.

As a family, research and write an emergency-response manual, which covers things like what to do in case of a hurricane or how to react when the smoke alarm goes off. Make sure everyone knows where the safety kit and manual are kept. Establish a strict rule about never opening the box or playing with the contents, but do hold a monthly inventory to update and review its contents.

Safety Video

Write, direct, and act in a safety video

Materials:
camcorder

6 years and up

Explain to your child what is involved in making a movie and develop an outline together for a video on safety. Topics may include what to do if approached by a stranger, how to be safe alone at home, and what to do in case of a fire. Be sure to help your child come up with the solutions herself, perhaps through books or by interviewing police or firefighters.

When the video is complete, encourage your child to show it to friends, her class, or younger children. This will reinforce what she learned as well as build her self-esteem.

Tricks for the Tricksters

Materials:
index cards

3 to 12 years

Familiarize your child with the way people trick children to do them harm

With your child, list the ways an adult might try to trick a child into following him. Examples are: "I lost my puppy. Could you help me find her?" or "Your mommy has been hurt and needs you right now, she asked me to get you." Write one statement on each card. Then make a second deck of cards with assertive and effective responses such as "Check your instincts" (which means, if something doesn't feel right, it probably isn't); "Run fast and get help"; "Scream loudly"; and "Check first with someone you can trust."

Place the response cards in front of your child and read a trick card. Ask him to counter the trick by selecting a response card. Have your child explain his choice. This is another exercise that works well with either one child or with a group of children.

Play Kit

2 to 8 years

Allows your child to explore safe and dangerous situations in an age-appropriate way

Fill a small box with toy versions of items that would be used in emergency situations, like toy telephones, flashlights, bandages, police hats, doctor kits, and dolls. Have this box of play items available to your child so that they can be used for imaginary play. Encourage your child to play out his understanding of danger and safety. Take time to observe and/or participate in the play. On occasion you can intervene or redirect the activity when the child's perceptions are inaccurate. You can inspire a child's curiosity and lend some direction by coming up with play themes and story lines that address your safety concerns such as "Let's pretend the boy was home alone and smelled smoke . . . or the baby bear is lost in the store . . . let's pretend to call the police."

911

3 to 12 years

Teach your child how to use 911

The more you practice using 911 calmly, the sharper your child's coping skills will be in the event of a real emergency. Use a toy telephone and pretend that you are hurt and can't reach the phone. (Do this in a playful way so you don't scare your child.) Your child should know which numbers to dial, how to identify herself and state her age, address, and a description of the emergency. You might want to mark the 9 and the 1 on the real telephone with red permanent marker or stickers.

Children younger than four may not be ready to learn how to use 911, but you can teach them to memorize their phone number, address, and parents' full names. Make this easy and fun by setting these pieces of information to a tune.

Helping People

Helps children identify who to turn to when parents aren't available   2 to 12 years

On excursions with your child, point out the people to approach for help in the event you become separated. These helping people would include sales clerks in stores (identifiable usually by the name tag on their clothes), police officers, neighbors, and friends.

Also, if your child sees footage of a tragedy on the television news, point out all the people who join together to help out. This will help your child focus less on the bad things that happen, and more on the good within people.

Okay and Not Okay

Teaches children that they are in charge of their bodies   2 to 12 years

Use a doll to point out different parts of the body. Make it clear to very young children which areas are private and off-limits to everyone unless permission is given by the child himself or herself. Older children can use the okay-and-not-okay game to set their own boundaries for other body parts.

For instance, your child may not like having his head patted. The okay-and-not-okay game allows him to set the rule that no one is allowed to touch his head without his permission. This emphasizes that he is ultimately in control of his body.

Seize the Moment

All ages *Be on the lookout for teachable moments*

Years ago when we were shopping for bunk beds for the girls, the salesman asked Arielle and Emily to follow him for a balloon. Much to our chagrin, the girls unquestioningly trailed after this man. When Denise called out, "Excuse me! Do you know this man?" all three turned around and the girls grinned sheepishly. Although we tell our children that people wearing badges with their name on it and who work at the store are "helping people," we still encourage them to use good judgment when they follow sales clerks.

Arielle looked at the salesman and said, "Excuse me, I don't know you and you're going to take me and I don't know where you're going." The salesman turned pink, but our daughters got a quick life lesson about going off with strangers. (We thanked the poor gentleman for the sacrifice he made.)

We found out how well our teachable moment worked months later when, in a store, Denise followed a fellow shopper who offered to help her find an item. Arielle said, "Excuse me! Do you know this woman?"

Buddy System

2 to 14 years *Teach your children to buddy-up for safety*

This is a system well known to abuse-prevention specialists. Essentially you teach your child that whenever he is out and about (walking to a friend's, walking to school, riding a bike to a game), he should always travel with another person—a buddy. Help a younger child understand this important safety measure by trying to pair him with a friend when he goes outside or moves around the neighborhood. Teach your children that there is safety in numbers.

Ask-First Rule

All ages *Emphasize the importance of asking permission*

Set a rule that your child must get your permission before going anywhere. (Examples of when your child needs to ask permission include: when an adult or child asks for help finding a lost pet; a neighbor invites your child over to see his new computer; a schoolmate offers your child a ride home with her mother). The ask-first rule is a safeguard that should put your child's mind at ease by putting decision-making responsibility on the parent.

Password

A word or phrase to be used when somebody other than a parent is picking your child up from school or elsewhere   2 years and up

Select or create a password so when someone other than you needs to pick up your child at school, soccer practice, and so on, your child will know to ask this person the prearranged password to verify that it is okay to get in the car. Make sure the password isn't obvious, and when it is used, change it so it becomes secret again.

Chapter 12

Humanity

Empathy
Appreciation
Respect
Tolerance for Diversity

Every holiday season our family volunteers at a community Christmas dinner given for people who are alone or have fallen on hard times. One year, we were pleased to see so many others helping out that we could barely squeeze into the kitchen. Rather than standing around, we went with our children into the dining area to mingle with the guests. Going from table to table, we began wishing everyone a happy holiday.

Our daughters were three and four at the time and were understandably shy at first. Then an interesting thing happened. As we approached the third table, an old woman who was by herself opened her arms to hug Arielle. Before we could react and to our surprise, Arielle slipped comfortably into this woman's arms and gave her a big, sweet hug. Both of our daughters are gifted huggers. They squeeze you "just right" into a soothing and pleasing embrace. This woman surely felt that.

Our first reaction naturally was protective. We've talked quite a bit with our daughters about their right to say no to an uncomfortable or unwanted touch, and about strangers. We were about to intervene when our other daughter, Emily, following her sister's lead, walked up to another elderly guest and gave him a hug. Resisting the instinct to put a stop to the hugging, we stood by and kept a watchful eye, as one by one, each guest at the table got a fantastic hug from our kids, leaving them smiling and, without a doubt, with that wonderfully warm feeling that one gets from a child's touch.

Before we approached the next table, Denise couldn't stop herself from intervening and told the girls that they didn't have to hug the guests if it made them uncomfortable. But before she could finish, Arielle interrupted. "Don't worry, Mommy, I know they're strangers. We can give warm food to make their bellies feel good, and we can give hugs to make their hearts feel good." Emily nodded in agreement. Being adept students, we joined our daughters in the merriment and also began to greet the guests, introducing ourselves and our daughters to each and every one. We shook delicately soft and aged hands, and accepted hugs of gratitude while we shared wishes for a happy holiday. We and our kids must have hugged one hundred people that day.

That day of volunteering turned out to be a learning experience for everyone, but most profoundly for us as parents and adults. We overcame the natural tendency adults have to keep a distance between ourselves and others, particularly the elderly, and we realized how little it takes to affect someone in a positive way. The years of helping prepare and serve food in the kitchen hadn't quite brought us to the place we had been aiming for. With our daughters' help, we were able to feed the hungry guests' hearts as well as their bellies, while learning a valuable lesson. To ensure that neither we nor our children forget this lesson, we have laid plans to begin a new category of the volunteers called "greeters and huggers," people whose sole job it will be to meet dinner guests and in some way reach out to them with a handshake, an embrace, or simply a warm smile.

As our daughters demonstrated, children have a natural ability to care for others, to share their love and touch the hearts and souls of people who need it most. Just as instinctive is their strong drive to satisfy their own wants and needs. Sometimes called egocentrism, this self-centered point of view is both normal and necessary, for it prepares the child to care for and care about himself. However, a child allowed to focus exclusively upon himself is unbalanced and selfish, resembling what is commonly known as a "spoiled brat."

To become a person with skills associated with humanity, every child must learn to empathize with others, appreciate their feelings and needs, and know when these are more important than their own. The skills associated with humanity—appreciation, empathy, and respect—do not overtake the focus upon self, they merge with it and complement it. The seeds of these skills are planted by a child's parents, caregivers, and teachers through their actions and attitude.

It is important to remember that the development of humanity is by nature slow and gradual, growing side by side with other important characteristics that the child will also need. These skills cannot be taught in concentrated lessons or at any particular stage in life. With mindful attention to everyday events and interactions, teaching opportunities make themselves available every day. Children engage in acts of respect, empathy, and appreciation all the time, but these skills are often overlooked or misunderstood. For example, when a child volunteers to help a harried parent with housework, cares lovingly for a stuffed animal who has become injured, helps out a child who has fallen, expresses appreciation with a gift or a hug, or voices an umprompted "thank-you" or "please," they are emulating the behavior of positive role models in their lives and learning to incorporate these skills into their personality.

Caregivers and educators must pay close attention to each and every attempt the child makes to establish these behaviors—finding and utilizing every teachable moment to point out to a child how his actions affected someone else, either positively or negatively. Our children did not graduate from character school that day, they simply achieved a milestone along the path of learning. Like all children, they lapse into periods of *"I want, I want,"* *"Gimme, gimme,"* and *"Who cares!"* At these times they desperately need us to inspire them to get back on track.

This chapter is about helping our children become skilled humanitarians capable of empathy, respect, and appreciation for others. It is last not because it is least important, but because it draws upon skills learned in many of the previous chapters.

Empathy

Empathy means to identify with and understand another's situation, feelings, and motives. This requires stepping inside another person's frame of reference, or as we often say to a child, "standing in their shoes." Once there, you see things as you imagine that person would. Empathy is not about feeling bad for someone else's plight; that is sympathy. When we empathize with someone, we utilize the ability to share another person's emotions, thoughts, or feelings.

Empathy alerts the child to another person's feelings, raising awareness and stirring her conscience. This trait equips a person to thwart impulses to act violently or hurtfully. Children or adults who have not developed this characteristic are prone to acting violently and selfishly. On the positive side, a child who can feel what others feel is also more likely to express meaningful appreciation, affection, and respect, because it is something he recognizes the other person will appreciate or needs.

Empathy helps a child become a better friend, a better leader, and a better member of society. In an environment where empathy is practiced, it becomes contagious, spreading to others who may not know it as well, leading to a more respectful and peaceful world.

Appreciation

Since our children were born, we've wanted to teach them to be appreciative and show gratitude to the waitress who brings them a glass of water, to us when we help them out, and to each other. Learning to appreciate these things is different from learning to say thank you, because, to be appreciative, the child must be able to understand and perceive the nature and quality of something. The something might be tangible like a toy, or one's home; or intangible like a parent's trust, or friendship. A child who understands the value of what others do for her will say thank you not because she has been told to a thousand times, but because she feels thankful and knows that saying thank you is a way to communicate her appreciation, and hold up her end of the relationship.

In order to be appreciative, children must have the knowledge that allows them to discern what holds value and what doesn't. This framework is passed down directly by a child's caregivers. For example, on the basketball court two children who have teamed up to score a point will react similarly—offering enthusiastic high fives; however, each will interpret and value different aspects of the situation according to what he has learned. One may be cheering the act of teamwork and accomplishment of the team, while the other may be reacting to his individual accomplishment of "twenty-five points so far this year."

In addition to this knowledge, children need to develop a repertoire of ways to express their appreciation, such as by saying thank you, taking care of a valued gift, and reciprocating expressions of love and concern to family, friends, and neighbors. These are learned through modeling, repetition, and practice.

Respect

Respect is often misunderstood to mean obedience, but the actual definition is to hold in esteem, to honor, regard, or love. The strong association between respect and obedience seems to exist because obedience has for a very long time been achieved through fear (you'll do this or else), and children respect the power that frightens them. The problem is that the child in this situation learns to respect power, strength, and size rather than people, knowledge, and relationships. Children who grow up in families where this dynamic exists often learn to bully others smaller or younger, for like all people they, too, seek respect, but know of only this way to get it.

To teach our children respect for people, social rules and customs, authority, and knowledge, we need to teach what we call "true respect" because it is about regard for others (empathy), and the values that guide the child's decisions and actions (morality), not about power and fear. A child who has learned true respect will value how others feel, what feels right and wrong, and the social rules of the environment. Therefore, he will usually behave and obey because he knows it's the right thing to do, he cares for how his actions might affect someone else, and he is able to think through the consequences of his actions. True respect is multifaceted for it includes respect for life, for property, for ourselves, for adults, for children, for our planet, and for the rights of others.

The quickest way to get respect is to give it. For those who believe that respect is solely based in power, this is a radical notion. A parent, teacher, or caregiver actually earns a child's respect by treating the child with respect and expecting it back. This adult not only models her definition of what respect is, but she also teaches reciprocity, caring, and sensitivity at the same time. Even a parent handing out a punishment can act respectfully, taking care to teach the child rather than shame or humiliate her.

A child treated disrespectfully will likely treat others similarly, whereas a child treated with respect and caring will be inspired to treat others this way. An example shared by a parent who described a common situation says it all. She told of a time when she overheard her husband yelling at their son, saying he was acting like an immature idiot because he was teasing his younger brother again and calling him names. This well-intentioned parent was delivering a rather confusing message of disrespect.

Tolerance for Diversity

This skill, like respect, is based in one's values and beliefs. To help our children build a more peaceful and respectful world, we must teach them to be tolerant and respectful of diversity. Vast differences exist between people and their cultures, appearance, religions, and lifestyles—the roots of misunderstanding, conflict, violence, and war. These differences are confusing for children and adults alike. Some adults deal with this confusion by attempting to classify those who are different as bad and immoral. A more constructive alternative is to teach children that diversity is a natural part of our life.

To develop this point of view, children need firsthand experience learning about people, customs, and cultures that are different from their own. With this exposure a child acquires knowledge that attacks prejudiced assumptions ("all _____ act this way"), because his experience tells him this is not so. With accurate information our children are prepared to examine things and people that are different more effectively. Tolerance should not suggest permissiveness or compliancy. It is actually the opposite, because this skill forces the child to reach her opinions and decisions in a disciplined and moral way, instead of basing them on shallow issues such as how a person dresses, speaks, prays, looks, eats, and so on.

How to Evalute If Your Child Needs to Develop Skills in Humanity

Review the "Over the Years Guidelines" to be sure that your expectations are in line with the child's age and developmental capabilities. Use the "Questions to Ask Yourself" as a way of evaluating the child's strengths and weaknesses. If you answer yes to any of these questions, it will be beneficial to help the child develop these skills further.

Questions to Ask Yourself

Does the child act selfishly, have difficulty sharing his possessions, or hog the spotlight? (When another child is the focus of attention, your child acts pouty, or tries to call attention to himself.)

Is the child cruel or insensitive to those who are weaker or less capable than he, such as animals, smaller children, or the elderly? Is he bossy or bullying without any awareness of how his actions might hurt others? (When playing with younger children he intimidates them into doing what he wants without regard for their feelings.)

Does the child treat her possessions and those of others with no regard for their worth, cost, or sentimental value? (This child might say, "I don't like it anymore, it's old and dirty," or "It's just a bike.")

Does the child seem to be directed not by an internal sense of right and wrong, but rather by material rewards and avoidance of negative consequences? (His way of thinking is "If I won't get in trouble or caught then it is okay to do.")

Note: This guide is meant to serve as a general orientation to what you can expect and when to expect it. While there are no absolute norms or limitations regarding how and when characteristics within a developmental period appear, and every child is unique, there is a range of similar and expectable periods of development, each marked by patterns of behavior and capabilities. Keep in mind that the nature of personality development is dynamic and repetitive, meaning that it is ever-changing and traits and/or skills seem to appear, disappear, and then reappear throughout development.

Humanity—Empathy, Appreciation, Respect, and Tolerance for Diversity

Stage I Infancy: Birth to 24 months
The stage of life from newborn through toddlerhood

Foundation period in which many behavior patterns, attitudes, and patterns of emotional expression are being established. Much of the first 12 months of this period are affected by instinctual drives for nurturing, food, and basic care.

Expect baby to: be by nature self-centered ("I want, I want"), unable to relate to what others feel (annoying a pet, pulling its tail), and cognitively too immature to understand the concepts behind these traits; show precursors of empathy when imitating the nurturing behavior of her caregivers toward a younger sibling, stuffed animal, doll, or another adult.

Do not expect baby to: understand or show overt signs of appreciation, empathy, or respect, as these skills rely upon a high level of self-awareness, objectivity, insight, and perspective, and will not develop until the end of the preschool stage (ages 3–4).

Stage II Early Childhood—The Preschool Years: Ages 2 to 6
The stage of life from toddlerhood through kindergarten

This is often called the play age because it is the peak period of interest in play and toys, marked by exploration, discovery play, creativity, magical thinking, fierce strivings for independence, and acquisition of social skills. This is a time of preparation for learning the foundations of social behavior needed for the school years to come.

Between ages 2–4, expect children to: be egocentric and self-centered—focused exclusively on themselves, with little concern or understanding of how others may be feeling ("I don't care," "what about me," "it's my turn"); appreciate people and objects in terms of how much they meet their interests or bring them pleasure; associate respect with an individual's level of authority and power to reward and punish, size and physical strength, status among peers, and relationship to the child.

Do not expect children to: understand the feelings and thoughts of others until age 3; appreciate the thoughts and meaning behind a gift or favor; pay respect to someone who does not show them respect.

Between ages 4–6, expect children to: begin to recognize the value of their relationships and associations with family, teachers, and close friends; exhibit more generosity and a willingness to share; begin to understand the feelings of others; begin to respect people for their skills and talents.

Do not expect children to: exhibit these developing understandings consistently or under adverse conditions (when tired, cranky, stressed, overexcited) without preparation and reminder cues from a caregiver.

Stage III Late Childhood—The School Years: Ages 6 to 11
This stage of life begins with entrance into first grade and extends into the beginning of adolescence

This period is marked by major interest and concern for social involvement with peers, participation in rule-based group play, and increased motivation to learn, acquire technical knowledge, information, and achieve academic success. This stage is very important for establishing attitudes and habits about learning, work, and personal potential.

Expect children to: make only small strides in developing these skills and traits; experience cruelty and disrespect at the hands of their peers; tune out the empathy alert when it is convenient to them; invest more energy in caring and appreciating friends than they do siblings; demonstrate a commitment to humanity skills in a disciplined environment that stresses morality and kindness.

Do not expect children to: pay attention to these issues if they are not reflected in the actions of their caregivers, older siblings, and educators; develop respect or empathy through fear and force.

Stage IV Early Adolescence: Ages 11 to 15
This stage of life begins around the time a child finishes elementary school and concludes by the time he graduates middle school (junior high school) and enters the world of high school

This period is marked by change and turmoil, the onset of puberty, growth spurts, increased interest in peer relationships and the opposite sex, and fierce strivings for self-identity and independence.

Expect young adolescents to: become more attentive to the nature of relationships between people, more aware of prejudice and discrimination and the disparities between rich and poor, and motivated to take action to help those who have been mistreated or oppressed (i.e., new immigrants, animals, sea life, children); convey an attitude of contempt toward adult customs and sensibilities; act scornfully toward, mistreat, and undervalue their family members, in particular their siblings.

Do not expect young adolescents to: put effort into treating family members with respect and empathy unless parents have taken the time to understand their adolescents' cultural values and interests—even if they do not wholeheartedly approve of them.

Is the child disrespectful toward adults and authority figures? Does he ignore or laugh at teachers or his elders, call them by their first names without being given permission to do so? (He believes that he knows more than these adults and has not developed a respect for their position within the community.)

Does the child express preconceived views and generalizations about anyone who is different, whether the difference is skin color, religious affiliation, size, or appearance because the other person wears glasses? (This child expresses simplistic opinions such as "All kids who wear glasses are smart," or "All fat kids are stupid.")

Do the child's expressions of gratitude and appreciation seem strategic or manipulative? (She sends a thank-you note to Grandpa so that he will send a bigger present next year.)

Does a school-aged child fail to show interest or concern about other people, almost as if their experience were not real? (He is not moved by the plight of the homeless, or children living amidst war or poverty.)

Does the child need frequent reminders about using manners? (She needs constant reminders to use social conventions such as table etiquette, waiting her turn in line, saying hello, please, or thank you.)

Does the child rarely delight in the opportunity to take care of and serve others, such as helping to set the table, care for Mom on Mother's Day, or sing to another child on his birthday? (She will say more often than not, "I don't want to do that, it's no fun. When is it going to be my birthday?")

How to Enhance a Child's Humanity

1. Live and breathe the art of humanity by constantly challenging yourself and your family to think outside of yourselves. Show by example how important others are to you by going the extra mile as often as you can, even when you think you can't, for the betterment of humanity. Simple things like thanking the waitress for her service and efforts go a long way to opening your child's eyes to these skills. If you want your child to be accepted, loved, and cared for not just by you but by others, than see to it that he sends out messages that he'll want to come his way in return.

2. We often speak about setting limits and dishing out punishments in a loving manner. This may sound like a contradiction, but when parents set lim-

its with respect and compassion, children will be less inclined to blame their parents and more likely to consider their own responsibility. When enforcing a punishment or loss of a privilege, let the child know that you believe in what you are doing—"It's Mom's [Dad's] job to make you miserable so that you can learn how to get your work done"; and that you feel for her—"I remember how much I hated missing dessert or going to sleep early." You will convey what it is to care and to live responsibly.

3. We teach respect when we afford children opportunities to work things out on their own. By doing this we are respecting their abilities and need for independence. Caregivers can begin this practice with children as young as two, by balancing their caregiving with times when the child is allowed to care for herself.

4. Help children develop a sense of appreciation by not jumping to fulfill their every request, need, or personal timetable. In the course of everyday life, many situations present teaching opportunities to accomplish this. For example, when you are speaking on the telephone, instead of letting your child interrupt you (since every child in the world seems to want your attention at that moment) be clear that he will need to wait until you are finished speaking to the *person* on the telephone. Let them know that your attention is something you choose to give, something of value to be treated with respect. The frustration the child will feel while waiting for you to finish helps develop her sense of appreciation for you and others and what you do for her. The child whose every need is met without wait or struggle will not grow to appreciate what others do for her, limiting her to a state of self-centered living. Certainly do not withhold love and affection, but put a limit on the amount of gift giving and "giving in" you do to teach your child to appreciate these acts of kindness.

   Respect your child's thoughts, feelings, and personal rights. This leads to a collective respect and appreciation and a shared consideration for each other, which builds trust and strengthens the parent-child relationship.

5. When evaluating your child's skills in humanity, consider her temperament, disposition, developmental stage, and environmental stressors. Use this knowledge to understand better why the child struggles with skills in empathy, respect, and appreciation that keep her from instinctively doing as well as you'd like.

6. Teaching children to think with empathy and respect for others takes time and patience. Maturation controls how quickly it can develop. Along the

way, a child will make many mistakes, but to grasp this complicated concept and hone her empathy skills, she needs to take chances and practice in an environment of acceptance and love. Share what you have learned from your own mistakes, and help the child confront her own (i.e., when she has been thoughtless, selfish, or unappreciative) to learn from these.

7. Show your love openly, not only for your child, but also toward your partner or spouse. Through your actions you will give the message that overt affection and love is good and that it need not be hidden or restricted to private moments. This may be difficult or awkward for many parents particularly if your parents were not demonstrative. Start early and take advantage of your relationship with your children to become more comfortable with public displays of affection. If you feel particularly conspicuous, look around; you'll find that most times people are not watching, and when they are, they are looking approvingly. Children need physical expressions of love.

8. Teach tolerance for diversity by recognizing how others are different from you rather than shying away or staring in silence. For example, take advantage of a time that you catch yourself or your child staring at someone or something unfamiliar, and talk about what you both noticed with interest, respect, and curiosity. Answer your child's questions factually, and if you don't know the facts, take the time to educate yourself and your child accurately.

9. Help your child see that there exists a great big world beyond herself by sharing information about issues and matters that affect people both in your community and on other continents. Take every opportunity to bring her the knowledge and experiences she needs to gain insight into other people and their customs and way of life. Sometimes seeing that there are tremendous problems in other parts of the world (health, education, malnutrition, war) will help expand the consciousness of an older school-age child who is becoming mature enough to handle some of these realities, particularly if there is something she can do to become part of the solution.

10. As parents, we must give ourselves permission to have children who will make mistakes, misbehave at times, and act selfishly. Part of learning is making mistakes.

Activities That Teach Empathy

Poster People

A humorous way to teach your child how it feels to be somebody else

Draw a life-size body of someone you want your child to empathize with, perhaps a physically challenged person, an ethnic minority, the neighborhood kid he's been teasing—even an animal or an endangered species. Leave a hole for the face. Have your child stick his head through the hole and talk about how it feels to be in that body. Present scenarios that the poster person might encounter and encourage your child truly to experience that person's feelings. For example, if the poster person is a shy classmate, describe a situation in which this person is rejected and ridiculed. Ask your child how it feels to be teased and cast aside by peers. Encourage your child to talk about what he would do about being teased. Switch places with your child to see what kind of scenarios he presents to you.

Materials:
child-size sheet of paper or poster board

4 to 10 years

Awareness-Through-Empathy Books

Encourage empathy by reading your child books that allow her to experience a character's feelings

Books are a wonderful way to try out someone else's world (in the security of your own). Review the list of books in the Appendix. Choose stories that may have little in common with your child's life but can give him the opportunity to consider another's.

All ages

Everybody Cooks Rice

A story of cultural differences and likeness

This book by Norah Dooley is about a little girl named Carrie who searches from house to house for her younger brother. At each culturally different home she samples that night's dinner and realizes that everybody eats rice, yet each dish is slightly different.

This book can launch you and your child on a multicultural adventure similar to Carrie's. Take your child to several ethnic markets and shop for rice. While you're there, compare food differences and similarities. Bring your rice home and cook up different dishes from each culture. Sample each and compare and contrast. Point out to your child that even though each dish tastes different, the key ingredient is the same. Draw the analogy that though people seem different, we're all essentially the same.

4 to 10 years

Empathy Antenna

Materials:
headband, thick wire,
and small Styrofoam balls

3 to 12 years

Teach your child empathy by making her a special antenna to wear on her head

Make an empathy antenna by attaching two thick wires to a headband and Styrofoam balls at the end of the wire. Pretend with your child that the empathy antenna can pick up the "feelings waves" of another person. When your child hurts another child's feelings, for instance, by refusing to share her toys, have her wear the antenna and tune in to the other child's feelings. Reinforce this by asking her what information her antenna was receiving. Put the antenna on yourself when you want to model empathy for others.

Family Projects

2 years and up

Make empathy a way of life

Find an official means to express your care for those who are less fortunate, perhaps by working as a family for an organization like UNICEF, or a homeless shelter. Become regular volunteers for the cause, pledging a certain number of hours per week or month. Even an annual commitment (delivering holiday food baskets to the elderly) is better than none.

What's most important is that every family member become involved in the effort. Make sure your kids understand that you're doing it not to gain recognition or to assuage guilt, but for the joy of bringing happiness to others. To find a worthy cause to become involved with, contact your local churches, synagogues, schools, or a local, state, or national volunteer clearinghouse. One organization that helps families find projects to get involved in is the Points of Light Foundation at 1-800-879-5400.

Here are a few suggestions for family giving projects:

- Volunteer at a soup kitchen, preparing and serving meals to the homeless and the hungry.

- Help out at a food pantry by soliciting donations of food and money from neighbors and local businesses, stocking shelves, and distributing the food.

- Help set up a free clothing store in a church basement or other donated space in your community. Collect clothing, wash and mend the items, and organize them by size. There is always a need for baby and toddler clothes and maternity clothes. If possible, include donated children's toys in your store.

- Help your child understand the plight of animals by donating your time to a local shelter. You can even volunteer your home to raise very young kittens that need constant feeding.

When his family first moved to Palm Beach, Florida, Christian Miller found a dead baby sea turtle while walking along the beach. When he learned that the tiny creature was an endangered species, he volunteered to help other baby turtles survive. Though only seven years old, he underwent a year of training by the State Department of Environmental Resources to monitor endangered giant sea turtle nests. Christian became the youngest person in Florida to get a permit for working with sea turtles. His task was to patrol a three-mile stretch of beach, guarding the turtles' nests. For eight years, from April through October, Christian would hit the beach. He began early in the morning searching out nests by following the turtles' tracks. When he found a nest, he marked the location, then watched it for forty to sixty days. As soon as he saw evidence that the eggs had hatched, Christian dug up the nest and carried the tiny turtles to the water's edge.

He kept meticulous records of his findings, which he sent to the Department of Natural Resources.

"When I look at the ocean, I know there are seventeen thousand turtles out there that would not have had the chance to live if I hadn't helped them," said Christian, who is now a college student. "Whether all seventeen thousand are alive now, I don't know. But I do know that at least I gave them a chance."

- Encourage your church or synagogue to sponsor a family from a war-torn nation. Helping a refugee family resettle in America takes money and a true pooling of community resources. There's no better way to help our children understand how precious feedom is.

- Many charitable organizations hold holiday fund-raisers to buy toys for needy children. Volunteer to help, and also write letters as a family to your local newspapers urging others to contribute. Encourage your children to save money throughout the year to donate to the cause.

In Your Shoes
How it feels to be in somebody else's shoes

Everyone tries on another family member's shoes and describes what it must feel like to be that person. Role-play different situations. For example, "wear" your child's shoes and act the part of a selfish and demanding child. Your

Materials:
wear your shoes!

3 years and up

child, who will be wearing your shoes, will have to act like an adult and deal maturely with the childish behavior. Conversely, act out a scenario that shows that you understand what it is like to be in your child's shoes when he needs something from you.

Different for a Day

8 years and up   *Teaching children about diversity by experiencing it*

Denise taught an interesting class at a school that mainstreamed deaf and hard-of-hearing children into regular classrooms. In this ninth-grade class, Denise's primary goal was to get both deaf and hearing to accept their differences, work as a team, and have respect for each other. The class project was that hearing students had to "become deaf" and deaf students had to "become different" for seventy-two hours. A deaf and hearing student were paired together and each needed to help the other become "different." The experience was for the students to learn as much as they could about their newly acquired "difference" so that they would feel it fully and be believable for the seventy-two hours that it took. The hearing students learned sign language, deaf culture, how not to rely on sound for cues, how to use gadgets such as vibrating alarm clocks, and what the emotional struggles are that come from being deaf. Deaf students picked differences including being physically challenged, being from a different culture, and some adventurous ones chose being of the opposite sex! The process of preparing had as much influence and impact as the actual seventy-two-hour experience. The relationships between deaf and hearing had grown tremendously simply because their "research" into becoming different had caused them to learn about each other and more importantly forced the hearing to learn sign language in order to communicate. The deaf students had to learn patience and tolerance as their hearing counterparts acquired knowledge and sensitivity about being deaf.

Walking in another's shoes can be very enlightening. We think this activity should be included in every school's curriculum, but it can also be done at

When Sarah Acheson was eight years old, she was so moved during a visit to an AIDS hospice that she immediately donated the dollar allowance in her pocket. Then she looked for a more meaningful way to help the people she met there. Sarah began volunteering at the hospice, bringing drawings, handmade cards, and the proceeds from her lemonade stand. Back at school, she enlisted children and adults to bake cookies for the residents and draw pictures to hang on the walls.

Most of the patients Sarah befriended have died, but Sarah knows that she helped make their lives a little more pleasant.

"If I ever got AIDS, I'd want children to care about me, to draw me pictures," Sarah said. "I just figured that's how they felt, too."

home. For example, family members can become "blind" for an hour or so by blindfolding themselves. How do you all work your way through your own home, how do you travel, what's it like not to be able to watch television and only hear it? The experience could be as enlightening as it had been for Denise's ninth-grade class.

Then What Happens?

Talking and thinking activity that helps children understand that their actions have consequences

2 years and up

This is a ritual that should be used by parents and teachers when teaching children empathy. Whenever a child does something either positive or negative to another person it is important for him to understand what the consequences of his actions are. You can get your child to ponder this by asking him to imagine what happens to the person after he has done something. For example, after your child sends thank-you cards to those who gave him gifts, ask him what might happen to each person when they receive the card. Did it make them happy? Did they smile and feel good inside? Did the card make them feel appreciated? Another example would be, after your child calls another child a bad name, what happens to that child's feelings moments later, what happens days later?

Activities That Enhance Appreciation and Respect

Declaration of Respect

A declaration by all members of your family to treat one another as they wish to be treated themselves

3 years and up

Your declaration of respect should contain a description of behaviors that family members are expected to follow, as well as those that will not be tolerated. Model your declaration of respect after the Declaration of Independence:

"We hold these truths to be self-evident, that all family members are to be respected, that they are endowed with certain inalienable rights, that among these are the right to a 'thank-you,' a 'please,' and the pursuit of an 'excuse me.'"

Follow with a thorough list of respectful behavior, including waiting for others to be served before eating, giving up a seat to an older person, and never borrowing something without asking first. You'll really capture your children's attention if in your list of forbidden behaviors you include things like belching at the dinner table and picking your nose. Which reminds us, be sure to ask your child for input. It will get them thinking about how to act (and how not to act) around others.

Make sure everyone (including family pets) signs the document, then post it on the wall. When someone acts disrespectfully, remind them that they have put their John Hancock on the declaration of respect.

Manners or Finishing School

3 to 8 years *A fun way to teach your child manners*

Finishing school . . . what a funny phrase. But we think it is a great idea. Finishing in effect means "done, final, you've reached the end." In a way that's what having manners is all about. Becoming a "finished" person means having all the necessary skills in place—most definitely manners! So send your child to finishing school by giving him some old-fashioned training in manners. Create a dramatic play experience in which you explain to your child that he will be partaking in a special manners class. Explain that waiters, hotel employees, and others have to be trained to respond appropriately to their customers. Set up a situation, such as going to a restaurant, and playact the situation with your child using impeccable etiquette. Have your child be the "guest" and go out of the way to give him the royal treatment by opening the door, saying excuse me, thank you, please, and so on. Play out different situations including answering the phone and accepting gifts. Give your child a diploma for finishing the finishing school. Later, in real-life situations, remind your child about the training he went through earlier.

> Kristen Belanger considers herself fortunate. She has a nice house and sleeps in a comfortable bed. But she can't feel truly content knowing others are hungry and homeless.
>
> Before she was twelve, Kristen spearheaded a drive to supply a soup kitchen and stock a food bank; she organized a clothing drive, sending nearly half a ton of clothing to a Native American reservation, and she collected and distributed toys and seven hundred seventy children's books to sixty-five children who otherwise would have gone without.
>
> "These are people who need the same stuff as us," she said. "They're just like us but they don't have nice houses and comfy beds. I started these projects because I didn't see anybody doing anything about them."

The Manners Menu

5 to 12 years *Help children remember their manners*

List life's essential manners on a menu, including a description beside each one of how and when to use it. For example, "Thank you . . . What you say when somebody is helpful," or "Please . . . What you say to somebody when you want something." Post your manners menu on the wall.

Rainbow Box

Expose your child to different cultures, ethnicities, and races through toys and books

1 to 12 years

One way to introduce your child to cultural and ethnic differences is to fill a box with games and toys that represent the rainbow of human diversity. Include dolls of different skin colors, board games from other cultures, books and magazines that recognize ethnic diversity, and dress-up clothes and items from different countries. (Many of these can be found at specialty toy and educational-products stores, and in catalogs.) As a family, you can also celebrate a variety of religious and ethnic holidays.

By accustoming your child at an early age to human diversity, you are broadening her perspective on life.

A Real Thank-you

Take time to appreciate birthday and holiday presents

All ages

Nothing saps the joy of a birthday party or holiday celebration faster than the feeding-frenzy mentality that often accompanies the opening of presents. Sometimes it's so bad you can barely see the kid through all the flying bows and gift paper. They're barely done unwrapping one present when they toss it aside to tear into the next. There's nothing wrong with getting caught up in the excitement of a birthday or holiday, but it doesn't have to be at the expense of the gift-givers' feelings.

We came up with a thank-you process that taught our children to take a moment with each present to focus on the person it came from. Before the celebration, we talk with our children about the thought that goes into each gift. We remind them to take their time with each one, to read the card first, then talk about the present, how they plan to use it, and why it makes them happy. We also make sure the kids come up with a special way to express their thanks to the giver, usually a big hug and kiss.

Taking the time to acknowledge each present is a delightful way for your child to make this favorite part of a celebration last even longer.

Thank-you Cards

Design your own thank-you cards

Materials:
nice paper stock

Have your child design and create a greeting card, then get it professionally printed. Give these cards out generously. When a teacher takes a class on a

3 years and up

field trip, send her a family thank-you card. When a grandparent takes your child out for the day, give him a family thank-you card. Give your own child a thank-you card whenever he does something nice for you. Send it through the mail to make it seem even more special.

Doing the Unexpected (Random Acts of Kindness)

All ages   *Do nice things for the sake of being nice*

You've seen the bumper sticker: "Practice Random Acts of Kindness and Senseless Acts of Beauty." Pass the message along to your kids. Challenge them to act spontaneously to brighten someone's day. The best way to get your message across is to do it yourself. Feed an expired parking meter to save a stranger from getting a ticket. Carry your neighbor's trash cans back from the curb on the next pick-up day. Commit enough kind acts in front of your child, and he'll start spreading his own random kindness.

Appreciation Parties

3 years and up   *Throw a party for someone you appreciate*

We heard about this activity from a small day-care center in Massachusetts. Every few months, the center fetes someone in their community with an appreciation day. Past honorees include nurses, firefighters, teachers, moms, dads, and even the postal carrier who has been delivering mail for over thirty-five years. The center decorates a room with streamers and banners for the occasion, bakes a cake, and sings songs for their special guest. Each child presents the guest of honor with a homemade thank-you card and takes turns verbally expressing their appreciation.

> Teddy Andrews was perplexed. He was aware of all sorts of children's organizations, but noticed none had actual kids working for them. So, at the age of eight, he started SAY YAY! (Save American Youth, Youth Advocates for Youth!) in Berkeley, California, where he lives.
>
> SAY YAY! delivers school supplies to homeless kids so they can do homework. The organization also holds toy drives and works with Berkeley's Gray Panthers, providing respite for grandparents raising grandchildren.
>
> In addition to his work with SAY YAY! Teddy spent two hours a day after school fulfilling the duties of Berkeley Youth Commissioner, bringing substance to what had largely been an honorary post. As a commissioner, Teddy became a tireless campaigner for homeless kids and had special parks and recreation programs initiated on their behalf.

We think this is a marvelous idea, one that we would love to see implemented at schools.

Monday Presents

A just-because present that eases the transition into the school week or work week

All ages

Denise used to leave Monday presents for Mark when they first met. She would leave these small surprises at his desk at work, or on the front seat of his car. She would always include a card wishing him a happy week.

Giving Goodies

Make sharing a way of life

All ages

Get into the habit of sharing what you have with others. For instance, when you bake cookies, make some extra to give to neighbors. When you pack your children's lunch boxes, include some goodies for them to share with their classmates or teacher. We know a family that secretly does things for their neighbors. They fill bird feeders, bring trash barrels back from the curb, leave little gifts. . . . By doing this they are teaching their children the rewards of anonymous giving.

The Sharing Box

A box of toys that must be shared

Materials:
a large cardboard box and play items

3 to 9 years

Write the words "Sharing Box" on a cardboard box. Fill it with toys that your child may play with only if he shares. Include toys that require a friend, such as a board game and a large jump rope, but be sure to include things that can be used alone, like a doll or a puzzle. This challenges your child to negotiate shared play and turn taking. Twice a year we turn our sharing box into another activity in which we select toys and play items we would like to share, essentially, by giving them to a shelter or children's facility. We make sure the toys are in good condition and we are often delighted with how much our children are willing to share with others. This takes sharing to a much higher level and gives a different meaning to the word.

Golden Hearts

2 years and up   *Reward your child for caring about others*

Tell your children they were born with a golden heart, which enables them to spread sunshine to others. The more they give to others, the shinier their golden heart becomes. Reward your child's generosity with an official golden heart—a heart-shaped medal.

Whenever your children need a gentle hint to think of others, remind them of their golden hearts.

Activities That Teach Respect for the Body

My Incredible Body

4 years and up   *A full week of exploration into the wonders of the human body*

You'll find several good books available about the human body such as, *The Magic School Bus: Inside the Human Body* by Joanna Cole (Scholastic, 1987) and *The Body Book* by Sara Stein (Workman Publishing, 1992). These will help your child realize just how amazing her body is. The most basic facts about how the human body works and the ways it adjusts to injuries astonish children and teach them a new respect for themselves.

Round out the learning week by bringing your child to a museum with a human body exhibit.

Private Time

2 years and up   *For children who have difficulty respecting the privacy of others, the following activities will reinforce the need for some personal space*

   ◆ Make a doorknob sign like the ones hotels use, with Knock First—I Want Privacy on one side and Come on In—I Want Company on the other.

- Set aside a portion of each day for family members to enjoy private time. Depending on your child's age, establish fifteen minutes to an hour a day when everyone either goes to his room, selects a private space to sit, or is given permission to take a walk on his own.

- Teach your child the concept of boundaries by having him define the progressive degrees of privacy: beginning with the physical boundaries of your property (it's not respectful for people to step on your grass), the physical boundaries of your home (people who do not live here must ask permission to come inside), and the emotional boundaries of your body (you must have permission to touch someone's body). Play a game and see if your child can think of ten or twenty ways to express his wish for privacy, such as closing a door, lowering the shades, and wearing clothing.

- Give a younger child a box that will always be off-limits to you. Tell him he can store his private things in the box and you will never look inside. Give an older child a diary and promise you will never read it.

- Make a list of things in the home or on a person's body that are off-limits. Tape little signs saying Off-limits on these things and/or on a person for a short period of time to further reinforce the need to respect these private places or items.

- Teaching your child about privacy and boundaries through play will help her learn to protect herself from unwanted touching while building her sense of self-worth, social awareness, and assertiveness. A good book to read with your child regarding appropriate and inappropriate touching is called *My Body Is Private* by Linda Walvoord Girard (Albert Whitman & Company, 1984).

The Family Spa
Turn your home into a spa   3 years and up

Pretend with your child to spend the weekend in a spa, a place where people go to refresh their bodies and minds. For two days, duplicate as many spa amenities as possible, and get the whole family to participate. A nice massage, steam bath, nature walk, healthy meal, and afternoon nap should be included in your spa weekend. Take your child to get a haircut and style and a manicure. Go shopping for a favorite article of clothing (sneakers, jeans, etc.). At the end of the spa weekend, take photographs of your child's new appearance, complete with latest hairstyle and clothes. If you like, make this a quarterly or biannual activity and take turns with your child being the spa owner. (This way you can get a few naps and massages in.)

Handle with Care

3 years and up — *Let everyone know when you feel fragile*

Who among us hasn't felt a little fragile from time to time? You alert the post office when the contents of your package are breakable, so why can't you slap on a handle-with-care sticker when you need to be treated with kid gloves?

Keep a pack of these handle-with-care stickers on hand for these occasions. Family members can apply them to themselves to warn others of their brittle condition, or on others as a gentle reminder to be good to themselves.

Activities That Teach Respect for the Environment

Humanity is not just for humans but for our earth and the creatures that share it with us.

Seeing Beauty

All ages — *Take time to see the beauty in everyday things*

Children have a seemingly endless reserve of fascination and curiosity. Walking with a very young child is like going on a sight-seeing tour in a strange but wonderful land. An adult will walk across the yard and see grass that needs cutting while the two-year-old beside her will notice the way the wind ruffles the blades, stirring the lawn into a sea of motion.

Seize teachable moments, windows of opportunity to foster the values you want your child to embrace. Even the littlest things can count a lot. On a stroll with the children, Denise spotted an ant and casually picked it up before anyone could squash it. Denise let the tiny creature crawl on her finger and wondered aloud about its family. She pointed out the beauty of the insect, and let the ant go. Since then, the girls have stopped stepping on ants. When they spot one in the house, they stop and look at it, then carry it outside to rejoin its family.

It was through a playful moment that two children learned to feel empathy, and it only took fifteen seconds. It's up to you to seek out those shortcuts and make those playful stops en route to character development. Try to look at your surroundings from a two-year-old's perspective, and share your discoveries with your children. Maybe your ten-year-old's first inclination upon seeing an ant is to flatten it under the toe of his sneaker. Stop him and talk about the social structure of an ant colony. Point out the crumb it is carrying and wonder together how many other ants the crumb will feed.

There is beauty in everything. Sometimes we just have to ask the two-year-old inside us to point it out.

Beach/Park Cleanup
A seasonal activity

2 years and up

Twice a year, or four times if necessary, organize a community cleanup. You can put a notice in the local newspaper or just round up as many people as you know to clear trash and debris from a park or beach. You can even make it a family-only project. The great thing about these group cleanups, no matter how small the group, is that they're fun and yield visible results.

Bark, Flower, and Leaf Book
Make a nature book

2 to 8 years

If you're lucky enough to live where autumn paints trees with a palette of crimson and gold you're undoubtedly familiar with the urge to press a bouquet of leaves into a scrapbook. This activity expands that urge to include all leaves, regardless of color, and even makes room for bark, buds, and blossoms. The best part is that the scrapbook will become a storybook featuring your neighborhood trees as the main characters.

Grab a field guide and go out with your child to collect samples from different trees. At home, have your child "reconstruct" the trees she saw by pasting the leaves, bark, and blossoms on paper. Label the trees and write a story for each one detailing its growth and seasonal cycles and describing the animals, birds, and insects that make their homes in there.

The bark, flower, and leaf book will remind your child that trees are a lot more than just bark, flowers, and leaves.

Appendix

Children's Books That Enhance the Development of Your Child's Skills

Chapter 1

Brain Twisters. Paul Hayes. (Penworthy, 1987) Older. Word puzzles challenge children to use their thinking skills.

BrainQuest. Chris Welles Feder. (Workman Publishing) All ages. A series of fun flash cards, trivia games, and quizzes on the things kids need to know, when they need to know it.

Color Kittens. Margaret Wise Brown (included in *A Treasury of Little Golden Books*, Golden, 1982) Older. Two kittens mix up their paints and come up with new colors.

Colors and Numbers. Guy Smalley. (Mallard Press, 1989) Younger. Simple words and pictures help children learn colors and numbers.

D'Aulaire's Book of Greek Myths. Ingri and Edgar D'Aulaire. (Doubleday, 1962) Older. Well-known Greek myths are retold as exciting adventures and beautifully illustrated.

Fantastic Book of Logic Puzzles. Muriel Mandell. (Sterling, 1986) Older. Logic puzzles, set in outer space and medieval kingdoms, help kids develop thinking and reasoning skills.

How to Dig a Hole to the Other Side of the World. Faith McNulty. (Harper & Row, 1979) Younger. A child digs an eight-thousand-mile tunnel through the center of the earth and discovers what is inside.

The Magic School Bus (various titles). Joanna Cole. (Scholastic) Younger. In this well-known series, Ms. Frizzle takes her class on exciting field trips in their magic bus.

Make an Interactive Science Museum. Robert Gardner. (McGraw-Hill, 1985) Older. Book shows how to display and make science projects.

More about Dinosaurs. David Cutts. (Troll Associates, 1992) Younger. Where dinosaurs lived, what they ate, and what might have happened to them.

My First Book of Questions and Answers. Philip Steele. (Gallery, 1989) Older. Interesting information about nature, food, far-away places, the earth and sky, how things work, and other subjects.

Number Mysteries. Cyril and Dympna Hayes. (Penworthy, 1987) Older. Magic tricks and puzzles test children's knowledge of numbers and basic math.

A Quiz Book: Interesting Facts That Inform and Entertain. Bill Adler. (Grosset and Dunlap, 1977) Older. Fun animal, history, sports, geography, and miscellaneous facts.

Using Your Head: The Many Ways of Being Smart. Sara Gilbert. (Macmillan, 1984) Older. Helps children find the talents and skills they are best at, and make the most of what they have.

What's under the Ocean. Janet Craig. (Troll Associates, 1982) Younger. Children see the myriad life forms that inhabit the sea.

Word Teasers. Dympna Hayes and Melanie Lehmann. (Penworthy, 1987) All ages. The scrambled words, riddles, tongue twisters, secret codes, and other puzzles in this book exercise a child's language and thinking skills.

Chapter 2

Are You My Mother? P. D. Eastman. (Beginner Books, 1960) Younger. A young bird falls from its nest and searches for his mother.

The Little House. Virginia Lee Burton. (Houghton Mifflin, 1969) Younger. A small house atop a hill is encroached upon by the city, then brought back to the quiet countryside.

My Mom Travels a Lot. Caroline Feller Bauer. (F. Warne, 1981) Younger. Even though some parents may have to be away from home a lot, they always love and miss their children.

My Mother's House, My Father's House. C. B. Christiansen. (Atheneum, 1989) Younger. A little girl lives with her mother during the week and with her father on weekends, and imagines what her house will be like when she grows up, where she will live every day of the week.

The Rooster Who Set Out to See the World. Eric Carle. (Franklin Watts, 1972) Younger. A rooster and several companions set out to see the world, then decide they would rather be safe at home.

Chapter 3

Bub, or, The Very Best Thing. Natalie Babbit. (HarperCollins, 1994) Younger. The king and queen aren't sure what the very best thing is for the prince, but he knows that it is love.

Don't Die, My Love. Lurlene McDaniel. (Bantam, 1995) Older. A story about the power of love during a terminal illness.

Even If I Did Something Awful? Barbara Shook Hazen. (Atheneum, 1981) Younger. A little girl learns that her mother will always love and forgive her.

Love You Forever. Robert Munsch. (Firefly, 1990) Younger. A mother promises her son that she will love him forever and always take care of him no matter how old he gets.

Mama, Do You Love Me? Barbara M. Joosse. (Chronicle, 1991) Younger. A young Eskimo girl is reassured that her mother will love her forever.

On Mother's Lap. Ann Herbert Scott. (Clarion, 1992) Younger. Michael's favorite place to be is on his mother's lap, rocking back and forth in the rocking chair.

The Runaway Bunny. Margaret Wise Brown. (Harper & Row, 1977) Younger. Mother Rabbit assures her little bunny that no matter where he may run to, she will always be there to take care of him.

Thistle. Walter Wangerin, Jr. (Augsburg, 1995) All ages. A modern fairy tale about how powerful love and compassion can be.

Waiting for Hannah. Marisabina Russo. (Greenwillow, 1989) Younger. Hannah's mother tells her about the excitement and happiness her parents felt while waiting for her to be born.

The Wild Baby. Barbro Lindgren and Jack Prelutsky. (Greenwillow, 1980) Older. Baby Ben is never where he should be, but Mama loves him, and when he gets into trouble, she is right there to help him out of it.

Chapter 4

Acts of Courage. Stef Donev and others. (Penworthy, 1986) Older. Martin Luther King, Jr., Clara Barton, and John F. Kennedy are some of the people profiled in this collection.

Armed With Courage. May McNeer and Lynd Ward. (E. M. Hale and Co., 1957) Older. Biographies of people who strived to help others; includes Florence Nightingale, Jane Addams, and Mahatma Gandhi.

Daring Deed. Teri Kelly. (Penworthy, 1986) Older. Stories of famous men and women who risked their lives to help others.

The Diary of a Young Girl. Anne Frank. (Pocket Books, 1952) Older. Anne Frank's diary, found after her death in a concentration camp, chronicles the life of a Jewish family hiding from the Nazis during World War II.

Elizabeth Blackwell, First Woman Doctor. Carol Greene. (Children's Press, 1991) Younger. The story of the first woman in the United States to receive a medical degree.

Girls to the Rescue. Bruce Lansky. (Meadowbook, 1995) Older. Ten stories about courageous girls from around the world.

Go Free or Die. Jeri Ferris. (Carolrhoda, 1988) Older. The story of Harriet Tubman, a slave who escaped and led more than three hundred other slaves to freedom on the Underground Railroad.

"Great Achievers" Series. (Chelsea House, 1995) Older. Highlights accomplishments by members of ethnic minorities, the physically challenged, and Native Americans of North America.

Jim Abbott. John Rolfe. (Warner Juvenile Books, 1991) Older. The story of Jim Abbott, who became a major league baseball pitcher despite having been born without a right hand.

Louis Braille, the Boy Who Invented Books for the Blind. Margaret Davidson. (Hastings House, 1971) Older. Left blind from an accident at the age of three, twelve-year-old Louis developed a system of printing and writing for the blind.

Martin Luther King, Jr.: Dreams for a Nation. Louise Quayle. (Ballantine, 1989) Older. The story of the minister who led thousands of people in peaceful protests against prejudice and segregation and galvanized the civil rights movement.

Samantha Smith, Young Ambassador. Patricia Stone Martin. (Rourke Enterprises, 1987) Younger. The story of Samantha Smith, who was only ten years old when she wrote to Yuri Andropov of the Soviet Union, asking for peace between his nation and the U.S.

The Story of My Life. Helen Keller. (Dell, 1961) Older. The story of the author and lecturer, blind and deaf since the age of two, who lived in silent darkness until a teacher, Anne Sullivan, taught her to communicate with others.

Chapter 5

All Kinds of Families. Norma Simon. (Albert Whitman & Co., 1976) Younger. There are many kinds of families, and this book illustrates lots of them.

Come a Tide. George Ella Lyon. (Orchard, 1990) Younger. When a small town is flooded the families tough it out together, illustrating the meaning of community.

Fathers, Mothers, Sisters, Brothers: A Collection of Family Poems. Mary Ann Hoberman. (Joy Street, 1991) All ages. A poem for every kind of family member, including parents, siblings, aunts and uncles, only children, grandparents, cousins, stepbrothers, stepsisters, and more!

Free to Be—a Family. Marlo Thomas, editor. (Bantam, 1987) All ages. This collection of stories, poems, and songs by today's best children's writers addresses the many meanings of family.

Gingerbread Days. Joyce Carol Thomas. (HarperCollins, 1995) All ages. Poems and stories celebrating life and love.

Horace. Holly Keller. (Greenwillow, 1991) Younger. Horace, an adopted child, leaves home in order to find a family where he looks the same as the others, but soon realizes that family is about love, not looks.

Megan's Two Houses. Erica Jong. (Dove Kids, 1995) All ages. A girl adjusts to divorce.

I Know a Lady. Charlotte Zolotow. (Greenwillow, 1984) Younger. An old woman is a friend to all the children in the town.

The Patchwork Quilt. Valerie Flournoy. (Dial Books for Young Readers, 1985) Younger. When Grandma gets sick, Tanya, her mother, and the rest of the family finish the quilt that Grandma has been making.

Sisters. David McPhail. (Harcourt Brace Jovanovich, 1984) Younger. The story of two sisters who in some ways are very different, but in other ways are very much alike.

Sisters. Tricia Tusa. (Crown, 1995) Younger. What it is like to fight, love, and live with a sister.

Tanya's Reunion. Valerie Flournoy. (Del Ray, 1995) Younger. This sequel to *The Patchwork Quilt* shows Tanya preparing for a family reunion.

Tess. Hazel Hutchins. (Annick Press, 1995) Older. Story set in the 1930s in Canada about a family making a home for themselves.

Whose Mouse Are You? Robert Kraus. (Macmillan, 1970) Younger. A little mouse is all alone until he decides to rescue his family.

Chapter 6

All by Myself. Anna Grossnickle Hines. (Clarion, 1985) Younger. One night, Josie goes to the bathroom all by herself—in the dark!

Arthur, for the Very First Time. Patricia MacLachlan. (Harper & Row, 1980) Older. Arthur is not happy about spending the summer at his aunt and uncle's farm, until he learns that it is okay to be different.

Brave Irene. William Steig. (Farrar Straus & Giroux, 1993) Younger. Irene braves a blizzard to deliver a dress her mother has made for the duchess.

Don't Feed the Monster on Tuesdays! The Children's Self-esteem Book. Adolph Moser. (Landmark Editions, 1991) All ages. Teaches children how to shrink the little monster in their heads that whispers negative thoughts.

Don't Worry Grandpa. Nick Ward. (Barrons, 1995) Younger. Charlie reassures his grandfather during a thunder and lightning storm.

I Like Me! Nancy Carlson. (Puffin, 1988) Younger. The protagonist of this story has a best friend—herself!

I Never Did That Before. Lillian Moore. (Simon & Schuster, 1995) Younger. Poems and pictures that show children's excitement about new accomplishments.

The Little Engine That Could. Watty Piper. (Platt & Munk, 1976) Younger. The classic about the small blue engine who says, "I think I can, I think I can." And sure enough, she does!

Mike Mulligan and His Steam Shovel. Virginia Lee Burton. (Houghton Mifflin, 1993) Younger. Mike and his steam shovel, Mary Anne, are thought to be outdated, but they know better.

My Friend Harry. Kim Lewis. (CandleWick, 1995) Younger. School starts and James must leave his stuffed animal at home.

Rockhopper. Errol Broome. (Allen & Unwin, 1995) Older. A timid boy asserts his independence.

Saint George and the Dragon. Margaret Hodges. (Little, Brown & Co., 1984) Older. A courageous knight battles a dragon that is destroying the land.

Sid and Sol. Arthur Yorinks. (Farrar Straus & Giroux, 1971) Younger. Sol the giant towers over skyscrapers, but little Sid refuses to be intimidated.

Speak Up, Chelsea Martin! Becky Thoman Lindberg. (Albert Whitman & Co., 1991) Older. Chelsea doesn't like drawing attention to herself, but one day she takes a stand.

Tuck in the Pool. Martha Weston. (Clarion, 1995) Younger. A rubber spider helps a pig overcome his fears of swimming.

What Is Beautiful? Mayjean Watson Avery and David Avery. (Tricycle, 1995) Younger. This story comes with a mirror and shows how there is something beautiful in everyone.

Where the Wild Things Are. Maurice Sendak. (Harper & Row, 1983) Younger. When Max is sent to his room without supper, he runs away to where the wild things are.

Chapter 7

Addie Meets Max. Joan Robins. (Harper & Row, 1985) Younger. There's a new boy next door, but Addie wishes he would move to the moon—and stay there!

Amos and Boris. William Steig. (Farrar Straus & Giroux, 1971) Younger. A mouse and a whale are loyal friends who come to each other's rescue.

Bialosky's Best Behavior: A Book of Manners. Leslie McGuire. (Golden, 1986) Younger. Bialosky always minds his manners, behaves well, and is considerate of others.

Big Pumpkin. Erica Silverman. (Macmillan, 1992) Younger. The witch has grown a huge pumpkin for her Halloween pie, but it is so big she can't get it off the vine!

Care and Share: A Book about Manners. Rita Golden Gelman. (Marvel, 1986) Younger. Children learn that it is polite to take turns, say please and thank you, and share, even though they may not always want to!

Chuck Wood and the Woodchucks in the Big Game. Marilyn Sadler. (Western, 1988) Younger.

Everyone on Chuck's team wants to be the pitcher, but when the team doesn't do very well, they learn that *every* position is important.

Communication. Aliki. (Greenwillow, 1983) Younger. There are all kinds of ways to communicate—not just by speaking, listening, and writing, but also by using pictures, symbols, sign language, body language, and more.

Do I Have to Say Hello? Delia Ephron. (Viking Press, 1989) All ages. "Aunt Delia" quizzes children on their manners in all kinds of situations—at the table, in school, on the phone, and even at a baseball game!

The Hating Book. Charlotte Zolotow. (Harper & Row, 1969) Younger. Two friends are angry with each other, but are too stubborn to ask why.

Helping Out. George Ancona. (Clarion, 1985) Younger. Children help their parents with jobs and chores, and have fun!

Herman the Helper. Robert Kraus. (Windmill, 1974) Younger. Herman the octopus puts his eight hands to work helping others.

How Kids Make Friends: Secrets for Making Lots of Friends, No Matter How Shy You Are. Lonnie Michelle. (Freedom Publishing Co., 1995) Older. A fun guide on how to make friends.

I Have a New Friend. Kathleen Allan-Meyer. (Barrons, 1995) Younger. Despite the language barriers a Japanese girl and an American girl become friends.

The Incredible Journey. Sheila Burnford. (Bantam, 1960) Older. Two dogs and a cat set out across the wilderness to find their family.

The Magic Friend Maker. Mary C. Olson. (Western, 1987) Younger. Kate is the only child in her apartment building, until one day she sees another girl sitting on the steps.

Making Friends. Fred Rogers. (G. P. Putnam's Sons, 1987) Younger. Mr. Rogers talks about the joys and challenges of friendship.

Manners. Aliki. (Greenwillow, 1990) All ages. Humorous illustrations of how kids should act—and shouldn't act—and why everyone should use their manners.

Manners Matter. Norah Smaridge. (Abingdon, 1980) All ages. Poems that amuse children while teaching them the proper way to act around other people.

My Mama Needs Me. Mildred Pitts Walter. (Lothrop Lee & Shepard, 1983) Younger. Jason's mother is very tired since the new baby came, and Jason is more than willing to help her out!

Navajo ABC. Luci Tapahonso and Eleanor Schick. (Simon & Schuster, 1995) All ages. Each letter represents a part of Navajo life.

No Friend of Mine. Ann Turnbull. (CandleWick, 1995) Older. The friendship of two boys from opposite sides of the tracks.

The Quarreling Book. Charlotte Zolotow. (Harper & Row, 1963) Younger. When one person is having a bad day, it can put everyone in a bad mood!

Richard Scarry's Please and Thank You. Richard Scarry. (Random House, 1973) Younger. Each of the short stories in this book addresses a different aspect of children's life, and the proper way to behave in each.

Signing Is Fun. Mickey Flodin. (Berkley, 1995) All ages. Guide to American Sign Language.

Who Can Boo the Loudest? Harriet Ziefert. (Harper & Row, 1990) Younger. Two ghosts have a contest to see who can boo the loudest.

Chapter 8

Alexander and the Terrible, Horrible, No Good, Very Bad Day. Judith Viorst. (Atheneum, 1972) Younger. Alexander is having one of those days when nothing goes right, and he wishes he could move to Australia.

A Baby Sister for Frances. Russell Hoban. (Harper & Row, 1964) Younger. Now that Frances has a baby sister, her parents don't have as much time for Frances as they used to, so Frances decides to run away (to under the dining room table).

Feelings. Aliki. (Greenwillow, 1984) Younger. Short illustrated vignettes depicting the many emotions children experience.

Feelings A to Z. Sally Masteller. (Modern, 1988) Younger. From Angry to Zonked, this book illustrates an alphabet of emotions that all kids have experienced.

Go Away, Bad Dreams! Susan Hill. (Random House, 1985) Younger. Tom's mother helps him realize that his bad dreams are only part of his imagination, and Tom can make them disappear.

I Was So Mad! Norma Simon. (Albert Whitman & Co., 1974) Younger. Parents explain to their children that everyone gets mad once in a while.

Noisy Nora. Rosemary Wells. (Dial, 1973) Younger. Nora feels left out when her parents spend time with her older sister and baby brother, but don't seem to have time for her.

One of Us. Nikki Amdur. (Dial, 1981) Older. Nora has just moved to a new town, and hates being the new girl at school.

Sometimes I Get Angry. Jane Werner Watson and others. (Crown, 1986) Younger. All children get angry, often because they can't have their own way.

Sometimes I'm Afraid. Jane Werner Watson and others. (Crown, 1986) Younger. Unfamiliar situations, bad dreams, and scary noises are frightening, but a little explanation and a lot of love from parents can help take a child's fear away.

Tristan's Temper Tantrum. Caroline Formby. (Children's Press, 1995) Younger. Granny deals with Tristan's tantrums.

The Temper Tantrum Book. Edna Mitchell Preston. (Puffin, 1969) Younger. Children jump up and down, and stomp their feet because they hate it when they don't get their way!

Will I Have a Friend? Miriam Cohen (Macmillan, 1967) Younger. It is Jim's first day at a new school and when he gets there it seems all the friends have been taken.

Chapter 9

Aesop's Fables. Retold by Tom Paxton. (Morrow Junior Books, 1988) All ages. Ten of Aesop's most famous fables retold in rhyme.

All-of-a-Kind Family. Sydney Taylor. (Dell, 1989) Younger. Five sisters, alike, learn moral lessons from their loving parents.

Bear's Picture. Manus Pinkwater. (Dutton, 1984) Younger. A young bear paints a picture and thinks it's a masterpiece despite the criticisms of others.

The Berenstain Bears and the Truth. Stan and Jan Berenstain. (Random House, 1983) Younger. Brother and Sister Bear break a lamp and make up a story to cover their mistake.

The Book of Virtues. William Bennett, editor. (Simon & Schuster, 1993) All ages. Classic literature for children (and adults) of all ages and reading levels illustrating character traits such as honesty, compassion, courage, and perseverance.

Ella. Bill Peet. (Houghton Mifflin, 1964) Younger. A spoiled elephant quits the circus and ends up in the hands of a mean old farmer who sets her to work.

Farmer Duck. Martin Waddell. (CandleWick Press, 1991) Younger. A lazy farmer stays in bed all day, leaving all the farm work to a duck.

Franklin Fibs. Paulette Bourgeois. (Scholastic, 1991) Younger. Franklin tells his friends he can eat sixty-seven flies in the blink of an eye—but what will he do when they want him to prove it?

The Gorilla Did It. Barbara Shook Hazen. (Atheneum, 1974) Younger. A boy tells his mother a gorilla messed up his room, so why should he have to clean up?

Horton Hatches the Egg. Dr. Seuss. (Random House, 1940) Younger. A bird persuades an elephant to sit on her nest and hatch her egg while she goes off to play.

Homecoming. Cynthia Voigt. (Atheneum, 1981) Older. When thirteen-year-old Dicey and her younger siblings are abandoned by their mother, Dicey leads the family from Cape Cod to Maryland, mostly on foot, in search of relatives who will take them in.

The Hundred Dresses. Eleanor Estes. (Harcourt Brace & Co., 1944) Older. A young girl works up the courage to defend her friend against teasing.

If I Were in Charge of the World. Judith Viorst. (Atheneum, 1982) All ages. A collection of humorous poems about life, its worries, and responsibilities.

I Just Forgot. Mercer Mayer. (Western, 1988) Younger. Little Critter remembers to do all the fun stuff, but forgets about little things, like chores, that need to be done.

Marcella's Guardian Angel. Evaline Ness. (Holiday House, 1973) Younger. A young girl grows tired of her guardian angel and tries to get rid of it.

Sometimes I Have To. David Ridyard. (Gareth Stevens, 1985) Younger. Sally knows that even though she may not like the rules, it is important to follow them.

Tacky the Penguin. Helen Lester. (Houghton Mifflin, 1988) Younger. Tacky's unusual ways make him an outcast among the penguins until he saves them from hunters.

Tillie and the Wall. Leo Lionni. (Knopf, 1989) Younger. Of all the mice who live next to the wall, only Tillie, the youngest, wonders about what is on the other side.

The Young Artist. Thomas Locker. (Dial Books for Young Readers, 1989) Younger. Adrian faces a dilemma when the king appoints him to paint the royal court.

Chapter 10

And to Think That I Saw It on Mulberry Street. Dr. Seuss. (Vanguard, 1937) Younger. As he walks home from school, all Marco sees is a horse and wagon. But by the time he gets there his imagination has turned it into a story that no one can beat!

Cloudy with a Chance of Meatballs. Judi Barrett. (Atheneum, 1978) Younger. In the town of Chewandswallow good falls from the sky until one day the weather takes a turn for the worse!

The Day Jimmy's Boa Ate the Wash. Trinka Nobel. (Dial Books for Young Readers, 1980) Younger. Jimmy sneaks his pet snake along on a class trip.

Don't Pop Your Cork on Mondays! The Children's Anti-stress Book. Adolph Moser. (Landmark Edition, 1988) All ages. Helps children deal with stress.

Flat Stanley. Jeff Brown. (Harper & Row, 1964) All ages. A bulletin board has flattened Stanley Lambchop, but Stanley doesn't mind!

Florence and Eric Take the Cake. Jocelyn Wild. (Dial Books for Young Readers, 1987) Younger. Florence and Eric are spending their vacation with their granny, doing everything they can to help her out.

Goodnight Moon. Margaret Wise Brown. (Harper & Row, 1947) Younger. A little bunny says good-night to all the things in his room.

If You Give a Mouse a Cookie. Laura Joffe Numeroff. (HarperCollins, 1985) Younger. If you give a mouse a cookie, he will want a glass of milk. If you give him some milk, you never know what he will want next!

Jamberry. Bruce Degen. (Harper & Row, 1983) Younger. Every kind of berry—including raspberries, jazzberries, and razamatazzberries are used to make jam for a bear and his friends.

My Little Red Car. Chris L. Demarest. (Boyds Mills Press, 1992) Younger. A young boy imagines driving around the world in the toy he receives for his birthday.

The Random House Book of Humor for Children. Pamela Pollack. (Random House, 1988) All ages. Thirty-four short stories and excerpts by Roald Dahl, Judy Blume, Beverly Cleary, Robert McCloskey, and others.

The Rubber Chicken Book: A Fine Collection of Bad Skits, Goofball Stunts, Frontyard Acrobatics and Really Dumb Jokes by the editors of Klutz Press. (Klutz Press, 1995) Older. The title tells it all!

Shake My Sillies Out. Raffi. (Crown, 1987) Younger. Three animals can't get to sleep and roam the forest looking for people to help them shake their sillies out, clap their crazies out, and wiggle their waggles away.

Simple Pictures Are Best. Nancy Willard. (Harcourt Brace Jovanovich, 1976) Younger. When the shoemaker and his wife have their picture taken, the photographer tells them that simple pictures are best, but the couple keeps adding one crazy thing after another.

The Stupids Step Out. Harry Allard. (Houghton Mifflin, 1974) Younger. The Stupid family and their dog, Kitty, spend the day together, wearing their socks (on their ears, of course), eating mashed potato sundaes, and walking home—on their hands.

Wackiest Jokes in the World. Michael J. Pellowski. (Sterling, 1994) All ages. Hundreds of jokes and crazy illustrations.

World's Toughest Tongue Twisters. Joseph Rosenbloom. (Sterling, 1986) All ages. Even if they can't say any of these five-hundred-plus tongue twisters, kids will have a great time trying!

Chapter 11

Bored—Nothing to Do! Peter Spier. (Doubleday, 1978) Younger. When two boys are sent out by their mother to find something to do, they keep themselves occupied by building an airplane from stuff lying around in the house!

The Brave Little Toaster. Thomas M. Disch. (Doubleday, 1986) Younger. Five small appliances set out on a journey to the big city to find their young master.

The Clever Carpenter. R. W. Alley. (Random House, 1988) Younger. The carpenter builds things that "don't look the way they should," but his inventions turn out to be more useful than the conventional ones.

The Contrary Kid. Matt Cilula. (Zino Press, 1995) All ages. A child who delights in his individuality.

The Emperor and the Kite. Jane Yolen. (World, 1967) Younger. No one pays attention to Djeow

Seow, the youngest of the emperor's eight children, until the emperor is kidnapped, and Djeow Seow is the only one who can rescue him.

The Fool of the World and the Flying Ship. Arthur Ransome. (Farrar Straus & Giroux, 1968) Older. A simple peasant wins the hand of the czar's daughter by paying attention to good advice and making the most of what he has learned.

Franklin in the Dark. Paulette Bourgeois. (Scholastic, 1987) Younger. Franklin the turtle won't go inside his shell—he's afraid of the dark!

Frej the Fearless (The Secret World of Frej). Marie Olofsdotter. (Franklin Watts, 1995) All ages. Alternative to violence.

From the Mixed-up Files of Mrs. Basil E. Frankweiler. E. L. Konigsburg. (Atheneum, 1967) Older. Claudia runs away and decides to live in the Metropolitan Museum of Art.

Googles! Ezra Jack Keats. (Macmillan, 1969) All ages. Peter, his friend, Archie, and his dog, Willie, have to think quickly to outwit the neighborhood bullies.

Harald and the Great Stag. Donald Carrick. (Clarion, 1988) Older. Harald is so excited when he sees the legendary Great Stag that he runs and tells everybody—including all the hunters.

Harold and the Purple Crayon. Crockett Johnson. (HarperCollins, 1955) Younger. A young boy draws his own adventures on a nighttime walk.

Hugh Can Do. Jennifer Armstrong. (Crown, 1992) Younger. Hugh wants to go to the city, but first he must find a way to pay the toll bridge.

Island of the Blue Dolphins. Scott O'Dell. (Houghton Mifflin, 1960) Older. When Karana's Native American tribe evacuates the island on which they live, she is left behind. For eighteen years, Karana survives on her own, with only a wild dog as a companion.

Listen and Look! A Safety Book. Rita Golden Gelman. (Marvel, 1986) Younger. Children learn what they should do in situations that require safety skills.

One Hundred and Two Steps. Donna Guthrie. (Cool Kids, 1995) Younger. A girl shares a story about how she found her way home after being lost.

Safety First: Fire. Eugene Baker. (Creative Education, Inc., 1980) Younger. Children learn how to prevent fires, and what they should do if they ever find themselves in one.

A School for Pompey Walker. Michael Rosen. (Harcourt Brace, 1995) Older. A slave's search for freedom leads to a dream of starting a school for African-American children.

The Sign of the Beaver. Elizabeth George Speare. (Houghton Mifflin, 1983) Older. When Matt is left alone in the woods to guard his family's cabin, he must learn to live on his own.

Stone Fox. John Reynolds Gardiner. (Crowell, 1980) Older. Ten-year-old Willy lives with his grandfather on their old farm. When his grandfather becomes ill and the farm is threatened, Willy is determined to find a way to save them.

The Story about Ping. Marjorie Flack. (Penguin, 1977) Younger. Ping and his family spend every day on the river shore, and return to their boat at night until one night, Ping is left behind.

The Trek. Ann Jonas. (Greenwillow, 1985) Younger. A little girl walks to school each day, and imagines she is trekking through the wilderness, encountering all kinds of wild animals.

What to Do When Your Mom or Dad Says "Be Prepared". Joy Wilt Berry. (Children's Press, 1981) Younger. Children learn what they should do in case of an emergency.

Yikes! Alison Lester. (Houghton Mifflin, 1995) Younger. Readers guess resolutions to adventures prior to turning the page.

Chapter 12

All in a Day. Mitsumasa Anno. (Philomel, 1986) Younger. Picture book about the similarities in children in eight different parts of the world.

Charlotte's Web. E. B. White. (Harper & Row, 1952) Older. Wilbur the pig learns the true meaning of friendship when Charlotte the spider saves his life.

Children Just Like Me. Barabus and Anabel Kindersley. (Disney Press, 1995) All ages. Photography celebrating children from around the world, copublished with UNICEF to commemorate its fiftieth year.

Corduroy. Don Freeman. (Scholastic, 1968) Younger. Corduroy sits on the shelf at the toy store, but no one seems to want a teddy bear in green overalls with one button missing.

Dogger. Shirley Hughes. (Lothrop Lee & Shepard, 1988) Younger. Dave's favorite stuffed dog shows up at the school fair, but a little girl buys him and refuses to give him back.

From Far Away. Robert Munsch and Saoussan Askar. (Annick Press, 1995) Younger. A girl's humorous experience of adapting to a new culture.

The Giving Tree. Shel Silverstein. (Harper & Row, 1964) All ages. A tree watches a boy grow from a young child to a man, offering everything he can. The boy takes and takes, but never gives.

It Could Be Worse. Eleanor Chroman. (Children's Press, 1972) Younger. Ivan and his family live in a very small house. When Ivan gets fed up with this, he asks an old wise man for some advice.

Kids Can Make a Difference! Steven Dashefsky. (McGraw-Hill, 1995) Older. Environmental projects children can tackle while learning about science.

The Little Snake. Edda Reinl. (Neugebauer Press USA, 1982) Younger. The little snake is lonely because everyone is afraid of her, until one day she finds a friend who is not afraid—a beautiful flower.

The Lorax. Dr. Seuss. (Random House, 1971) All ages. The man who cut down all the beautiful truffula trees entrusts the very last truffula seeds to a young man in a final effort to right his wrong.

The Man Who Kept His Heart in a Bucket. Sonia Levitin. (Dial Books for Young Readers, 1991) Younger. Jack's heart has been broken, so he carries his heart around in a bucket so it won't happen again.

Molly's Pilgrim. Barbara Cohen. (Bantam, 1990) Older. The Pilgrim doll that Molly makes for her school assignment looks different than the other children's dolls.

Mufaro's Beautiful Daughters: An African Tale. John Steptoe. (Lothrop Lee & Shepard, 1987) Older. When the king decides to choose a wife, both Nyasha and Manyara are invited to appear before him. Nyasha is loving and considerate, while Manyara is selfish and impatient. Manyara devises a plan to ensure that she is chosen by the king but it is Nyasha's kindness that is rewarded in the end.

The Velveteen Rabbit. Margery Williams. (Doubleday, 1971) All ages. A small boy's love for his stuffed rabbit makes the toy into a real rabbit.

Problem-Solving Worksheet

Step 1 to 5 problem-solving worksheet to be used in conjunction with a "recipe."

Step 1: Define the Problem

The adult(s) in this family see the problem as:_____

_____

_____

The child(ren) in this family see the problem as: _____

_____

_____

We all agree that the problem we want to solve is: _____

_____

_____

Step 2: Identify Skills—What are the "Skillutions"?

Make a list of all the skills, talents, personality traits, capabilities, and abilities of the child(ren) in the family in solving the problem.

1. _____   7. _____
2. _____   8. _____
3. _____   9. _____
4. _____   10. _____
5. _____   11. _____
6. _____   12. _____

Step 3: Write Your Goal

"We can solve our _____

_____
                                    (problem discussed in step 1)

_____

_____ by using our skills _____
                                              (skills discussed in step 2)

_____

_____

_____ to become a happier family!"

Signed,

_____   _____

_____   _____

Step 4: Practice and Play

Put your skillutions into play to reach your goal.

Step 5: Review and Recognize Efforts

Yea! Hooray! Whoopeee! If you made it this far, it is an accomplishment. Take the time to recognize efforts and accomplishments both big and small:

1. _____

2. _____

3. _____

4. _____

Ask yourselves:

A. Did you reach your goal?   Yes _____   No_____

B. Do you need more practice?

   Do you need to try another recipe to   Yes _____   No_____

   solve the problem?   Yes _____   No_____

C. What did each of you learn from the recipe?

_____

_____

More Than 450 Skills, Talents, and Abilities in Children

Body Related

body care
  washes self
  brushes teeth well
  combs hair nicely
  nail cleaning
takes care of clothing
nice dresser
eats healthy foods
finishes a meal
knows when is full
uses bathroom right
nice hair
nice nails
muscular
nice eyes
cute dimples
friendly face
great freckles
strong arms
  legs
  stomach
  hands
great smile
smells nice
petite
tall

Physical Abilities

(Gross motor)

jumps high
runs fast
walks quickly
moves nice and slowly
holds breath long
spins around
can balance
graceful
throws well
catches well
flexible
leaps high
good tree climber

good rope climber
swings high
can hop well
can skip well
can gallop well

Physical Abilities

(Fine motor)

nice handwriting
puzzles
drawing
carpentry
model building

Artistic Ability

Good at:
  painting
  coloring
  cutting
  pasting
  doodling
  drawing lines, circles,
    squares
  clay molding
  ceramics
  cake decorating
  candlemaking
  cartoon drawing
  doll making
  knitting
  macramé
  fabric art
  calligraphy
  weaving
  woodcraft
  sewing
  quilting
  photography
  origami
  needlepoint
  pottery
  print making
  tie-dyeing
  embroidery

  crocheting
  sculpting
  moviemaking

Personality Traits

creative
friendly
careful
brave
curious
alert
active
happy
humorous
funny
silly
smart
giving
fearless
powerful
imaginative
charming
sweet
caring
athletic
artistic
happy-go-lucky
free spirited
tries hard
patient
learns quickly
applies self
takes his time
follows directions
watches carefully
does things safely
kind
appreciative
doesn't give up
mature
responsible
peacemaker
cooperative
quick thinker

assertive
gifted
agile
noncompetitive
good mood
respectful
accepting
excitable
independent
forgiving
generous
gift of gab
intriguing
joyful
good memory
determined
negotiator
trustworthy
self-confident
sure of self
organizer
flexible
handles emergencies well
accepts criticism
accepts praise
calm
gentle
private
thoughtful
physical
insightful
understanding
tells the truth
good storyteller
speaks nicely
well-mannered
proud
empathic
easy going
great joker
terrific laugh
good problem solver
motivated

Social Skills

leader
follower
plays nicely
good loser
good winner
introduces self nicely
says thank you
says you're welcome
shares
listens to others
sits nicely
nice manners
polite
apologizes
waits turn
good pen pal
participates in clubs
    (Girl or Boy Scouts)
  good member
  joins activities
  earns badges
  follows rules of club
helps others
supports others
plays quietly
remembers names
says hello
says good-bye
gives good hugs, kisses
talks nicely about others
nice party guest
good host
nice phone skills
good sister/brother/cousin
plays fair

Performance Ability

Good at:
  dramatics
  mime
  chorus
  improvisation
  puppetry
  role-playing

ventriloquism
playwriting
costuming
face painting
magic tricks, card tricks
set constructions
play production and
    direction
dancing
  ballet
  jazz
  modern
  tap

Nature and Outdoor Abilities

Good at:
  caring for animals
  astronomy
  bird-watching
  backpacking
  camping
  hiking
  rock climbing
  studying butterflies
  collecting rocks
  mountain climbing
  gardening
  playground playing
  shell collecting
  whale watching
  traveling
  environmentalist
  recycling
  wildlife protector
  explorer
  farming

Sports Ability

Good at:
  aerobics
  archery
  badminton
  baseball
  baton twirling
  basketball

bicycling
boating
canoeing
sailing
skiing
dart throwing
fencing
field hockey
ice hockey
skating
football
golf
horseback riding
jogging
tennis
soccer
surfing
windsurfing
swimming
skateboarding
rollerskating
kite flying
karate
judo
jumping rope
self-defense
softball
cheerleading
wrestling
yoga
water-skiing
track and field
racquetball

Musical Abilities

can play an instrument
good ear
good songwriter
good band player
good in marching band
singing
chorus/choir
reading music

School Abilities

math

science
history
spelling
reading
writing
concentrating
staying in seat
handwriting
foreign language
home economics
computers
geography
religious studies
researching
taking tests
neatly done papers
good reports
good speaker
raises hand
answers questions
joins class discussion
remembers to bring home
    books
good on bus
respects teacher
loves learning
studies hard
does homework
turns in papers on time
good library skills
on time
good grades
hardly absent

Special Abilities

board games
crosswords
cooking
video games
collecting things like:
  baseball cards
  stamps
  railroad cars
  dollhouse furniture
learning about:
  cars

dinosaurs
electricity
music groups
saving money
gift giving
dog walking
map reading
pet care
fixing things

putting things together
taking things apart
reading directions

Home Abilities

Good at:
  cleaning up
  cleaning dishes
    room

bathroom
outside
windows
closets
polishing
vacuuming
wiping
spraying
dusting

remembering chores
taking out garbage
folding clothes
hanging clothes
making things shiny
putting things away
turning off lights

Note: With a little creative adjustment, each of these skills can become a heading for a group of related skills. For example, "brushes teeth well" can be extended to gargles well, flosses well, puts cap on toothpaste, listens to dentist, nice breath, etc.

Special Resources

Catalogs of quality toys, play supplies, videos, books, and special music that playfully enhance your child's problem-solving skills.

Childswork, Childsplay
Center for Applied Psychology, Inc.
P.O. Box 1586
King of Prussia, PA 19406
(1-800-962-1141)

Constructive Playthings
1227 East 119th Street
Grandview, MO 64030
(1-800-255-6124)

Childcraft
P.O. Box 29149
Mission, KS 66201-9149
(1-800-367-3255)

The Great Kids Company
P.O. Box 609
Lewisville, NC 27023-0609
(1-800-533-2166)

Troll Learn & Play
100 Corporate Drive
Mahwah, NJ 07430
(1-800-247-6106)

Sensational Beginnings
300 Detroit Ave. #E
P.O. Box 2009
Monroe, MI 48161
(1-800-444-2147)

Hearth Song
6519 N. Galena Road
Peoria, IL 61614-3125
(1-800-325-2502)

Hand-in-Hand
Route 26
RR1, Box 1425
Oxford, ME 04270
(1-800-872-9745)

Play Fair Inc.
1690 28th St.
Boulder, CO 80302
(1-800-824-7255)
This catalog of toys and games focuses on nonviolent, noncompetitive educational toys.

Positive Promotions
222 Ashland Place
Brooklyn, NY 11217
(1-800-635-2666)

Uniquity
P.O. Box 6
Galt, CA 95632
(1-800-521-7771)
The items in this catalog focus on personal growth and are widely used by play therapists.

J. L. Hammett Co.
P.O. Box 9057
Braintree, MA 02184
(1-800-333-4600)

Galt, Inc.
63 North Plains Highway
Wallingford, CT 06492
(1-800-966-GALT)

Environments, Inc.
P.O. Box 1348
Beaufort Industrial Park
Beaufort, SC 29901
(1-800-EI CHILD)

Kaplans
P.O. Box 609
Lewisville, NC 27023
(1-800-4KAPLAN)

Flaghouse, Inc.
150 N. MacQuesten Parkway
Mt. Vernon, NY 10550
(1-800-793-7900)

Nasco
901 Janesville Avenue
Fort Atkinson, WI 53538
(1-800-558-9595)

Discovery Toys
12530 Arnold Drive
Martinez, CA 94553
(1-800-426-4777)

World Book Catalog
2515 East 43rd St.
P.O. Box 182246
Chattanooga, TN 37422

S&S World Wide
P.O. Box 513
Colchester, CT 06415
(1-800-243-9232)

Toys to Grow On
P.O. Box 17
Longbeach, CA 90801
(1-800-542-8338)

School Catalogs
The following are school-supply catalogs that have wonderful play items
and educational material such as board
games for teaching academics and
poster kits that reinforce body care.

Lakeshore Learning Material
2695 E. Dominguez
P.O. Box 6261
Carson, CA 90749
(1-800-421-5354)

Up with Learning
Catalog Division
19 Ridge Street
Pawtucket, RI 02860

Chasell, Inc.
9645 Gerwig Lane
Columbia, MD 21046
(1-800-242-7355)

Educational Insights
19560 S. Rancho Way
Dominguez Hills, CA 90220
(1-800-933-3277)

Chime Time Catalog
One Spotime Way
Atlanta, GA 30340
(1-800-477-5075)

The Giraffe Project

The Giraffe Project is a nonprofit organization that recognizes people for sticking their necks out for the common good. Members report instances of such behavior to a volunteer jury, which decides who will receive Giraffe commendations. Commendations are awarded based upon both the personal risk taken by the nominees, and their desire, through their actions, to make the world a better place.

The Project's "Standing Tall" curriculum helps teachers and youth leaders build courage, caring, and responsibility in kids six to eighteen years old and guide them in designing and implementing their own service projects.
For more information, call or write:

> The Giraffe Project
> P.O. Box 759
> Langley, WA 98260
> (360) 221-7989
> e-mail:
> http://www.giraffe.org/giraffe/